331-8510

SAM SHEPARD has written over forty plays and won ten Obie Awards, one Pulitzer Prize for Drama in 1979 for *Buried Child*, and an Oscar nomination in 1984 for his part as Chuck Yeager in *The Right Stuff*. He was born Samuel Shepard Rogers on November 5, 1943, in Fort Sheridan, Illinois. His career as a playwright began in New York in 1964 with the Theater Genesis production of two one-act plays, *Cowboys* and *The Rock Garden*, at St. Mark's Church in the Bowery. His first full-length play, *La Turista*, was performed at the American Place Theater and won an Obie in 1967. *The Tooth of Crime*, a rock-drama written during the four years he lived in London, was staged in its American premiere at Princeton University in 1972; *Curse of the Starving Class* first appeared at the New York Shakespeare Festival in 1978. Mr. Shepard spent several successful seasons with Off-Off-Broadway groups such as La Mama and Caffe Cino and was playwright-in-residence at the Magic Theater in San Francisco for a number of years. His works produced at the Magic include *Action*, *Killer's Head*, *Inacoma*, *Tongues*, *Suicide in B♭*, and *True West*. As an actor Mr. Shepard has performed in the movies *Days of Heaven*, *Resurrection*, *Raggedy Man*, *Frances*, and *Country*. Most recently he has written the screenplay for Wim Wenders's *Paris, Texas*, which won the Golden Palm Award at the 1984 Cannes Film Festival.

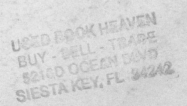

Also by Sam Shepard
Seven Plays

FOOL FOR LOVE
And Other Plays

by Sam Shepard

*Introduction
by Ross Wetzsteon*

BANTAM BOOKS
Toronto • New York • London • Sydney • Auckland

FOOL FOR LOVE AND OTHER PLAYS

A Bantam Book / December 1984

FOOL FOR LOVE *copyright © 1983 by Sam Shepard.*
ANGEL CITY *copyright © 1976 by Sam Shepard.*
MELODRAMA PLAY *copyright © 1967, 1981 by Sam Shepard.*
COWBOY MOUTH *copyright © 1976 by Sam Shepard and Patti Smith.*
ACTION *copyright © 1976 by Sam Shepard.*
SUICIDE IN B♭ *copyright © 1978, 1979 by Sam Shepard.*
SEDUCED *copyright © 1976, 1977 by Sam Shepard.*
GEOGRAPHY OF A HORSE DREAMER *copyright © 1974 by Sam Shepard.*

Library of Congress Cataloging in Publication Data

Shepard, Sam, 1943–
   Fool for love and other plays.

   Contents: Fool for love — Angel city — Melodrama play — [etc.]
   I. Title.
PS3569.H394A6   1984   812'.54   84-45182
ISBN 0-553-34129-4 (pbk.)

Published simultaneously in the United States and Canada

To Jessica

CONTENTS

FOOL FOR LOVE
And Other Plays

INTRODUCTION

by Ross Wetzsteon

"One story's as good as another," says the Howard Hughes character in *Seduced*. "It's all in the way you tell it." The way Sam Shepard tells his stories is in dazzling bursts of light, momentarily blinding us, but leaving a radiant afterimage silhouetted in our minds.

I can still recall the first moment I was stunned by Shepard's stagecraft—the final image of *La Turista*, the American Place Theater, 1967. Yes, the language of the play had a kind of fevered lyricism, its bizarre characters seemed strangely familiar, its fractured structure was oddly coherent—yes, I sat there thinking, here's yet another promising young American playwright. There was something more, though, something in the play's atmosphere, an elusive, elliptical, almost dreamlike disorientation that was as enthralling as it was bewildering. But just as when we awaken we try to reduce our dreams to their meanings, so in the theater we instinctively ask "what is the playwright trying to *say*?" and, in spite of my increasing enchantment, I didn't have the vaguest idea what it was. Then, at the end of the play, at the very moment that Shepard's fragmentary glimpses seemed about to come into focus, providing some sort of illumination at last, that flash of lightning came instead—the hero, in a panicked flight for freedom, turned his back to the audience, raced full speed toward the rear of the stage, and crashed through the wall, leaving only the outline of his body before our startled eyes. And staring at that image, an image that dramatized the themes of the play far more precisely than could any words, an image that communicated the emotional texture of

1

the characters' lives far more vividly than could any speech, at that instant I realized that Sam Shepard was more than just another promising young American playwright, he was the most instinctive, the most purely theatrical playwright of his generation.

Again and again in his plays, Shepard uses stage images not merely to illustrate his themes but to *embody* them. Although he has an extraordinary facility with language, the climactic moments of most of his plays are wordless. Think of the final scene of *Angel City*, for instance, in which slimy green ooze slowly seeps across the stage—has anyone ever captured the corruption of Hollywood with such succinct disgust? Or recall the end of *Melodrama Play*, the captor standing menacingly over his captive, beaten, tortured, insane with pain, mouth dripping with blood, slowly circling the stage on his hands and knees, wailing like a dying animal in anguished sobs—the most visceral image in our theater of the brutality of power. And could any words convey the decline of the Old West more dramatically than the image of Eddie, in *Fool for Love,* cooped up in a seedy motel on the edge of the Mojave Desert, bursting with pent-up energy, making a loop in a rope, tensely spinning it above his head, and angrily lassoing the bedposts? This is not staged prose, this is *theater*.

"I would have . . . a picture, and just start from there," Shepard once said of his plays. This impulse to visualize "is mistakenly called an idea by those who have never experienced it," he wrote somewhat later. "I can't even count how many times I've heard the line, 'where did the idea for this play come from?' I never can answer it because it seems totally ass backwards. Ideas emerge from plays—not the other way around." On other occasions, he has spoken disdainfully of "ideas which speak only to the mind," and warily of "interpretation" since "once it goes off into the so-called *meaning* of it, then it's lost, it's gone away." Asked to "explain" one of his plays, he says simply, "I think explanation destroys it and makes it less than it is." Or, in the words of Jacques Levy, who directed several of Shepard's early plays: "Sam is more interested in *doing* something to audiences than in saying something to them."

But of course it's necessary to ask, what is this "something" he's trying to "do"? Even Levy begins by describing what Shepard is *not* trying to do: it "has no relationship to the purging of emotions through identification or total involvement"; he then calls metaphor to the rescue: "it is more like the way changing a room's temperature does something to the people in it." Others answer the question by saying that Shepard's genius lies not so much in helping us understand what we don't know as in making us feel what we know all too well, and that's true enough, as far as it goes. Symptoms, Shepard wrote in *La Turista*, are "things that show on the outside what the inside might be up to," and it's probably more to the point to say that he provides us not with the symptoms but with the disease itself, not with the outside but with the inside, not with ideas but with the feelings that are their source.

There's a quality in Shepard's work that can only be conveyed by referring to dreams once more, the feeling that we have entered a world at once beyond rational comprehension and yet utterly familiar. "I feel something here that's going on that's deeply mysterious," Shepard has said of the way he approaches a play. "I know that it's true, but I can't put my finger on it." "The fantastic thing about theater," he has said elsewhere, "is that it can make something be seen that's invisible, and that's where my interest in theater is—that you can be watching this thing happening with actors and costumes and light and set and language, and even plot, and something emerges from beyond that, and that's the image part that I'm looking for, that sort of added dimension." In *Angel City* the filmmakers realize that their script doesn't need a new character or a new story angle, but something else, something magical, some "force." And it is precisely this something deeply mysterious, this added dimension, this magical force that finally distinguishes Shepard's plays.

Now the problem with all this, of course, is that if he can't put his finger on it, neither can critics or theatergoers. As a result, critics too often attempt to reduce his plays to their "meanings" and thus miss their "force" (the very quality that makes them worth discussing in the first place), and, more important, theatergoers too often feel intimidated by the plays' apparent inaccessibility and thus fail to submit to their magic.

For years, even people who acknowledged the power of Shepard's work spoke of its obscurity without realizing that there might be a connection between the two. But to say that his work resists analysis is not the same as to say that it is vague or unfocused or incomprehensible. Think of the plays as music, for instance, something Shepard himself has repeatedly suggested: "A play's like music—ephemeral, elusive, appearing and disappearing all the time." No one ever left a Rolling Stones concert confused.

But it's not necessary to resort to analogy to explain his apparent difficulty. A more direct explanation lies in the fact that while his plays are saturated with the familiar myths of popular culture, they deal with them in the unfamiliar methods of modernist art. If the plays seem elliptical and disjointed, this is because, like so many contemporary artists, he has abandoned the conventions of co-herence—traditional means of characterization, narrative, dialogue, structure, and so on—and has attempted to create a theater in which emotional, psychological, or spiritual states are presented directly to the audience. Shepard's characters often seem unmo-tivated, implausible, and inconsistent at first—not because they are untrue to life but because we confuse "true to life" with the conventions of psychological realism. Similarly, when Shepard aban-dons conventional methods of narration—sequential events, conti-nuity of time and space, clear-cut distinctions between realism and fantasy, and so on—theatergoers are confused not so much by his apparent distortion of experience as by his refusal to follow the formulas in which experience is usually packaged. "Stick with the actual moment by moment thing of it," he advises—stick with the always unstable ebb and flow of character, experience, consciousness. As critic Michael Smith once wrote of Shepard's work: "It's like real life. You can't tell what's going on."

Shepard's work can be roughly divided into three periods. The early plays, mostly one-acters, from 1964 to the early 1970s—"vibrations" the poet Michael McClure has called them—were abstract collages, elusive but intensely concentrated sketches, frag-mentary but resonantly linked anecdotes, characterized by lyrical monologues, abrupt shifts of focus and tone, and stunningly visual-ized climaxes. These plays (*Red Cross, Chicago, Icarus's Mother*, to name three) didn't seem to be "about" anything; that is, unlike most plays, they weren't about their characters (who didn't have that bundle of recognizable traits and tics that we add together and label "personality"), and they weren't about their stories (which seemed random, disconnected, even nonexistent). But once one realized that they were actually about their highly charged atmospheres—terrified loneliness, for example, or sexual betrayal, or paranoid despair—their surreal dislocations perfectly conveyed Shepard's sense of the psychic pressures of contemporary life.

The second group of plays deal with the ways the artist pursues his identity and freedom even if it results in isolation and betrayal, the ways the artist is at once essential and intolerable to his society. These works invariably see the writer as a visionary, sometimes in parable form (the Howard Hughes character in *Seduced*, the man in *Geography of a Horse Dreamer* who dreams the winners of horse races), often obliquely (the musicians in *Melodrama Play*, *Cowboy Mouth*, *The Tooth of Crime*, and *Suicide in B♭*), and twice directly (the screenwriters in *Angel City* and *True West*). One of the characteristic figures of the media century—from Franz Kafka to J. D. Salinger to Woody Allen—has been the artist who publicly exposes his deepest feelings while at the same time ruthlessly concealing his private life. Shepard discovered in this theme a profound metaphor for contemporary life, brilliantly exploring our paradoxical need for both individuality and belonging.

Again and again in Shepard's plays, the characters are shaman figures—those pop heroes embodying our national obsessions, cowboys, criminals, rock stars—who confront the psychic traumas that result when the integrity of the self comes into conflict with the compromises of community. Striving to escape the confinements of the flesh, the family, the culture, these heroes—who frequently refer to themselves as "escape artists"—are either victimized by a civilization that turns our history into cultural debris or spiritually kidnapped, their gifts corrupted, their souls poisoned. ("You got the genius," the gambler tells the dreamer in *Geography*, "somebody else got the power.") The shaman figure thus allows Shepard to explore the paradoxes at the core of the American experience—the contradictory desires for self and community, for freedom and roots, for escape and family. These paradoxes contain their *own* paradoxes, for he realizes that self, freedom, and escape may disorient as well as liberate, and community, roots, and family may nourish as well as confine. So to say that Shepard's major theme is a lament for the Old West is to overlook the fact that his plays imaginatively link the nineteenth-century obsession with the frontier spirit and the twentieth-century obsession with the alienated self. In this sense Shepard is at once as quintessentially American as Melville or Whitman and as quintessentially modernist as Beckett or Handke. Sam Shepard—existential cowboy.

Of course, the conflict takes place both between and within individuals. It often happens in his plays—culminating in the relationship of the brothers in *True West*—that two characters do battle over the turf of the soul, and the shifts of identity between them, the shifts of power, so bewildering to the rational mind, make perfect sense when regarded not as struggles between separate characters so much as contradictions within the solitary spirit. "I think we're split in a much more devastating way than psychology can ever reveal," Shepard has said. So it follows that he is not interested in constructing narrative questions to which he can supply the denouement (the well-made play) nor in raising intellectual questions to which he can suggest solutions (the play of ideas). He is committed instead to exploring the eternally urgent conflict between head and heart, between self and society. And since they are at once interdependent and irreconcilable, it's no wonder these plays seem at once so passionately engaged and so restlessly inconclusive. It's no wonder, also, that they frequently end in stage images that intensify rather than resolve their dilemmas. As he says simply, "I think it's a cheap trick to resolve things."

Third, there are Shepard's two great "family plays," *Curse of the Starving Class* and *Buried Child* (and to a certain extent *True West*, which combines the themes of artistic corruption and family disintegration). In these plays, the hero, after his visionary quest, returns home, to the place from which he originally escaped, to confront the desolating paradox at the heart of the family—the fact that it simultaneously defines our being and denies our existence.

"I have American scars on my brain," Shepard has said. But it was only in England—where he lived in the years just before writing his family plays—that he "found out what it really means to be an American. The more distant you are from it, the more the implications of what you grew up with start to emerge. You can't escape, that's the whole thing, you can't. You finally find yourself in a situation where . . . that's the way it is—you can't get out of it. But there's always that impulse toward another kind of world."

The odyssey, as we've known since the Greeks, is a circle, and Shepard's heroes have finally realized that the trip outward eventually, inevitably, becomes a trip backward, that the quest for spiritual liberation must circle back to its beginnings. The hero has no choice but to accept his past ("that's the way it is—you can't get out of it"), while still striving to transcend it ("there's always that impulse toward another kind of world")—he has no choice, yet his freedom lies in this very recognition.

One of the most characteristically American aspects of Shepard's sensibility is that he has altered the conventions of theater as radically as Brecht or Beckett without an accompanying theoretical rationale. His work is based on the spontaneous outpouring of feeling, on the refusal to be confined by inherited cultural or intellectual forms. In this sense, his lineage includes Jackson Pollock as well as the Rolling Stones and Walt Whitman. What better way to convey the on-the-go restlessness, the raw vitality, of his frontier-jukebox vision of American life than through process, energy, song? I'd like to suggest four ways in particular in which his theater has transformed the rigid categories of naturalism in order to achieve a kind of hyperrealism.

First, in Shepard's theater *space is emotional rather than physical.* This is made clear in the stage directions to such plays as *Angel City* and *Seduced,* but even a play with an apparently realistic location such as *Fool for Love* takes place within the feelings of the characters as much as within the confines of the set. The scenes with the father, for instance, are not momentary switches to fantasy (in the manner of dream sequences) but are as present in space as they are in time. In other plays characters wander on and off stage with no concern for spatial plausibility (in *Suicide in B♭* they even wander unnoticed among the other characters), for their space conforms only to their dramatic function. Never ask "where are we?" in a Shepard play—we're in a theater.

Second, in Shepard's theater *time is immediate rather than sequential.* Again and again, apparently "realistic" passages of time are shattered by eruptions of discontinuity, as "real time" is either condensed or elongated, as scenes or events are cut short or lingered over beyond chronological plausibility to reflect the dramatic rhythms of the actions on stage. The time-span of *Melodrama Play* or *Fool for Love* (or almost any other Shepard play, for that matter) seems almost ludicrously improbable by the standards of naturalism, yet we never leave a Shepard play feeling that only by the playwright's contrivance did all this take place in an hour and a half.

Third, in Shepard's theater *narrative is a matter of consciousness rather than behavior.* "Actions" and "events" are frequently metaphoric crystallizations of the characters' inner lives rather than characteristic activities from which we deduce their emotions. Jim in *Red Cross,* for instance, doesn't cry out for help or show by his actions that he's in pain—he simply sits with his back to the audience, then slowly turns to reveal a stream of blood trickling down his forehead. Or think of the "implausible" events in *Angel City* (Wheeler's skin turning green) or *Seduced* (Henry Hackamore's refusal to die even after he's been shot several times); while these scenes violate our expectations of "believable" plot development, they instantly clarify the mental and emotional states of the characters. Furthermore, Shepard's frequent fragmentation of the story line, his abrupt shifts of focus, even the way he'll occasionally have the apparent hero of the play disappear halfway through or have an apparently secondary character take over near the end, reflect an emphasis on continuity of consciousness rather than consistency of behavior.

Fourth, and perhaps most important, in Shepard's theater *character is spontaneous rather than coherent.* "You have this personality," he has said, "and somehow feel locked into it, jailed by all of your cultural influences and your psychological ones from the family . . . And somehow I feel that that isn't the whole of it." As a result, Shepard rejects such staples of conventional theater as sociological context and psychological biography in favor of a more existential view of character. In one of his rare comments on his own work, he wrote in the introduction to *Angel City:* "Instead of the idea of a 'whole' character with logical motives behind his behavior which the actor submerges himself into, he should consider instead a fractured whole with bits and pieces of character flying off the central theme. In other words, more in terms of collage construction or jazz improvisation." This emphasis accounts for the fact that Shepard has not created memorable characters so much as a provocative view of the nature of character itself. We rarely say of a Shepard character, "that's just the way so-and-so often acts," but we almost always say, "that's exactly how I sometimes feel." (In fact, we remember the mood, the atmosphere, the feeling of his plays longer than the people in them.) Shepard has even gone so far as to say that "personality is everything that is false in a human being," by which he means that the behavioral mannerisms that supposedly define our individuality have little to do with the inner impulses that actually define our humanity.

This view of character relates to the theme of uncertain identity. How often in his plays characters attempt to find their true nature by adopting roles, by performing, by hoping to become (like that quintessential American, Jay Gatsby) what they fantasize they are. To act "naturally," Shepard implies, is usually to act in conformity to socially determined rituals, while to act "uncharacteristically," as his characters so frequently do, is often to obey our deepest impulses. In other words, to stress consistency of character is often to miss the immediacy of experience. *We make ourselves up as we go along,* his plays suggest, for, in yet another paradox, that kind of spontaneity of self is the only way to discover the integrity of self. What could be more American than this sense of eternal renewal?

*   *   *

With all this in mind, it seems futile to try to analyze the plays in this collection in terms of what they are about, or what they mean, or what statement Shepard is trying to make. Like his characters, his plays are not whole and logical but fractured and improvised. So it would be more useful to follow his own method—bits and pieces flying off a central theme.

Fool for Love

For the first time in his forty-odd plays, Shepard has focused on sexual connection. (His work, in fact, has been almost totally concerned with male experience.) It's hardly surprising, though, that in dealing with love he has once again depicted passionately divided emotions: Eddie can't live with May, but he can't live without her either, and May almost simultaneously throws Eddie out and begs him not to leave. And what better way to capture the paradox of sexual attraction as freely chosen and yet ruthlessly fated than to write about incest?

Many of Shepard's familiar symbols are present (horses in particular), but notice especially the way in which the stage directions stress the walls of the motel. Over and over in his plays, walls symbolize confinement, and the way Eddie and May constantly bang against them perfectly conveys their claustrophobic sense of entrapment, the futility of their desire to escape (a word that keeps coming up in Shepard's work).

In almost all of Shepard's plays there's at least one long monologue. His "arias," in fact, have become a Sam Shepard signature. In his later plays, however, he has muted his earlier rhapsodic tendencies, choosing lean, spare language and staccato rhythms. In *Fool for Love* Eddie's long monologue explaining his relationship to May is almost prosaic, gaining its power not so much from his language as from the way he relentlessly paces in a circle throughout the entire speech—reminding us once more how important it is to *see* Shepard's plays as well as hear them.

Shepard has occasionally directed his own plays, and *Fool for Love* in particular gives specific clues as to how he wants his texts staged: violent emotions constantly on the verge of going out of control. Eddie and May, for instance, *slam* against those walls, Eddie's pacing in a circle is disturbingly ominous, and even Eddie's teasing of Martin is full of menace.

So it's particularly important, in reading this play, to pay attention to Shepard's stage images. The opening image of May, for instance, "legs apart, elbows on knees, hands hanging limp and crossed between her knees, head hanging forward, face staring at floor," is held for several minutes in the production Shepard himself directed, vividly establishing from the beginning, before she even speaks, her sense of weary, vulnerable desolation. And when Eddie tells the story of first seeing May, it's crucial to visualize "the bathroom door very slowly and silently [swinging] open revealing May, standing in the door frame back-lit with yellow light in her red dress"; wordlessly, the image captures the voluptuous rapture that has made them both fools for love.

Angel City

Shepard's plays often seem like interlocking fragments of a larger whole. *True West*, for example, in its treatment of brothers, creativity, and identity, almost seems like a rewrite of *Melodrama Play*, while *Geography of a Horse Dreamer*, in its theme of the tortured artist-shaman, prefigures *Suicide in B Flat*. But *Angel City* in particular is a virtual labyrinth of cross-references to other Shepard plays, most obviously calling to mind *True West* (art and commerce) and *Geography* (the kidnapped visionary), but also subtly evoking The *Tooth of Crime* (the deadlock scene), *Melodrama Play* (the shift of power), *Seduced* (the shaman's risk of madness), and, in its abrupt reversals of roles, its stalking of "twins," any number of Shepard plays ("They were one being with two opposing parts," Wheeler says of the characters in his movie—and it isn't hard to figure out who must have been the screenwriter). This almost obsessive sense of scenic and thematic cross-reference, in fact, is one of the clearest indications of how intuitively Shepard writes—a jazz musician improvising multitudes of moods from the same few melodies.

Shepard often constructs his plays (*Melodrama Play* being the best example) by starting with an apparently simple, almost sociological concept, which almost immediately takes on a larger, less realistic, more metaphoric scope. Here, for instance, we seem at first to be watching yet another "corruption of Hollywood" play ("We don't get smog in here," Lanx says, that is, real life doesn't intrude; or the name Wheeler, as in wheeler-dealer), but

Shepard quickly moves from the industry of imagination to the soul of imagination, with a stunningly original treatment of that often hackneyed theme, "the relationship between image and reality."

Melodrama Play

"The real quest of a writer," Shepard has written, "is to penetrate into another world. A world behind the form. The contradiction is that as soon as that world opens up, I tend to run the other way. It's scary because I can't answer to it from what I know." When Shepard wrote *Melodrama Play* in the late 1960s, he was at that stage in his career when audiences were beginning to pay attention, when people were starting to ask "what are you doing next?" so it's no wonder that he felt compelled to deal with the pressures of creativity, the fear of once more penetrating into that other world. (Is there a hint of self-mockery in the title?)

Notice once more the realistic beginning (the sociologist's letter), the theme of captivity and escape (we're even imprisoned by our reputations), the shift of focus (the early disappearance of the person we think is going to be the main character), and especially the emphasis on uncertain identity (anybody can pretend to be Duke Durgens, Dana warns, and yet Duke himself has been pretending to be Duke Durgens—and Peter confuses Drake and Cisco to such an extent that they virtually turn into one another). The transfer of power is particularly important here—the artist has the vision, but he can't keep it to himself. As Shepard has said about his early work, "I was very uptight about making a whole public thing out of something that you do privately. I felt that by having the play become public, it was almost like giving it away or something."

Cowboy Mouth

Fragments of autobiography are scattered through Shepard's work, from casual references (Rabbit, in *Angel City*, refuses to fly, just like his creator) to recurring types (the remote father), and Shepard occasionally deals with immediate personal crises in extended metaphoric situations (see the comments on *Melodrama Play* and *Geography*). But *Cowboy Mouth* is his most directly autobiographical play, not only thematically (the temptation to become a rock star), but in plot as well (his relationship with rock singer Patti Smith, with whom he cowrote and coperformed the play—"I have a wife and a life of my own," Slim says in angry remorse, again just like his creator). Making ourselves up as we go along, trying out various roles for size. . . .

So it's hardly surprising that "playacting" forms a significant part of the action of *Cowboy Mouth*—changing the time of year by an act of will, for instance—culminating in the key line, "now what'll we do," with its echo of *Waiting for Godot*. There are other Shepard signatures: "I always felt the rhythm of what it means," Cavale says, linking Shepard's two great loves, rock and roll and playwriting, "but I never translated it to words." Cavale also says, speaking of Nerval (Slim?), that he's "always banging into walls." When this play was first anthologized, by the way, among the people Shepard dedicated the book to was Jackson Pollock. And notice in particular the last word of the play.

Action

No one who was part of the Off-Broadway community in the 1960s and early 1970s can forget the excitement with which each new Shepard play was greeted—with a single exception. Almost universally dismissed when it opened, rarely revived, *Action* at first seems one of Shepard's most inaccessible, absurdist plays. Yet, if we abandon our conventional expectations of what theater is "about," we can see it as one of his most direct and realistic. "Stick with the actual moment by moment thing of it."

The title is not just a clue, it's a specific announcement. But what "actions" take place? Functional actions (eating), gratuitous behavior (chewing on one's arm), isolated performance (the dancing bear), communal ritual (the Christmas dinner), even frustrated outbursts of violence (the shattered chair), all of which fail to give the characters any sense of identity. There's no stasis in *Action*, yet the *feeling* is one of stasis, for none of the characters' activities seem to them to have any relationship to who they *are*. ("I'm looking forward to my life" is the play's first line.) They feel a profoundly disturbing disconnection between their outer and inner beings;

they're as lost in their lives as they are in the plot (the "action") of the novel they're reading. They're even thrown back on phenomenological descriptions of their behavior because psychological or sociological explanations seem so detached from their emotions.

Superficially spare, random, entropic, and pointless, *Action*—in its examination of the gaps between action, meaning, and self—is in fact one of the most richly textured, tightly constructed, passionately engaged, and intellectually provocative plays of the 1970s.

Suicide in B♭

"Now that you've seen me on the street," Niles tells an admirer scornfully, "you think that just by coming in contact with me that your asslicking life will be saved from hopelessness." If we remember the pressure the artist in *Melodrama Play* felt when he had to penetrate into that other world once more, when we recall the burden placed on the artist in *Cowboy Mouth* by followers who demanded that he become their rock-and-roll savior, it's easier to understand Niles's anguish. Too much is demanded of the visionary, Shepard suggests; he's always in danger of becoming the captive of his own legend.

Much of the play recapitulates familiar Shepard themes, this time expressed, appropriately enough, in jazzlike riffs: confused identity, the invented self, the disparity between creativity and power, the sterility of inherited forms ("What's the point in messing around in the same old dimension all the time?"). But the stress here is on the artist's need to disappear periodically, to escape the confining concepts people have of him. And not just the artist, of course, for we all sometimes feel imprisoned in our habits, in our roles, in other people's expectations of us. So it's not too much to suggest that the suicide in the title is in a sense the playwright's also, that he is killing off his various aesthetic identities (that cowboy persona, for example, turns out to be nothing but a costume) in hopes of disappearing, of escaping, of being left free to make himself up once more.

Seduced

Shepard has occasionally been accused of privatism, of avoiding politics, of ignoring social issues, but his work has touched on murder, ambition, betrayal, media manipulation, dread of war, government conspiracy, the corruption of democratic values, the role of myth in sustaining culture, the distintegration of the family, and the conflict between individual need and communal forms—a catalogue of concerns far broader in scope than that of any of the so-called committed writers of his generation. And here he deals with "the nightmare of the nation." "I was taken by the dream and all the time I thought I was taking it," the Howard Hughes figure moans. "I'm the demon they invented. Everything they ever aspired to."

Seduced begins in an almost satirical way, oddly reminiscent of *Angel City* (when Henry Hackamore begins moving trees around, we're reminded of Lanx keeping out the smog—even nature is controlled), and, like *Angel City,* it immediately expands into a larger, almost savage metaphor. There are even intimations of Prospero, but again details are crucial: could any speech convey the obsessive paranoia of our times more vividly than the simple image of Hackamore carefully spreading sheets of Kleenex over his entire body?

Geography of a Horse Dreamer

Ostensibly dealing with gamblers, *Geography* is actually another extended metaphor for the dilemma of the artist—more specifically, the conflict between personal vision and social exploitation. Cody (echoing Buffalo Bill, another western visionary whose dreams were cheapened) dreams the winners of horse races (writes plays), is kidnapped by gamblers (cultural entrepreneurs), and loses his gift until he shifts to dog racing (a new artistic persona). He longs for escape (that word again) and is finally rescued by his brothers from Wyoming (the return to the freedom of the West). The text is full of references to the artistic nature of Cody's dreams (he's even called Mr. Artistic Cowboy), and numerous details come straight out of Shepard's own life (he wrote the play in England, where he became fascinated with dog racing, where he became interested in a leaner style, and where he felt increasingly ill at ease—in the second act Cody lapses into an Irish accent, the accent of the outsider). Despite the ambiguity, even despair, beneath the superficially "happy ending," Shepard continues the struggle of a steadily maturing artist.

*   *   *

It's a peculiarly American irony that this playwright who has so frequently dealt with the captivity of the artist by commerce, who has so often shown how our myths have been corrupted by our media, should at last come to widespread public attention as a movie star. The irony is mitigated in part by the fact that Shepard has consistently defined the self as a process of performance, but more so by the fact that his work itself shows not the slightest sign of captivity or corruption. This is one American life at least—in contradiction of F. Scott Fitzgerald's famous lament—that seems destined to have a second act. Indeed, if his career denies one of our most common myths, the inevitable debasement of talent by popular success, it has the potential to fulfill another, our search for the Great American Playwright.

I keep thinking of that electrifying final image in *La Turista*, that silhouette etched in the wall at the back of the stage. "One story's as good as another. It's all in the way you tell it," the Hughes character says, adding, "If I don't actually get the *feeling* of it, then there's no point in tellin' it. Am I right?"

FOOL FOR LOVE

for Billy Pearson

"The proper response to love is to accept it. There is nothing to do."
—Archbishop Anthony Bloom

Fool for Love was first performed at the Magic Theater in San Francisco on February 8, 1983. It was directed by Sam Shepard.

The cast was as follows:

MAY:	Kathy Baker
EDDIE:	Ed Harris
MARTIN:	Dennis Ludlow
THE OLD MAN:	Will Marchetti

This play is to be performed relentlessly without a break.

SCENE: *Stark, low-rent motel room on the edge of the Mojave Desert. Faded green plaster walls. Dark brown linoleum floor. No rugs. Cast iron four poster single bed, slightly off center favoring stage right, set horizontally to audience. Bed covered with faded blue chenille bedspread. Metal table with well-worn yellow Formica top. Two matching metal chairs in the fifties "S" shape design with yellow plastic seats and backs, also well-worn. Table set extreme down left (from actor's p.o.v.). Chairs set upstage and down right of table. Nothing on the table. Faded yellow exterior door in the center of the stage-left wall. When this door is opened, a small orange porch light shines into room. Yellow bathroom door up right of the stage-right wall. This door slightly ajar to begin with, revealing part of an old style porcelain sink, white towels, a general clutter of female belongings and allowing a yellow light to bleed onto stage. Large picture window dead center of upstage wall, framed by dirty, long, dark green plastic curtains. Yellow-orange light from a streetlamp shines thru window.*

Extreme down left, next to the table and chairs, is a small extended platform on the same level as the stage. The floor is black and it's framed by black curtains. The only object on the platform is an old maple rocking chair facing upstage right. A pillow with no slipcover rests on the seat. An old horse blanket with holes is laced to the back of the rocker. The color of the blanket should be subdued—grays and blacks.

Lights fade to black on set. In the dark, Merle Haggard's tune "Wake Up" from his The Way I Am *album is heard. Lights begin to rise slowly on stage in the tempo of the song. Volume swells slightly with the lights until they arrive at their mark. The platform remains in darkness with only a slight spill from the stage lights. Three actors are revealed.*

Characters

THE OLD MAN *sits in the rocker facing up right so he's just slightly profile to the audience. A bottle of whiskey sits on the floor beside him. He picks up bottle and pours whiskey into a Styrofoam cup and drinks. He has a scraggly red beard, wears an old stained "open-road" Stetson hat (the kind with the short brim), a sun-bleached, dark quilted jacket with the stuffing coming out at the elbows, black-and-white checkered slacks that are too short in the legs, beat up, dark western boots, an old vest and a pale green shirt. He exists only in the minds of* MAY *and* EDDIE, *even though they might talk to him directly and acknowledge his physical presence.* THE OLD MAN *treats them as though they all existed in the same time and place.*

MAY *sits on the edge of bed facing audience, feet on floor, legs apart, elbows on knees, hands hanging limp and crossed between her knees, head hanging forward, face staring at floor. She is absolutely still and maintains this attitude until she speaks. She wears a blue denim full skirt, baggy white T-shirt and bare feet with a silver ankle bracelet. She's in her early thirties.*

EDDIE *sits in the upstage chair by the table, facing* MAY. *He wears muddy, broken-down cowboy boots with silver gaffer's tape wrapped around them at the toe and instep, well-worn, faded, dirty jeans that smell like horse sweat. Brown western shirt with snaps. A pair of spurs dangles from his belt. When he walks, he limps slightly and gives the impression he's rarely off a horse. There's a peculiar broken-down quality about his body in general, as though he's aged long before his time. He's in his late thirties. On the floor, between his feet, is a leather bucking strap like bronc riders use. He wears a bucking glove on his right hand and works resin into the glove from a small white bag. He stares at* MAY *as he does this and ignores* THE OLD MAN. *As the song nears the end of its fade, he leans over, sticks his gloved hand into the handle of the bucking strap and twists it so that it makes a weird stretching sound from the friction of the resin and leather. The song ends, lights up full. He pulls his hand out and removes glove.*

EDDIE: (*seated, tossing glove on the table. Short pause*) May, look.
May? I'm not goin' anywhere. See? I'm right here. I'm not gone.
Look. (*she won't*) I don't know why you won't just look at me.
You know it's me. Who else do you think it is. (*pause*) You want
some water or somethin'? Huh? (*he gets up slowly, goes cautiously to
her, strokes her head softly, she stays still*) May? Come on. You can't
just sit around here like this. How long you been sittin' here
anyway? You want me to go outside and get you something?
Some potato chips or something? (*she suddenly grabs his closest leg
with both arms and holds tight burying her head between his knees*) I'm
not gonna' leave. Don't worry. I'm not gonna' leave. I'm stayin'
right here. I already told ya' that. (*she squeezes tighter to his leg, he
just stands there, strokes her head softly*) May? Let go, okay? Honey?
I'll put you back in bed. Okay? (*she grabs his other leg and holds on
tight to both*) Come on. I'll put you in bed and make you some
hot tea or somethin'. You want some tea? (*she shakes her head
violently, keeps holding on*) With lemon? Some Ovaltine? May, you
gotta' let go of me now, okay? (*pause, then she pushes him away and
returns to her original position*) Now just lay back and try to relax.
(*he starts to try to push her back gently on the bed as he pulls back the
blankets. She erupts furiously, leaping off bed and lashing out at him
with her fists. He backs off. She returns to bed and stares at him
wild-eyed and angry, faces him squarely*)
EDDIE: (*after pause*) You want me to go?

(*She shakes her head.*)

MAY: No!

EDDIE: Well, what do you want then?

MAY: You smell.

EDDIE: I smell.

MAY: You do.

EDDIE: I been drivin' for days.

MAY: Your fingers smell.

EDDIE: Horses.

MAY: Pussy.

EDDIE: Come on, May.

MAY: They smell like metal.

EDDIE: I'm not gonna' start this shit.

MAY: Rich pussy. Very clean.

EDDIE: Yeah, sure.

MAY: You know it's true.

EDDIE: I came to see if you were all right.

MAY: I don't need you!

EDDIE: Okay. (*turns to go, collects his glove and bucking strap*) Fine.

MAY: Don't go!

EDDIE: I'm goin'.

(*He exits stage-left door, slamming it behind him; the door booms.*)

MAY: (*agonized scream*) Don't go!!!

(*She grabs pillow, clutching it to her chest, then throws herself face down on bed, moaning and moving from one end of bed to the other on her elbows and knees. EDDIE is heard returning to stage-left door outside. She leaps off bed clutching pillow, stands upstage right of bed, facing stage-left door. EDDIE enters stage-left door, banging it behind him. He's left the glove and bucking strap offstage. They stand there facing each other for a second. He makes a move toward her. MAY retreats to extreme upstage-right corner of room clutching pillow to her chest. EDDIE stays against left wall, facing her.*)

EDDIE: What am I gonna' do? Huh? What am I supposed to do?

MAY: You know.

EDDIE: What.

MAY: You're gonna' erase me.

EDDIE: What're you talkin' about?

MAY: You're either gonna' erase me or have me erased.

EDDIE: Why would I want that? Are you kidding?

MAY: Because I'm in the way.

EDDIE: Don't be stupid.

MAY: I'm smarter than you are and you know it. I can smell your thoughts before you even think 'em.

(EDDIE *moves along wall to upstage-left corner.* MAY *holds her ground in opposite corner.*)

EDDIE: May, I'm tryin' to take care of you. All right?
MAY: No, you're not. You're just guilty. Gutless and guilty.
EDDIE: Great.

(*He moves down left to table, sticking close to wall. Pause.*)

MAY: (*quietly, staying in corner*) I'm gonna' kill her ya' know.
EDDIE: Who?
MAY: Who.
EDDIE: Don't talk like that.

(MAY *slowly begins to move downstage right as* EDDIE *simultaneously moves up left. Both of them press the walls as they move.*)

MAY: I am. I'm gonna' kill her and then I'm gonna' kill you. Systematically. With sharp knives. Two separate knives. One for her and one for you. (*she slams wall with her elbow. Wall resonates*) So the blood doesn't mix. I'm gonna' torture her first though. Not you. I'm just gonna' let you have it. Probably in the midst of a kiss. Right when you think everything's been healed up. Right in the moment when you're sure you've got me buffaloed. That's when you'll die.

(*She arrives extreme down right at the very limits of the set.* EDDIE *in the extreme up left corner. Pause.*)

EDDIE: You know how many miles I went outa' my way just to come here and see you? You got any idea?
MAY: Nobody asked you to come.
EDDIE: Two thousand, four hundred and eighty.
MAY: Yeah? Where were you, Katmandu or something?
EDDIE: Two thousand, four hundred and eighty miles.
MAY: So what!

(*He drops his head, stares at floor. Pause. She stares at him. He begins to move slowly down left, sticking close to wall as he speaks.*)

EDDIE: I missed you. I did. I missed you more than anything I ever missed in my whole life. I kept thinkin' about you the whole time I was driving. Kept seeing you. Sometimes just a part of you.

MAY: Which part?

EDDIE: Your neck.

MAY: My neck?

EDDIE: Yeah.

MAY: You missed my neck?

EDDIE: I missed all of you but your neck kept coming up for some reason. I kept crying about your neck.

MAY: Crying?

EDDIE: (*he stops by stage-left door. She stays down right*) Yeah. Weeping. Like a little baby. Uncontrollable. It would just start up and stop and then start up all over again. For miles. I couldn't stop it. Cars would pass me on the road. People would stare at me. My face was all twisted up. I couldn't stop my face.

MAY: Was this before or after your little fling with the Countess?

EDDIE: (*he bangs his head into wall. Wall booms*) There wasn't any fling with any Countess!

MAY: You're a liar.

EDDIE: I took her out to dinner once, okay?

MAY: Ha!

(*She moves upstage-right wall.*)

EDDIE: Twice.

MAY: You were bumping her on a regular basis! Don't gimme that shit.

EDDIE: You can believe whatever you want.

MAY: (*she stops by bathroom door, opposite Eddie*) I'll believe the truth! It's less confusing.

(*Pause.*)

EDDIE: I'm takin' you back, May.

(*She tosses pillow on bed and moves to upstage-right corner.*)

MAY: I'm not going back to that idiot trailer if that's what you think.

EDDIE: I'm movin' it. I got a piece of ground up in Wyoming.

MAY: Wyoming? Are you crazy? I'm not moving to Wyoming. What's up there? Marlboro Men?

EDDIE: You can't stay here.

MAY: Why not? I got a job. I'm a regular citizen here now.

EDDIE: You got a job?

MAY: (*she moves back down to head of bed*) Yeah. What'd you think, I was helpless?

EDDIE: No. I mean—it's been a long time since you had a job.

MAY: I'm a cook.

EDDIE: A cook? You can't even flip an egg, can you?

MAY: I'm not talkin' to you anymore!

(*She turns away from him, runs into bathroom, slams door behind her.* EDDIE *goes after her, tries door, but she's locked it.*)

EDDIE: (*at bathroom door*) May, I got everything worked out. I been thinkin' about this for weeks. I'm gonna' move the trailer. Build a little pipe corral to keep the horses. Have a big vegetable garden. Some chickens maybe.

MAY'S VOICE: (*unseen, behind bathroom door*) I hate chickens! I hate horses! I hate all that shit! You know that. You got me confused with somebody else. You keep comin' up here with this lame country dream life with chickens and vegetables and I can't stand any of it. It makes me puke to even think about it.

EDDIE: (EDDIE *has crossed stage left during this, stops at table*) You'll get used to it.

MAY: (*enters from bathroom*) You're unbelievable!

(*She slams bathroom door, crosses upstage to window.*)

EDDIE: I'm not lettin' go of you this time, May.

(*He sits in chair upstage of table.*)

MAY: You never had ahold of me to begin with. (*pause*) How many times have you done this to me?

EDDIE: What.

MAY: Suckered me into some dumb little fantasy and then dropped me like a hot rock. How many times has that happened?

EDDIE: It's no fantasy.

MAY: It's all a fantasy.

EDDIE: And I never dropped you either.

MAY: No, you just disappeared!

EDDIE: I'm here now aren't I?

MAY: Well, praise Jesus God!

EDDIE: I'm gonna' take care of you, May. I am. I'm gonna' stick with you no matter what. I promise.

MAY: Get outa' here.

(*Pause.*)

EDDIE: What'd you have to go and run off for anyway.

MAY: Run off? Me?

EDDIE: Yeah. Why couldn't you just stay put. You knew I was comin' back to get you.

MAY: (*crossing down to head of bed*) What do you think it's like sittin' in a tin trailer for weeks on end with the wind ripping through it? Waitin' around for the butane to arrive. Hiking down to the Laundromat in the rain. Do you think that's thrilling or somethin'?

EDDIE: (*still sitting*) I bought you all those magazines.

MAY: What magazines?

EDDIE: I bought you a whole stack of those fashion magazines before I left. I thought you liked those. Those French kind.

MAY: Yeah, I especially liked the one with the Countess on the cover. That was real cute.

(*Pause.*)

EDDIE: All right.

(*He stands.*)

MAY: All right, what.

(*He turns to go out stage-left door.*)

MAY: Where are you going?

EDDIE: Just to get my stuff outa' the truck. I'll be right back.

MAY: What're you movin' in now or something?

EDDIE: Well, I thought I'd spend the night if that's okay.

MAY: Are you kidding?

EDDIE: (*opens door*) Then I'll just leave, I guess.

MAY: (*she stands*) Wait.

(*He closes door. They stand there facing each other for a while. She crosses slowly to him. She stops. He takes a few steps toward her. Stops. They both move closer. Stop. Pause as they look at each other. They embrace. Long, tender kiss. They are very soft with each other. She pulls away from him slightly. Smiles. She looks him straight in the eyes, then suddenly knees him in the groin with tremendous force.* EDDIE *doubles over and drops like a rock. She stands over him. Pause.*)

MAY: You can take it, right. You're a stunt man.

(*She exits into bathroom, stage right, slams the door behind her. The door is amplified with microphones and a bass drum hidden in the frame so that each time an actor slams it, the door booms loud and long. Same is true for the stage-left door.* EDDIE *remains on the floor holding his stomach in pain. Stage lights drop to half their intensity as a spot rises softly on* THE OLD MAN. *He speaks directly to* EDDIE.)

THE OLD MAN: I thought you were supposed to be a fantasist, right? Isn't that basically the deal with you? You dream things up. Isn't that true?

EDDIE: (*stays on floor*) I don't know.

THE OLD MAN: You don't know. Well, if you don't know I don't know who the hell else does. I wanna' show you somethin'. Somethin' real, okay? Somethin' actual.

EDDIE: Sure.

THE OLD MAN: Take a look at that picture on the wall over there. (*he points at wall stage-right. There is no picture but* EDDIE *stares at the wall.*) Ya' see that? Take a good look at that. Ya' see it?

EDDIE: (*staring at wall*) Yeah.

THE OLD MAN: Ya' know who that is?

EDDIE: I'm not sure.

THE OLD MAN: Barbara Mandrell. That's who that is. Barbara Mandrell. You heard a' her?

EDDIE: Sure.

THE OLD MAN: Well, would you believe me if I told ya' I was married to her?

EDDIE: (*pause*) No.

THE OLD MAN: Well, see, now that's the difference right there. That's realism. I am actually married to Barbara Mandrell in my mind. Can you understand that?

EDDIE: Sure.

THE OLD MAN: Good. I'm glad we have an understanding.

(THE OLD MAN *drinks from his cup. Spot slowly fades to black as stage lights come back up full. These light changes are cued to the opening and closing of doors.* MAY *enters from bathroom, closes door quietly. She is carrying a sleek red dress, panty hose, a pair of black high heels, a black shoulder purse and a hairbrush. She crosses to foot of bed and throws the clothes on it. Hangs the purse on a bedpost, sits on foot of bed her back to* EDDIE *and starts brushing her hair.* EDDIE *remains on floor. She finishes brushing her hair, throws brush on bed, then starts taking off her clothes and changing into the clothes she brought onstage. As she speaks to* EDDIE *and changes into the new clothes, she gradually transforms from her former tough drabness into a very sexy woman. This occurs almost unnoticeably in the course of her speech.*)

MAY: (*very cold, quick, almost monotone voice like she's writing him a letter*) I don't understand my feelings. I really don't. I don't understand how I could hate you so much after so much time. How, no matter how much I'd like to not hate you, I hate you even more. It grows. I can't even see you now. All I see is a picture of you. You and her. I don't even know if the picture's real anymore. I don't even care. It's a made-up picture. It invades my head. The two of you. And this picture stings even more than if I'd actually seen you with her. It cuts me. It cuts me so deep I'll never get over it. And I can't get rid of this picture either. It just comes. Uninvited. Kinda' like a little torture. And I blame you more for this little torture than I do for what you did.

EDDIE: (*standing slowly*) I'll go.

MAY: You better.

EDDIE: Why?

MAY: You just better.

EDDIE: I thought you wanted me to stay.

MAY: I got somebody coming to get me.

EDDIE: (*short pause, on his feet*) Here?

MAY: Yeah, here. Where else?

EDDIE: (*makes a move toward her upstage*) You been seeing somebody?

MAY: (*she moves quickly down left, crosses right*) When was the last time we were together, Eddie? Huh? Can you remember that far back?

EDDIE: Who've you been seeing?

(*He moves violently toward her.*)

MAY: Don't you touch me! Don't you even think about it.

EDDIE: How long have you been seeing him!

MAY: What difference does it make!

(*Short pause. He stares at her, then turns suddenly and exits out the stage-left door and slams it behind him. Door booms.*)

MAY: Eddie! Where are you going? Eddie!

(*Short pause. She looks after* EDDIE, *then turns fast, moves upstage to window. She parts the Venetian blinds, looks out window, turns back into room. She rushes to upstage side of bed, gets down on hands and knees, pulls a suitcase out from under bed, throws it on top of bed, opens it. She rushes into bathroom, disappears, leaving door open. She comes back on with various items of clothing, throws stuff into suitcase, turns as if to go back into bathroom. Stops. She hears* EDDIE *off left. She quickly shuts suitcase, slides it under bed again, rushes around to downstage side of bed. Sits on bed. Stands again. Rushes back into bathroom, returns with hairbrush, slams bathroom door. Starts brushing her hair*

*as though that's what she's been doing all along. She sits on bed brushing
her hair.* EDDIE *enters stage left, slams door behind him, door booms.
He stands there holding a ten gauge shotgun in one hand and a bottle of
tequila in the other. He moves toward bed, tosses shotgun on bed beside
her.*)

MAY: (*she stands, moves upstage, stops brushing her hair*) Oh, wonderful.
What're you gonna' do with that?
EDDIE: Clean it.

(*He opens the bottle.*)

EDDIE: You got any glasses?
MAY: In the bathroom.
EDDIE: What're they doin' in the bathroom?

(EDDIE *crosses toward bathroom door with bottle.*)

MAY: I keep everything in the bathroom. It's safer.
EDDIE: You want some a' this?
MAY: I'm on the wagon.
EDDIE: Good. 'Bout time.

(*He exits into bathroom.* MAY *moves back to bed, stares at shotgun.*)

MAY: Eddie, this is a very friendly person who's coming over here.
He's not malicious in any way. (*pause*) Eddie?
EDDIE'S VOICE: (*off right*) Where's the damn glasses?
MAY: In the medicine cabinet!
EDDIE'S VOICE: What the hell're they doin' in the medicine cabinet!

(*Sound of medicine cabinet being opened and slammed shut off right.*)

MAY: There's no germs in the medicine cabinet!
EDDIE'S VOICE: Germs.
MAY: Eddie, did you hear me?

(EDDIE *enters with a glass, pouring tequila into it slowly until it's full as
he crosses to table down left.*)

MAY: Did you hear what I said, Eddie?
EDDIE: About what?
MAY: About the man who's coming over here.
EDDIE: What man?
MAY: Oh, brother.

(EDDIE *sets bottle of tequila on table then sits in upstage chair. Takes a
long drink from glass. He ignores* THE OLD MAN.)

EDDIE: First off, it can't be very serious.

MAY: Oh, really? And why is that?

EDDIE: Because you call him a "man."

MAY: What am I supposed to call him?

EDDIE: A "guy" or something. If you called him a "guy," I'd be worried about it but since you call him a "man" you give yourself away. You're in a dumb situation with this guy by calling him a "man." You put yourself below him.

MAY: What in the hell do you know about it.

EDDIE: This guy's gotta' be a twerp. He's gotta' be a punk chump in a two dollar suit or somethin'.

MAY: Anybody who doesn't half kill themselves falling off horses or jumping on steers is a twerp in your book.

EDDIE: That's right.

MAY: And what're you supposed to be, a "guy" or a "man"?

(EDDIE *lowers his glass slowly. Stares at her. Pause. He smiles then speaks low and deliberately.*)

EDDIE: I'll tell you what. We'll just wait for this "man" to come over here. The two of us. We'll just set right here and wait. Then I'll let you be the judge.

MAY: Why is everything a big contest with you? He's not competing with you. He doesn't even know you exist.

EDDIE: You can introduce me.

MAY: I'm not introducing you. I am definitely not introducing you. He'd be very embarrassed to find me here with somebody else. Besides, I've only just met him.

EDDIE: Embarrassed?

MAY: Yes! Embarrassed. He's a very gentle person.

EDDIE: Is that right. Well, I'm a very gentle person myself. My feelings get easily damaged.

MAY: What feelings.

(EDDIE *falls silent, takes a drink, then gets up slowly with glass, leaves bottle on table, crosses to bed, sits on bed, sets glass on floor, picks up shotgun and starts dismantling it.* MAY *watches him closely.*)

MAY: You can't keep messing me around like this. It's been going on too long. I can't take it anymore. I get sick everytime you come around. Then I get sick when you leave. You're like a disease to me. Besides, you got no right being jealous of me after all the bullshit I've been through with you.

(*Pause.* EDDIE *keeps his attention on shotgun as he talks to her.*)

EDDIE: We've got a pact.

MAY: Oh, God.

EDDIE: We made a pact.

MAY: There's nothing between us now!

EDDIE: Then what're you so excited about?

MAY: I'm not excited.

EDDIE: You're beside yourself.

MAY: You're driving me crazy. You're driving me totally crazy!

EDDIE: You know we're connected, May. We'll always be connected. That was decided a long time ago.

MAY: Nothing was decided! You made all that up.

EDDIE: You know what happened.

MAY: You promised me that was finished. You can't start that up all over again. You promised me.

EDDIE: A promise can't stop something like that. It happened.

MAY: Nothing happened! Nothing ever happened!

EDDIE: Innocent to the last drop.

MAY: (*pause, controlled*) Eddie—will you please leave? Now.

EDDIE: You're gonna' find out one way or the other.

MAY: I want you to leave.

EDDIE: You didn't want me to leave before.

MAY: I want you to leave now. And it's not because of this man. It's just—

EDDIE: What.

MAY: Stupid. You oughta' know that by now.

EDDIE: You think so, huh?

MAY: It'll be the same thing over and over again. We'll be together for a little while and then you'll be gone.

EDDIE: I'll be gone.

MAY: You will. You know it. You just want me now because I'm seeing somebody else. As soon as that's over, you'll be gone again.

EDDIE: I didn't come here because you were seein' somebody else! I don't give a damn who you're seeing! You'll never replace me and you know it!

MAY: Get outa' here!

(*Long silence.* EDDIE *lifts his glass and toasts her, then slowly drinks it dry. He sets glass down softly on floor.*)

EDDIE: (*smiles at her*) All right.

(*He rises slowly, picks up the sections of his shotgun. He stands there looking down at the shotgun pieces for a second.* MAY *moves slightly toward him.*)

MAY: Eddie—

(*His head jerks up and stares at her. She stops cold.*)

EDDIE: You're a traitor.

(*He exits left with shotgun. Slams door. Door booms.* MAY *runs toward door.*)

MAY: Eddie!!

(*She throws herself against stage-left door. Her arms reach out and hug the walls. She weeps and slowly begins to move along the stage-left wall upstage to the corner, embracing the wall as she moves and weeps.* THE OLD MAN *begins to tell his story as* MAY *moves slowly along the wall. He tells it directly to her as though she's a child.* MAY *remains involved with her emotion of loss and keeps moving clear around the room, hugging the walls during the course of the story until she arrives in the extreme downstage-right corner of the room. She sinks to her knees.*)

(*Slowly, in the course of* MAY'S *mourning, the spotlight softly rises on* THE OLD MAN *and the stage lights decrease to half again.*)

THE OLD MAN: Ya' know, one thing I'll never forget. I'll never forget this as long as I live—and I don't even know why I remember it exactly. We were drivin' through southern Utah once, I think it was. Me, you and your mother—in that old Plymouth we had. You remember that Plymouth? Had a white plastic hood ornament on it. Replica of the *Mayflower* I think it was. Some kind a' ship. Anyway, we'd been drivin' all night and you were sound asleep in the front. And all of a sudden you woke up crying. Just bustin' a gut over somethin'. I don't know what it was. Nightmare or somethin'. Woke your mom right up and she climbed over the seat in back there with you to try to get you settled down. But you wouldn't shut up for hell or high water. Just kept wailing away. So I stopped the Plymouth by the side of the road. Middle a' nowhere. I can't even remember where it was exactly. Pitch black. I picked you up outa' the back seat there and carried you into this field. Thought the cold air might quiet you down a little bit. But you just kept on howling away. Then, all of a sudden, I saw somethin' move out there. Somethin' bigger than both of us put together. And it started to move toward us kinda' slow.

(MAY *begins to crawl slowly on her hands and knees from down-right corner toward bed. When she reaches bed, she grabs pillow and embraces*

it, still on her knees. She rocks back and forth embracing pillow as THE
OLD MAN *continues.*)

And then it started to get joined up by some other things just
like it. Same shape and everything. It was so black out there I
could hardly make out my own hand. But these things started to
kinda' move in on us from all directions in a big circle. And I
stopped dead still and turned back to the car to see if your
mother was all right. But I couldn't see the car anymore. So I
called out to her. I called her name loud and clear. And she
answered me back from outa' the darkness. She yelled back to
me. And just then these things started to "moo." They all
started "mooing" away.

(*He makes the sound of a cow.*)

And it turns out, there we were, standin' smack in the middle of
a goddamn herd of cattle. Well, you never heard a baby pipe
down so fast in your life. You never made a peep after that. The
whole rest of the trip.

(MAY *stops rocking abruptly. Suddenly* MAY *hears* EDDIE *off left. Stage
lights pop back up. Spot on* THE OLD MAN *cuts to black. She leaps to her
feet, completely dropping her grief, hesitates a second, then rushes to
chair upstage of table and sits. She takes a drink straight from the
bottle, slams bottle down on table, leans back in the chair and stares at
the bottle as though she's been sitting like that the whole time since he left.*
EDDIE *enters fast from stage-left door carrying two steer ropes. He
slams door. Door booms. He completely ignores* MAY. *She completely
ignores him and keeps staring at the bottle. He crosses upstage of bed,
throws one of the ropes on bed and starts building a loop in the other
rope, feeding it with the left hand so that it makes a snakelike zipping
sound as it passes through the honda. Now he begins to pay attention to*
MAY *as he continues fooling with the rope. She remains staring at the
bottle of tequila.*)

EDDIE: Decided to jump off the wagon, huh?

(*He spins the rope above his head in a flat horn-loop, then ropes one of
the bedposts, taking up the slack with a sharp snap of the right hand. He
takes the loop off the bedpost, rebuilds it, swings and ropes another
bedpost. He continues this right around the bed, roping every post and
never missing.* MAY *takes another drink and sets bottle down quietly.*)

MAY: (*still not looking at him*) What're you doing?

EDDIE: Little practice. Gotta' stay in practice these days. There's kids out there ropin' calves in six seconds dead. Can you believe that? Six and no change. Flyin' off the saddle on the right hand side like a bunch a' Spider Monkeys. I'm tellin' ya', they got it down to a science.

(*He continues roping bedposts, making his way around the bed in a circle.*)

MAY: (*flatly, staring at bottle*) I thought you were leaving. Didn't you say you were leaving?

EDDIE: (*as he ropes*) Well, yeah, I was gonna'. But then it suddenly occurred to me in the middle of the parking lot out there that there probably isn't any man comin' over here at all. There probably isn't any "guy" or any "man" or anybody comin' over here. You just made all that up.

MAY: Why would I do that?

EDDIE: Just to get even.

(*She turns to him slowly in chair, takes a drink, stares at him, then sets bottle on table.*)

MAY: I'll never get even with you.

(*He laughs, crosses to table, takes a deep drink from bottle, cocks his head back, gargles, swallows, then does a backflip across stage and crashes into stage-right wall.*)

MAY: So, now we're gonna' get real mean and sloppy, is that it? Just like old times.

EDDIE: Well, I haven't dropped the reins in quite a while ya' know. I've been real good. I have. No hooch. No slammer. No women. No nothin'. I been a pretty boring kind of a guy actually. I figure I owe it to myself. Once a once.

(*He returns to roping the bedposts. She just stares at him from the chair.*)

MAY: Why are you doing this?

EDDIE: I already told ya'. I need the practice.

MAY: I don't mean that.

EDDIE: Well, say what ya' mean then, honey.

MAY: Why are you going through this whole thing again like you're trying to impress me or something. Like we just met. This is the same crap you laid on me in high school.

EDDIE: (*still roping*) Well, it's just a little testimony of my love, see, baby. I mean if I stopped trying to impress you, that'd mean it was all over, wouldn't it?

MAY: It *is* all over.

EDDIE: You're trying to impress me, too, aren't you?

MAY: You know me inside and out. I got nothing new to show you.

EDDIE: You got this guy comin' over. This new guy. That's very impressive. I woulda' thought you'd be hung out to dry by now.

MAY: Oh, thanks a lot.

EDDIE: What is he, a "younger man" or something?

MAY: It's none of your damn business.

EDDIE: Have you balled him yet?

(*She throws him a mean glare and just pins him with her eyes.*)

EDDIE: Have you? I'm just curious. (*pause*) You don't have to tell me. I already know.

MAY: You're just like a little kid, you know that? A jealous little snot-nosed kid.

(EDDIE *laughs, spits, makes a snot-nosed-kid face, keeps roping bedposts.*)

EDDIE: I hope this guy comes over. I really hope he does. I wanna' see him walk through that door.

MAY: What're you gonna' do?

(*He stops roping, turns to her. He smiles.*)

EDDIE: I'm gonna' nail his ass to the floor. Directly.

(*He suddenly ropes chair downstage, right next to* MAY. *He takes up slack and drags chair violently back toward bed. Pause. They stare at each other.* MAY *suddenly stands, goes to bedpost, grabs her purse, slings it on her shoulder and heads for stage-left door.*)

MAY: I'm not sticking around for this.

(*She exits stage-left door, leaving it open.* EDDIE *runs offstage after her.*)

EDDIE: Where're you goin'?

MAY: (*off left*) Take your hands offa' me!

EDDIE: (*off left*) Wait a second, wait a second. Just a second, okay?

(MAY *screams.* EDDIE *carries her back onstage screaming and kicking. He sets her down, slams door shut. She walks away from him stage right, straightening her dress.*)

EDDIE: Tell ya' what. I'll back off. I'll be real nice. I will. I promise. I'll be just like a little ole pussycat, okay? You can introduce me to him as your brother or something. Well—maybe not your brother.

MAY: Maybe not.

EDDIE: Your cousin. Okay? I'll be your cousin. I just wanna' meet him is all. Then I'll leave. Promise.

MAY: Why do you want to meet him? He's just a friend.

EDDIE: Just to see where you stand these days. You can tell a lot about a person by the company they keep.

MAY: Look. I'm going outside. I'm going to the pay phone across the street. I'm calling him up and I'm telling him to forget about the whole thing. Okay?

EDDIE: Good. I'll pack up your stuff while you're gone.

MAY: I'm not going with you, Eddie!

(*Suddenly headlights arc across the stage from upstage right, through the window. They slash across the audience, then dissolve off left. These should be two intense beams of piercing white light and not "realistic" headlights.*)

MAY: Oh, great.

(*She rushes upstage to window, looks out.* EDDIE *laughs, takes a drink.*)

EDDIE: Why don't ya' run out there. Go ahead. Run on out. Throw yourself into his arms or somethin'. Blow kisses in the moonlight.

(EDDIE *laughs, moves to bed, pulls a pair of old spurs off his belt. Sits. Starts putting spurs on his boots. It's important these spurs look old and used, with small rowels—not cartoon "cowboy" spurs.* MAY *goes into bathroom, leaving door open.*)

MAY: (*off right*) What're you doing?

EDDIE: Puttin' my hooks on. I wanna' look good for this "man." Give him the right impression. I'm yer cousin, after all.

MAY: (*entering from bathroom*) If you hurt him, Eddie—

EDDIE: I'm not gonna' hurt him. I'm a nice guy. Very sensitive, too. Very civilized.

MAY: He's just a date, you know. Just an ordinary date.

EDDIE: Yeah? Well, I'm gonna turn him into a fig.

(*He starts laughing so hard at his own joke that he rolls off the bed and crashes to the floor. He goes into a fit of laughter, pounding his fists into the floor.* MAY *makes a move toward the door, then stops and turns to* EDDIE.)

MAY: Eddie! Do me a favor. Just this once, okay?

EDDIE: (*laughing hard*) Anything you want, honey. Anything you want.

(*He goes on laughing hysterically.*)

MAY: (*turning away from him*) Shit.

(*She goes to stage-left door and throws it open. Pitch black outside with only the porch light glowing. She stands in the doorway, staring out. Pause as* EDDIE *slowly gains control of himself and stops laughing. He stares at* MAY.)

EDDIE: (*still on floor*) What're you doing? (*Pause.* MAY *keeps looking out*) May?

MAY: (*staring out open door*) It's not him.

EDDIE: It's not, huh?

MAY: No, it's not.

EDDIE: Well, who is it then?

MAY: Somebody else.

EDDIE: (*slowly getting up and sitting on bed*) Yeah. It's probably not ever gonna' be "him." What're you tryin' to make me jealous for? I know you've been livin' alone.

MAY: It's a big, huge, extra-long, black Mercedes-Benz.

EDDIE: (*pause*) Well, this is a motel, isn't it? People are allowed to park in front of a motel if they're stayin' here.

MAY: People who stay here don't drive a big, huge, extra-long, black Mercedes-Benz.

EDDIE: You don't, but somebody else might.

MAY: (*still at door*) This is not a black Mercedes-Benz type of motel.

EDDIE: Well, close the damn door then and get back inside.

MAY: Somebody's sitting out there in that car looking straight at me.

EDDIE: (*stands fast*) What're they doing?

MAY: It's not a "they." It's a "she."

(EDDIE *drops to floor behind bed.*)

EDDIE: Well, what's she doing, then?

MAY: Just sitting there. Staring at me.

EDDIE: Get away from the door, May.

MAY: (*turning toward him slowly*) You don't know anybody with a black Mercedes-Benz by any chance, do you?

EDDIE: Get away from the door!

(*Suddenly the white headlight beams slash across the stage through the open door.* EDDIE *rushes to door, slams it shut and pushes* MAY *aside.*

Just as he slams the door the sound of a large caliber magnum pistol explodes off left, followed immediately by the sound of shattering glass, then a car horn blares and continues on one relentless note.)

MAY: (*yelling over the sound of horn*) Who is that! Who in the hell is that out there!

EDDIE: How should I know.

(EDDIE *flips the light switch off by stage-left door. Stage lights go black. Bathroom light stays on.*)

MAY: Eddie!

EDDIE: Just get down will ya'! Get down on the floor!

(EDDIE *grabs her and tries to pull her down on the floor beside the bed.* MAY *struggles in the dark with him. Car horn keeps blaring. Headlights start popping back and forth from high beam to low beam, slashing across stage through the window now.*)

MAY: Who is that? Did you bring her with you! You sonofabitch!

(*She starts lashing out at* EDDIE, *fighting with him as he tries to drag her down on the floor.*)

EDDIE: I didn't bring anybody with me! I don't know who she is! I don't know where she came from! Just get down on the floor, will ya'!

MAY: She followed you here! Didn't she! You told her where you were going and she followed you.

EDDIE: I didn't tell anybody where I was going. I didn't know where I was going till I got here.

MAY: You are gonna' pay for this! I swear to God. You are gonna' pay.

(EDDIE *finally pulls her down and rolls over on top of her so she can't get up. She slowly gives up struggling as he keeps her pinned to the floor. Car horn suddenly stops. Headlights snap off. Long pause. They listen in the dark.*)

MAY: What do you think she's doing?

EDDIE: How should I know.

MAY: Don't pretend you don't know her. That's the kind of car a Countess drives. That's the kind of car I always pictured her in. (*she starts struggling again*)

EDDIE: (*holding her down*) Just stay put.

MAY: I'm not gonna' lay here on my back with you on top of me and get shot by some dumb rich twat. Now lemme up, Eddie!

(*Sound of tires burning rubber off left. Headlights arc back across the stage again from left to right. A car drives off. Sound fades.*)

EDDIE: Just stay down!

MAY: I'm down!

(*Long pause in the dark. They listen.*)

MAY: How crazy is this chick anyway?

EDDIE: She's pretty crazy.

MAY: Have you balled her yet? (*pause*)

(EDDIE *gets up slowly, hunched over, crosses upstage to window cautiously, parts Venetian blinds and peeks outside.*)

EDDIE: (*looking out*) Shit, she's blown the windshield outa' my truck. Goddammit.

MAY: (*still on floor*) Eddie?

EDDIE: (*still looking out window*) What?

MAY: Is she gone?

EDDIE: I don't know. I can't see any headlights. (*pause*) I don't believe it.

MAY: (*gets up, crosses to light switch*) Yeah, you shoulda' thought of the consequences before you got in her pants.

(*She switches the light back on.* EDDIE *whirls around toward her. He stands.*)

EDDIE: (*moving toward her*) Turn the lights off! Keep the lights off!

(*He rushes to light switch and turns lights back off. Stage goes back to darkness.* MAY *shoves past him and turns the lights back on again. Stage lit.*)

MAY: This is my place!

EDDIE: Look, she's gonna' come back here. I know she's gonna' come back. We either have to get outa' here now or you have to keep the fuckin' lights off.

MAY: I thought you said you didn't know her!

EDDIE: Get your stuff! We're gettin' outa' here.

MAY: I'm not leaving! This is your mess, not mine.

EDDIE: I came here to get you! Whatsa' matter with you! I came all this way to get you! Do you think I'd do that if I didn't love you!

Huh? That bitch doesn't mean anything to me! Nuthin'. I got no reason to be here but you.

MAY: I'm not goin', Eddie.

(*Pause.* EDDIE *stares at her.*)

(*Spot rises on* THE OLD MAN. *Stage lights stay the same.* EDDIE *and* MAY *just stand there staring at each other through the duration of* THE OLD MAN'S *words. They are not "frozen," they just stand there and face each other in a suspended moment of recognition.*)

THE OLD MAN: Amazing thing is, neither one a' you look a bit familiar to me. Can't figure that one out. I don't recognize myself in either one a' you. Never did. 'Course your mothers both put their stamp on ya'. That's plain to see. But my whole side a' the issue is absent, in my opinion. Totally unrecognizable. You could be anybody's. Probably are. I can't even remember the original circumstances. Been so long. Probably a lot a' things I forgot. Good thing I got out when I did though. Best thing I ever did.

(*Spot fades on* THE OLD MAN. *Stage lights come back up.* EDDIE *picks up his rope and starts to coil it up.* MAY *watches him.*)

EDDIE: I'm not leavin'. I don't care what you think anymore. I don't care what you feel. None a' that matters. I'm not leavin'. I'm stayin' right here. I don't care if a hundred "dates" walk through that door—I'll take every one of 'em on. I don't care if you hate my guts. I don't care if you can't stand the sight of me or the sound of me or the smell of me. I'm never leavin'. You'll never get rid of me. You'll never escape me either. I'll track you down no matter where you go. I know exactly how your mind works. I've been right every time. Every single time.

MAY: You've gotta' give this up, Eddie.

EDDIE: I'm not giving it up!

(*Pause.*)

MAY: (*calm*) Okay. Look. I don't understand what you've got in your head anymore. I really don't. I don't get it. *Now* you desperately need me. *Now* you can't live without me. *NOW* you'll do anything for me. Why should I believe it this time?

EDDIE: Because it's true.

MAY: It was supposed to have been true every time before. Every other time. Now it's true again. You've been jerking me off like this for fifteen years. Fifteen years I've been a yo-yo for you. I've never been split. I've never been two ways about you. I've either loved you or not loved you. And now I just plain don't love you. Understand? Do you understand that? I don't love you. I don't need you. I don't want you. Do you get that? Now if you can still stay, then you're either crazy or pathetic.

(*She crosses down left to table, sits in upstage chair facing audience, takes slug of tequila from bottle, slams it down on table. Headlights again come slashing across the stage from up right, across audience, then disappear off left.* EDDIE *rushes to light switch, flips it off. Stage goes black. Exterior lights shine through.*)

EDDIE: (*taking her by shoulder*) Get in the bathroom!
MAY: (*pulls away*) I'm not going in the bathroom! I'm not gonna' hide in my own house! I'm gonna' go out there. I'm gonna' go out there and tear her damn head off! I'm gonna' wipe her out!

(*She moves toward stage-left door.* EDDIE *stops her. She screams. They struggle as* MAY *yells at stage-left door.*)

MAY: (*yelling at door*) Come on in here! Come on in here and bring your dumb gun! You hear me? Bring all your weapons and your skinny silly self! I'll eat you alive!

(*Suddenly the stage-left door bursts open and* MARTIN *crashes onstage in the darkness. He's in his mid-thirties, solidly built, wears a green plaid shirt, baggy work pants with suspenders, heavy work boots.* MAY *and* EDDIE *pull apart.* MARTIN *tackles* EDDIE *around the waist and the two of them go crashing into the stage-right bathroom door. The door booms.* MAY *rushes to light switch, flips it on. Lights come back up onstage.* MARTIN *stands over* EDDIE *who's crumpled up against the wall on the floor.* MARTIN *is about to smash* EDDIE *in the face with his fist.* MAY *stops him with her voice.*)

MAY: Martin, wait!

(*Pause.* MARTIN *turns and looks at* MAY. EDDIE *is dazed, remains on floor.* MAY *goes to* MARTIN *and pulls him away from* EDDIE.)

MAY: It's okay, Martin. It's uh—it's okay. We were just having a kind of an argument. Really. Just take it easy. All right?

(MARTIN *moves back away from* EDDIE. EDDIE *stays on floor. Pause.*)

MARTIN: Oh. I heard you screaming when I drove up and then all the lights went off. I thought somebody was trying to—

MAY: It's okay. This is my uh—cousin. Eddie.

MARTIN: (*stares at* EDDIE) Oh. I'm sorry.

EDDIE: (*grins at* MARTIN) She's lying.

MARTIN: (*looks at* MAY) Oh.

MAY: (*moving to table*) Everything's okay, Martin. You want a drink or something? Why don't you have a drink.

MARTIN: Yeah. Sure.

EDDIE: (*stays on floor*) She's lying through her teeth.

MAY: I gotta' get some glasses.

(MAY *exits quickly into bathroom, stepping over* EDDIE. MARTIN *stares at* EDDIE. EDDIE *grins back. Pause.*)

EDDIE: She keeps the glasses in the bathroom. Isn't that weird?

(MAY *comes back on with two glasses. She goes to table, pours two drinks from bottle.*)

MAY: I was starting to think you weren't going to show up, Martin.

MARTIN: Yeah, I'm sorry. I had to water the football field down at the high school. Forgot all about it.

EDDIE: Forgot all about what?

MARTIN: I mean I forgot all about watering. I was halfway here when I remembered. Had to go back.

EDDIE: Oh, I thought you meant you forgot all about her.

MARTIN: Oh, no.

EDDIE: How far was halfway?

MARTIN: Excuse me?

EDDIE: How far were you when it was halfway here?

MARTIN: Oh—uh—I don't know. I guess a couple miles or so.

EDDIE: Couple miles? That's all? Couple a' lousy little miles? You wanna' know how many miles I came? Huh?

MAY: We've been drinking a little bit, Martin.

EDDIE: She hasn't touched a drop.

(*Pause.*)

MAY: (*offering drink to* MARTIN) Here.

EDDIE: Yeah, that's my tequila, Martin.

MARTIN: Oh.

EDDIE: I don't care if you drink it. I just want you to know where it comes from.

MARTIN: Thanks.

EDDIE: You don't have to thank me. Thank the Mexicans. They made it.

MARTIN: Oh.

EDDIE: You should thank the entire Mexican nation in fact. We owe everything to Mexico down here. Do you realize that? You probably don't realize that, do ya'. We're sittin' on Mexican ground right now. It's only by chance that you and me aren't Mexican ourselves. What kinda' people do you hail from anyway, Martin?

MARTIN: Me? Uh—I don't know. I was adopted.

EDDIE: Oh. You must have a lotta' problems then, huh?

MARTIN: Well—not really, no.

EDDIE: No? You orphans are supposed to steal a lot aren't ya'? Shoplifting and stuff. You're also supposed to be the main group responsible for bumping off our Presidents.

MARTIN: Really? I never heard that.

EDDIE: Well, you oughta' read the papers, Martin.

(*Pause.*)

MARTIN: I'm really sorry I knocked you over. I mean, I thought she was in trouble or something.

EDDIE: She is in trouble.

MARTIN: (*looks at* MAY) Oh.

EDDIE: She's in big trouble.

MARTIN: What's the matter, May?

MAY: (*moves to bed with drink, sits*) Nothing.

MARTIN: How come you had the lights off?

MAY: We were uh—just about to go out.

MARTIN: You were?

MAY: Yeah—well, I mean, we were going to come back.

(MARTIN *stands there between them. He looks at* EDDIE, *then back to* MAY. *Pause.*)

EDDIE: (*laughs*) No, no, no. That's not what we were gonna' do. Your name's Martin, right?

MARTIN: Yeah, right.

EDDIE: That's not what we were gonna' do, Marty.

MARTIN: Oh.

EDDIE: Could you hand me that bottle, please?

MARTIN: (*crossing to bottle at table*) Sure.

EDDIE: Thanks.

(MARTIN *moves back to* EDDIE *with bottle and hands it to him.* EDDIE *drinks.*)

EDDIE: (*after drink*) We were actually having an argument about you. That's what we were doin'.

MARTIN: About me?

EDDIE: Yeah. We were actually in the middle of a big huge argument about you. It got so heated up we had to turn the lights off.

MARTIN: What was it about?

EDDIE: It was about whether or not you're actually a man or not. Ya' know? Whether you're a "man" or just a "guy."

(*Pause.* MARTIN *looks at* MAY. MAY *smiles politely.* MARTIN *looks back to* EDDIE.)

EDDIE: See, she says you're a man. That's what she calls you. A "man." Did you know that? That's what she calls you.

MARTIN: (*looks back to* MAY) No.

MAY: I never called you a man, Martin. Don't worry about it.

MARTIN: It's okay. I don't mind or anything.

EDDIE: No, but see I uh—told her she was fulla' shit. I mean I told her that way before I even saw you. And now that I see you I can't exactly take it back. Ya' see what I mean, Martin?

(*Pause,* MAY *stands.*)

MAY: Martin, do you want to go to the movies?

MARTIN: Well, yeah—I mean, that's what I thought we were going to do.

MAY: So let's go to the movies.

(*She crosses fast to bathroom, steps over* EDDIE, *goes into bathroom, slams door, door booms. Pause as* MARTIN *stares at bathroom door.* EDDIE *stays on floor, grins at* MARTIN.)

MARTIN: She's not mad or anything is she?

EDDIE: You got me, buddy.

MARTIN: I didn't mean to make her mad.

(*Pause.*)

EDDIE: What're you gonna' go see, Martin?

MARTIN: I can't decide.

EDDIE: What d'ya' mean you can't decide? You're supposed to have all that worked out ahead of time aren't ya'?

MARTIN: Yeah, but I'm not sure what she likes.

EDDIE: What's that got to do with it? You're takin' her out to the movies, right?

MARTIN: Yeah.

EDDIE: So you pick the movie, right? The guy picks the movie. The guy's always supposed to pick the movie.

MARTIN: Yeah, but I don't want to take her to see something she doesn't want to see.

EDDIE: How do you know what she wants to see?

MARTIN: I don't. That's the reason I can't decide. I mean what if I take her to something she's already seen before?

EDDIE: You miss the whole point, Martin. The reason you're taking her out to the movies isn't to see something she hasn't seen before.

MARTIN: Oh.

EDDIE: The reason you're taking her out to the movies is because you just want to be with her. Right? You just wanna' be close to her. I mean you could take her just about anywhere.

MARTIN: I guess.

EDDIE: I mean after a while you probably wouldn't have to take her out at all. You could just hang around here.

MARTIN: What would we do here?

EDDIE: Well, you could uh—tell each other stories.

MARTIN: Stories?

EDDIE: Yeah.

MARTIN: I don't know any stories.

EDDIE: Make 'em up.

MARTIN: That'd be lying wouldn't it?

EDDIE: No, no. Lying's when you believe it's true. If you already know it's a lie, then it's not lying.

MARTIN: (*after pause*) Do you want some help getting up off the floor?

EDDIE: I like it down here. Less tension. You notice how when you're standing up, there's a lot more tension?

MARTIN: Yeah. I've noticed that. A lot of times when I'm working, you know, I'm down on my hands and knees.

EDDIE: What line a' work do you follow, Martin?

MARTIN: Yard work mostly. Maintenance.

EDDIE: Oh, lawns and stuff?

MARTIN: Yeah.

EDDIE: You do lawns on your hands and knees?

MARTIN: Well—edging. You know, trimming around the edges.

EDDIE: Oh.

MARTIN: And weeding around the sprinkler heads. Stuff like that.

EDDIE: I get ya'.

MARTIN: But I've always noticed how much more relaxed I get when I'm down low to the ground like that.

EDDIE: Yeah. Well, you could get down on your hands and knees right now if you want to. I don't mind.

MARTIN: (*grins, gets embarrassed, looks at bathroom door*) Naw, I'll stand. Thanks.

EDDIE: Suit yourself. You're just gonna' get more and more tense.

(*Pause.*)

MARTIN: You're uh—May's cousin, huh?

EDDIE: See now, right there. Askin' me that. Right there. That's a result of tension. See what I mean?

MARTIN: What?

EDDIE: Askin' me if I'm her cousin. That's because you're tense you're askin' me that. You already know I'm not her cousin.

MARTIN: Well, how would I know that?

EDDIE: Do I look like her cousin.

MARTIN: Well, she said that you were.

EDDIE: (*grins*) She's lying.

(*Pause.*)

MARTIN: Well—what are you then?

EDDIE: (*laughs*) Now you're really gettin' tense, huh?

MARTIN: Look, maybe I should just go or something. I mean—

(MARTIN *makes a move to exit stage left.* EDDIE *rushes to stage-left door and beats* MARTIN *to it.* MARTIN *freezes, then runs to window upstage, opens it and tries to escape.* EDDIE *runs to him and catches him by the back of the pants, pulls him out of the window, slams him up against stage-right wall, then pulls him slowly down the wall as he speaks. They arrive at down-right corner.*)

EDDIE: No, no. Don't go, Martin. Don't go. You'll just get all blue and lonely out there in the black night. I know. I've wandered around lonely like that myself. Awful. Just eats away at ya'. (*he puts his arm around* MARTIN'S *shoulder and leads him to table down left*) Now just come on over here and sit down and we'll have us a little drink. Okay?

MARTIN: (*as he goes with* EDDIE) Uh—do you think she's okay in there?

EDDIE: Sure she's okay. She's always okay. She just likes to take her time. Just to torture you.

MARTIN: Well—we were supposed to go to the movies.

EDDIE: She'll be out. Don't worry about it. She likes the movies.

(*They sit at table, down left.* EDDIE *pulls out the down-right chair and seats* MARTIN *in it, then he goes to the upstage chair and sits so that he's now partially facing* THE OLD MAN. *Spot rises softly on* THE OLD MAN *but* MARTIN *does not acknowledge his presence. Stage lights stay the same.* MARTIN *sets his glass on table.* EDDIE *fills it up with the bottle.* THE OLD MAN'S *left arm slowly descends and reaches across the table holding out his empty Styrofoam cup for a drink.* EDDIE *looks* THE OLD MAN *in the eye for a second, then pours him a drink, too. All three of them drink.* EDDIE *takes his from the bottle.*)

MARTIN: What exactly's the matter with her anyway?

EDDIE: She's in a state a' shock.

(THE OLD MAN *chuckles to himself. Drinks.*)

MARTIN: Shock? How come?

EDDIE: Well, we haven't seen each other in a long time. I mean—me and her, we go back quite a ways, see. High school.

MARTIN: Oh. I didn't know that.

EDDIE: Yeah. Lotta' miles.

MARTIN: And you're not really cousins?

EDDIE: No. Not really. No.

MARTIN: You're—her husband?

EDDIE: No. She's my sister. (*he and* THE OLD MAN *look at each other, then he turns back to* MARTIN) My half-sister.

(*Pause.* EDDIE *and* THE OLD MAN *drink.*)

MARTIN: Your sister?

EDDIE: Yeah.

MARTIN: Oh. So—you knew each other even before high school then, huh?

EDDIE: No, see, I never even knew I had a sister until it was too late.

MARTIN: How do you mean?

EDDIE: Well, by the time I found out we'd already—you know—fooled around.

(THE OLD MAN *shakes his head, drinks. Long pause.* MARTIN *just stares at* EDDIE.)

EDDIE: (*grins*) Whatsa' matter, Martin?

MARTIN: You fooled around?

EDDIE: Yeah.

MARTIN: Well—um—that's illegal, isn't it?

EDDIE: I suppose so.

THE OLD MAN: (*to* EDDIE) Who is this guy?

MARTIN: I mean—is that true? She's really your sister?

EDDIE: Half. Only half.

MARTIN: Which half?

EDDIE: Top half. In horses we call that the "topside."

THE OLD MAN: Yeah, and the mare's what? The mare's uh—"distaff," isn't it? Isn't that the bottom half? "Distaff." Funny I should remember that.

MARTIN: And you fooled around in high school together?

EDDIE: Yeah. Sure. Everybody fooled around in high school. Didn't you?

MARTIN: No. I never did.

EDDIE: Maybe you should have, Martin.

MARTIN: Well, not with my sister.

EDDIE: No, I wouldn't recommend that.

MARTIN: How could that happen? I mean—

EDDIE: Well, see—(*pause, he stares at* THE OLD MAN)—our daddy fell in love twice. That's basically how it happened. Once with my mother and once with her mother.

THE OLD MAN: It was the same love. Just got split in two, that's all.

MARTIN: Well, how come you didn't know each other until high school then?

EDDIE: He had two separate lives. That's how come. Two completely separate lives. He'd live with me and my mother for a while and then he'd disappear and go live with her and her mother for a while.

THE OLD MAN: Now don't be too hard on me, boy. It can happen to the best of us.

MARTIN: And you never knew what was going on?

EDDIE: Nope. Neither did my mother.

THE OLD MAN: She knew.

EDDIE: (*to* MARTIN) She never knew.

MARTIN: She must've suspected something was going on.

EDDIE: Well, if she did she never let on to me. Maybe she was afraid of finding out. Or maybe she just loved him. I don't know. He'd disappear for months at a time and she never once asked him where he went. She was always glad to see him when he came back. The two of us used to go running out of the house to meet him as soon as we saw the Studebaker coming across the field.

THE OLD MAN: (*to* EDDIE) That was no Studebaker, that was a Plymouth. I never owned a goddamn Studebaker.

EDDIE: This went on for years. He kept disappearing and reappearing. For years that went on. Then, suddenly, one day it stopped. He stayed home for a while. Just stayed in the house. Never went outside. Just sat in his chair. Staring. Then he started going on these long walks. He'd walk all day. Then he'd walk all night. He'd walk out across the fields. In the dark. I used to watch him from my bedroom window. He'd disappear in the dark with his overcoat on.

MARTIN: Where was he going?

EDDIE: Just walking.

THE OLD MAN: I was making a decision.

(EDDIE *gets* MARTIN *to his feet and takes him on a walk around the entire stage as he tells the story.* MARTIN *is reluctant but* EDDIE *keeps pulling him along.*)

EDDIE: But one night I asked him if I could go with him. And he took me. We walked straight out across the fields together. In the dark. And I remember it was just plowed and our feet sank down in the powder and the dirt came up over the tops of my shoes and weighed me down. I wanted to stop and empty my shoes out but he wouldn't stop. He kept walking straight ahead and I was afraid of losing him in the dark so I just kept up as best I could. And we were completely silent the whole time. Never said a word to each other. We could barely see a foot in front of us, it was so dark. And these white owls kept swooping down out of nowhere, hunting for jackrabbits. Diving right past our heads, then disappearing. And we just kept walking silent like that for miles until we got to town. I could see the drive-in movie way off in the distance. That was the first thing I saw. Just square patches of color shifting. Then vague faces began to appear. And, as we got closer, I could recognize one of the faces. It was Spencer Tracy. Spencer Tracy moving his mouth. Speaking without words. Speaking to a woman in a red dress. Then we stopped at a liquor store and he made me wait outside in the parking lot while he bought a bottle. And there were all these Mexican migrant workers standing around a pickup truck with red mud all over the tires. They were drinking beer and laughing and I remember being jealous of them and I didn't know why. And I remember seeing the old man through the glass door of the liquor store as he paid for the bottle. And I remember feeling sorry for him and I didn't know why. Then he came outside with the bottle wrapped in a brown paper sack and as soon as he came out, all the Mexican men stopped laughing. They just stared at us as we walked away.

(*During the course of the story the lights shift down very slowly into blues and greens—moonlight.*)

EDDIE: And we walked right through town. Past the donut shop, past the miniature golf course, past the Chevron station. And he opened the bottle up and offered it to me. Before he even took a drink, he offered it to me first. And I took it and drank it and handed it back to him. And we just kept passing it back and forth like that as we walked until we drank the whole thing dry. And we never said a word the whole time. Then, finally, we reached this little white house with a red awning, on the far side of town. I'll never forget the red awning because it flapped in the night breeze and the porch light made it glow. It was a hot, desert breeze and the air smelled like new-cut alfalfa. We walked right up to the front porch and he rang the bell and I remember getting real nervous because I wasn't expecting to visit anybody. I thought we were just out for a walk. And then this woman comes to the door. This real pretty woman with red hair. And she throws herself into his arms. And he starts crying. He just breaks down right there in front of me. And she's kissing him all over the face and holding him real tight and he's just crying like a baby. And then through the doorway, behind them both, I see this girl.

(*The bathroom door very slowly and silently swings open revealing* MAY, *standing in the doorframe backlit with yellow light in her red dress. She just watches* EDDIE *as he keeps telling story. He and* MARTIN *are unaware of her presence.*)

EDDIE: She just appears. She's just standing there, staring at me and I'm staring back at her and we can't take our eyes off each other. It was like we knew each other from somewhere but we couldn't place where. But the second we saw each other, that very second, we knew we'd never stop being in love.

(MAY *slams bathroom door behind her. Door booms. Lights bang back up to their previous setting.*)

MAY: (*to* EDDIE) Boy, you really are incredible! You're unbelievable! Martin comes over here. He doesn't know you from Adam and you start telling him a story like that. Are you crazy? None of it's true, Martin. He's had this weird, sick idea for years now and it's totally made up. He's nuts. I don't know where he got it from. He's completely nuts.

EDDIE: (*to* MARTIN) She's kinda' embarrassed about the whole deal, see. You can't blame her really.

MARTIN: I didn't even know you could hear us out here, May. I—

MAY: I heard every word. I followed it very carefully. He's told me that story a thousand times and it always changes.

EDDIE: I never repeat myself.

MAY: You do nothing but repeat yourself. That's all you do. You just go in a big circle.

MARTIN: (*standing*) Well, maybe I should leave.

EDDIE: NO! You sit down.

(*Silence.* MARTIN *slowly sits again.*)

EDDIE: (*quietly to* MARTIN, *leaning toward him*) Did you think that was a story, Martin? Did you think I made that whole thing up?

MARTIN: No. I mean, at the time you were telling it, it seemed real.

EDDIE: But now you're doubting it because she says it's a lie?

MARTIN: Well—

EDDIE: She suggests it's a lie to you and all of a sudden you change your mind? Is that it? You go from true to false like that, in a second?

MARTIN: I don't know.

MAY: Let's go to the movies, Martin.

(MARTIN *stands again.*)

EDDIE: Sit down!

(MARTIN *sits back down. Long pause.*)

MAY: Eddie—

(*Pause.*)

EDDIE: What?

MAY: We want to go to the movies.

(*Pause.* EDDIE *just stares at her.*)

MAY: I want to go out to the movies with Martin. Right now.

EDDIE: Nobody's going to the movies. There's not a movie in this town that can match the story I'm gonna' tell. I'm gonna' finish this story.

MAY: Eddie—

EDDIE: You wanna' hear the rest of the story, don't ya', Martin?

MARTIN: (*pause. He looks at* MAY, *then back to* EDDIE) Sure.

MAY: Martin, let's go. Please.

MARTIN: I—

(*Long pause.* EDDIE *and* MARTIN *stare at each other.*)

EDDIE: You what?

MARTIN: I don't mind hearing the rest of it if you want to tell the rest of it.

THE OLD MAN: (*to himself*) I'm dyin' to hear it myself.

(EDDIE *leans back in his chair. Grins.*)

MAY: (*to* EDDIE) What do you think this is going to do? Do you think this is going to change something?

EDDIE: No.

MAY: Then what's the point?

EDDIE: It's absolutely pointless.

MAY: Then why put everybody through this. Martin doesn't want to hear this bullshit. *I* don't want to hear it.

EDDIE: I know *you* don't wanna' hear it.

MAY: Don't try to pass it off on me! You got it all turned around, Eddie. You got it all turned around. You don't even know which end is up anymore. Okay. Okay. I don't need either of you. I don't need any of it because I already know the rest of the story. I know the whole rest of the story, see. (*she speaks directly to* EDDIE, *who remains sitting*) I know it just exactly the way it happened. Without any little tricks added onto it.

(THE OLD MAN *leans over to* EDDIE, *confidentially.*)

THE OLD MAN: What does she know?

EDDIE: (*to* THE OLD MAN) She's lying.

(*Lights begin to shift down again in the course of* MAY'S *story. She moves very slowly downstage, then crosses toward* THE OLD MAN *as she tells it.*)

MAY: You want me to finish the story for you, Eddie? Huh? You want me to finish this story?

(*Pause as* MARTIN *sits again.*)

MAY: See, my mother—the pretty red-haired woman in the little white house with the red awning—was desperately in love with the old man. Wasn't she, Eddie? You could tell that right away.

You could see it in her eyes. She was obsessed with him to the point where she couldn't stand being without him for even a second. She kept hunting for him from town to town. Following little clues that he left behind, like a postcard maybe, or a motel on the back of a matchbook. (*to* MARTIN) He never left her a phone number or an address or anything as simple as that because my mother was his secret, see. She hounded him for years and he kept trying to keep her at a distance because the closer these two separate lives drew together, these two separate women, these two separate kids, the more nervous he got. The more filled with terror that the two lives would find out about each other and devour him whole. That his secret would take him by the throat. But finally she caught up with him. Just by a process of elimination she dogged him down. I remember the day we discovered the town. She was on fire. "This is it!" she kept saying; "this is the place!" Her whole body was trembling as we walked through the streets, looking for the house where he lived. She kept squeezing my hand to the point where I thought she'd crush the bones in my fingers. She was terrified she'd come across him by accident on the street because she knew she was trespassing. She knew she was crossing this forbidden zone but she couldn't help herself. We walked all day through that stupid hick town. All day long. We went through every neighborhood, peering through every open window, looking in at every dumb family, until finally we found him.

(*Rest.*)

It was just exactly suppertime and they were all sitting down at the table and they were having fried chicken. That's how close we were to the window. We could see what they were eating. We could hear their voices but we couldn't make out what they were saying. Eddie and his mother were talking but the old man never said a word. Did he, Eddie? Just sat there eating his chicken in silence.

THE OLD MAN: (*to* EDDIE) Boy, is she ever off the wall with this one. You gotta' do somethin' about this.

MAY: The funny thing was, that almost as soon as we'd found him—he disappeared. She was only with him about two weeks before he just vanished. Nobody saw him after that. Ever. And my mother—just turned herself inside out. I never could understand that. I kept watching her grieve, as though somebody'd died. She'd pull herself up into a ball and just stare at the floor.

And I couldn't understand that because I was feeling the exact opposite feeling. I was in love, see. I'd come home after school, after being with Eddie, and I was filled with this joy and there she'd be—standing in the middle of the kitchen staring at the sink. Her eyes looked like a funeral. And I didn't know what to say. I didn't even feel sorry for her. All I could think of was him.

THE OLD MAN: (*to* EDDIE) She's gettin' way outa' line, here.

MAY: And all he could think of was me. Isn't that right, Eddie. We couldn't take a breath without thinking of each other. We couldn't eat if we weren't together. We couldn't sleep. We got sick at night when we were apart. Violently sick. And my mother even took me to see a doctor. And Eddie's mother took him to see the same doctor but the doctor had no idea what was wrong with us. He thought it was the flu or something. And Eddie's mother had no idea what was wrong with him. But my mother—my mother knew exactly what was wrong. She knew it clear down to her bones. She recognized every symptom. And she begged me not to see him but I wouldn't listen. Then she begged Eddie not to see me but he wouldn't listen. Then she went to Eddie's mother and begged her. And Eddie's mother—(*pause. She looks straight at* EDDIE)—Eddie's mother blew her brains out. Didn't she, Eddie? Blew her brains right out.

THE OLD MAN: (*standing. He moves from the platform onto the stage, between* EDDIE *and* MAY) Now, wait a second! Wait a second. Just a goddamn second here. This story doesn't hold water. (*To* EDDIE, *who stays seated*) You're not gonna' let her off the hook with that one are ya'? That's the dumbest version I ever heard in my whole life. She never blew her brains out. Nobody ever told me that. Where the hell did that come from? (*to* EDDIE, *who remains seated*) Stand up! Get on yer feet now goddammit! I wanna' hear the male side a' this thing. You gotta' represent me now. Speak on my behalf. There's no one to speak for me now! Stand up!

(EDDIE *stands slowly. Stares at* THE OLD MAN.)

THE OLD MAN: Now tell her. Tell her the way it happened. We've got a pact. Don't forget that.

EDDIE: (*calmly to* THE OLD MAN) It was your shotgun. Same one we used to duck-hunt with. Browning. She never fired a gun before in her life. That was her first time.

THE OLD MAN: Nobody told me any a' that. I was left completely in the dark.

EDDIE: You were gone.

THE OLD MAN: Somebody could've found me! Somebody could've hunted me down. I wasn't that impossible to find.

EDDIE: You were gone.

THE OLD MAN: That's right, I was gone! I was gone. You're right. But I wasn't disconnected. There was nothing cut off in me. Everything went on just the same as though I'd never left. (*to* MAY) But *your* mother—your mother wouldn't give it up, would she?

(THE OLD MAN *moves toward* MAY *and speaks directly to her.* MAY *keeps her eyes on* EDDIE, *who very slowly turns toward her in the course of* THE OLD MAN'S *speech. Once their eyes meet they never leave each other's gaze.*)

THE OLD MAN: (*to* MAY) She drew me to her. She went out of her way to draw me in. She was a force. I told her I'd never come across for her. I told her that right from the very start. But she opened up to me. She wouldn't listen. She kept opening up her heart to me. How could I turn her down when she loved me like that? How could I turn away from her? We were completely whole.

(EDDIE *and* MAY *just stand there staring at each other.* THE OLD MAN *moves back to* EDDIE. *Speaks to him directly.*)

THE OLD MAN: (*to* EDDIE) What're you doin'? Speak to her. Bring her around to our side. You gotta' make her see this thing in a clear light.

(*Very slowly* EDDIE *and* MAY *move toward each other.*)

THE OLD MAN: (*to* EDDIE) Stay away from her! What the hell are you doin'? Keep away from her! You two can't come together! You gotta' hold up my end a' this deal. I got nobody now! Nobody! You can't betray me! You gotta' represent me now! You're my son!

(EDDIE *and* MAY *come together center stage. They embrace. They kiss each other tenderly. Headlights suddenly arc across stage again from up right, cutting across the stage through window, then disappearing off left. Sound of loud collision, shattering glass, an explosion. Bright orange and blue light of a gasoline fire suddenly illuminates upstage window. Then sounds of horses screaming wildly, hooves galloping on pavement, fading, then total silence. Light of gas fire continues now to end of play.*

EDDIE *and* MAY *never stop holding each other through all this. Long pause. No one moves. Then* MARTIN *stands and moves upstage to window, peers out through Venetian blinds. Pause.*)

MARTIN: (*upstage at window, looking out into flames*) Is that your truck with the horse trailer out there?
EDDIE: (*stays with* MAY) Yeah.
MARTIN: It's on fire.
EDDIE: Yeah.
MARTIN: All the horses are loose.
EDDIE: (*steps back away from* MAY) Yeah, I figured.
MAY: Eddie—
EDDIE: (*to* MAY) I'm just gonna' go out and take a look. I gotta' at least take a look, don't I?
MAY: What difference does it make?
EDDIE: Well, I can't just let her get away with that. What am I supposed to do? (*moves toward stage-left door*) I'll just be a second.
MAY: Eddie—
EDDIE: I'm only gonna' be a second. I'll just take a look at it and I'll come right back. Okay?

(EDDIE *exits stage-left door.* MAY *stares at door, stays where she is.* MARTIN *stays upstage.* MARTIN *turns slowly from window upstage and looks at* MAY. *Pause.* MAY *moves to bed, pulls suitcase out from underneath, throws it on bed and opens it. She goes into bathroom and comes out with clothes. She packs the clothes in suitcase.* MARTIN *watches her for a while, then moves slowly downstage to her as she continues.*)

MARTIN: May—

(MAY *goes back into bathroom and comes back out with more clothes. She packs them.*)

MARTIN: Do you need some help or anything? I got a car. I could drive you somewhere if you want. (*pause.* MAY *just keeps packing her clothes*) Are you going to go with him?

(*She stops. Straightens up. Stares at* MARTIN. *Pause.*)

MAY: He's gone.
MARTIN: He said he'd be back in a second.
MAY: (*pause*) He's gone.

(MAY *exits with suitcase out stage-left door. She leaves the door open behind her.* MARTIN *just stands there staring at open door for a while.* THE OLD MAN *looks stage left at his rocking chair, then a little above it, in blank space. Pause.* THE OLD MAN *starts moving slowly back to platform.*)

THE OLD MAN: (*pointing into space, stage left*) Ya' see that picture over there? Ya' see that? Ya' know who that is? That's the woman of my dreams. That's who that is. And she's mine. She's all mine. Forever.

(*He reaches rocking chair, sits, but keeps staring at imaginary picture. He begins to rock very slowly in the chair. After* THE OLD MAN *sits in rocker, Merle Haggard's "I'm the One Who Loves You" starts playing as lights begin a very slow fade.* MARTIN *moves slowly upstage to window and stops. He stares out with his back to audience. The fire glows through window as stage lights fade.* OLD MAN *keeps rocking slowly. Stage lights keep fading slowly to black. Fire glows for a while in the dark, then cuts to black. Song continues in dark and swells in volume.*)

ANGEL CITY

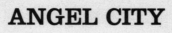

Angel City was first produced at the Magic Theatre, San Francisco, on July 2, 1976. It was directed by the author, with the following cast:

LANX:	Jack Thiebeau
WHEELER:	John Nesci
MISS SCOONS:	O-Lan Shepard
RABBIT:	Ebie Roe Smith
TYMPANI:	James Dean
SAX:	Bob Feldman

Original music composed and performed by Bob Feldman.

Note on the Music:

The dominant theme for the saxophone is the kind of lyrical loneliness of Lester Young's playing, occasionally exploding into Charlie Parker and Ornette Coleman. The musician should be free to explore his own sound within that general jazz structure and may find other places in the script, not indicated in the stage directions, to heighten or color the action. The saxophonist should remain cut off from the other characters in the play, even when he appears on stage. His presence is felt as a shadow to the other actors. His playing remains aloof and above the chaos for the most part. At moments when it does become chaotic it tends to explode right through the action and out the other side.

The actor who plays Tympani should either know how to play drums or at least be able to carry out some basic rhythm patterns without falling apart. Ideally his musicianship should be on the same level as the saxophonist's.

It might be useful for the musicians to listen to some of the recordings of Japanese theater to hear how the actor's voice is used in conjunction with the instruments—especially in the Act 2 contest between the generals.

Note to the Actors:

The term "character" could be thought of in a different way when working on this play. Instead of the idea of a "whole character" with logical motives behind his behavior which the actor submerges himself into, he should consider instead a fractured whole with bits and pieces of character flying off the central theme. In other words, more in terms of collage construction or jazz improvisation. This is not the same thing as one actor playing many different roles, each one distinct from the other (or "doubling up" as they call it), but more that he's mixing many different underlying elements and connecting them through his intuition and senses to make a kind of music or painting in space without having to feel the need to completely answer intellectually for the character's behavior. If there needs to be a "motivation" for some of the abrupt changes which occur in the play they can be taken as full-blown manifestations of a passing thought or fantasy, having as much significance or "meaning" as they do in our ordinary lives. The only difference is that here the actor makes note of it and brings it to life in three dimensions.

ACT 1

SCENE: *Basically bare stage. Upstage center is a large suspended blue neon rectangle with empty space in the middle. The rectangle is lit from time to time. Behind the rectangle the upstage wall is covered by a scrim which can be backlit in different colors. Upstage, directly behind the rectangle, is a narrow platform, raised about two feet above the stage floor and running horizontally the width of the stage. When the actors enter on this platform they become framed by the rectangle. Directly center, in front of the rectangle, is a large black swivel chair with the back of it facing the audience. The back is high enough to conceal whoever is sitting in it. There is a hand-held microphone attached to one arm of the chair which is used to amplify the narration sequences. There are two copper tympani drums placed at the very edge of the stage in the down-left corner. As the audience enters, the stage is set like this with the rectangle unlit and no color in the scrim. Lights go to black.* LANX *and* TYMPANI *enter in blackout.* LANX *seats himself in the swivel chair with the back still facing audience so he's unseen.* TYMPANI *stands facing audience behind the two drums and begins to play a slowly rising drum roll in the dark. The drumming rises in volume. The blue rectangle is lit with the rest of the stage dark. The drumming rises slowly, and with it the scrim slowly turns a pale yellow with the stage lighting still dark.* TYMPANI'S *form begins to be made out in the light. He is dressed in an English working-class cap, white T-shirt, suspenders, baggy pants and heavy construction boots. He is playing the drums with mallet type sticks. His expression is very serious as he watches the audience as he plays. Slowly yellow light begins to fill the stage area as* TYMPANI *begins to reach a thundering pitch on the drums. The drumming and light reach their*

63

full intensity. Suddenly TYMPANI *stops playing, and makes a short bow to the audience and exits left.* LANX *begins to speak immediately from the chair over the microphone. Still unseen.*

LANX: (*as though reading from a script*) "It's a great office. A great window. A great life. All hell passes before me, and I can watch it like a junkie. With no pain." (*flatly, as though contained in the speech*) Yes, come in.

(RABBIT BROWN *enters from right.* LANX *goes on talking, still unseen.* RABBIT *is dressed in a tattered detective's type suit and overcoat, hat and tennis shoes. He seems fatigued. He has bundles of various sizes attached to him by long leather thongs and dragging on the floor behind him. He makes his way to center stage and stops. He scans the space for the source of* LANX'S *voice.*

LANX: "From the blackest black to the lightest light. It's all happening. The amazing thing to me is that despite its desolate appearance, the city teems with living things. Things crawl across upholstered seats. Deals are made in remote glove compartments. And we exist, here, walled in. A booming industry. Self-sufficient. Grossing fifty million in just two weeks. Our own private police. Our own private food. Lawyers, doctors, technical staff, a laboratory of the highest caliber." Help yourself to anything. I'll be with you when the time comes.

(RABBIT *looks around the space for something to help himself to but finds nothing. He tries to locate the voice as* LANX *rambles on, getting more intense. Sax could be used underneath some of this.*)

LANX: "Outside, the smog strikes clean to the heart. Babies' eyes bleed from it. Paint blisters from it. Grown men keel over. Dogs go paralyzed. Used-car lots melt away into the black macadam. The Tar Pits squirm with animal life. And all along through the terrifying shopping centers the doom merchants whisper our fate. They hide behind the grape counters twisting their bony faces at us. Pointing their narrow hands and marking our death as though they themselves stood somehow out of time and judged us from eternity. Even so, it would seem that, after all these years, after all these plagues and holocausts, the city is finally being rebuilt."

(*The voice stops.* LANX *whirls the chair around facing front. He is short and powerfully built with his hair greased straight back, dark glasses,*

*black suit and shoes, starched white shirt with a high collar, gold cuff
links which he's constantly snapping and adjusting, a ball point pen
which he clicks continuously. In his lap he holds a few sheets of paper.
He puffs and chews violently on a huge cigar and cracks his knuckles.*
RABBIT *looks at him nervously.* LANX *just stares at him for a while.*)

LANX: So, as pure narration, what do you think of it?

RABBIT: (*looking around*) You're asking me?

LANX: You're the Rabbit aren't ya'?

(RABBIT *nods.*)

LANX: So, it's you I'm askin'. What do ya' think?

RABBIT: Terrible. Old time.

LANX: Exactly!

(LANX *rips the papers into shreds and then sits on them.*)

RABBIT: Worse than Jack Webb I'd say.

LANX: Very good, very smart. That's enough now. Shut up.

RABBIT: Did you write it?

LANX: No, I didn't write it! What do you think I am! What kind of
a question is that!

RABBIT: Sorry.

LANX: Don't apologize. And wet your lips.

RABBIT: What?

LANX: Your lips! Wet them! Run your tongue around the outside.

(RABBIT *does it.*)

LANX: That's better. What've you been, out in the elements or
something?

RABBIT: It's the smog.

LANX: Right. We don't get smog in here. You'll notice that.

RABBIT: Yeah.

LANX: We don't tolerate it in here. Out there, yes. (*indicating
toward rectangle*) It's necessary. But in here, no.

RABBIT: Right. It's very nice the way you've got it controlled.

LANX: Well, it's either we control it or it controls us. You know
what I mean? (*short tense laugh*)

RABBIT: Yeah.

LANX: (*suddenly serious*) So, you don't fly, huh?

RABBIT: No, I rode the buckboard down. I got a team a' horses.
Stopped off at all the missions.

LANX: The missions? What for? Missions are stupid.

RABBIT: To pray.

LANX: You stopped and prayed on the way down?

RABBIT: Yeah.

LANX: You stopped at all the missions?

RABBIT: Right.

LANX: Terrific. Well, it woulda' been faster a' course if you'd a' flown down. That's gonna' be a problem. I mean time-wise and money-wise.

RABBIT: Well, I don't fly.

LANX: That's what I understand. You don't have to repeat what I already understand. Would you like a drink or something?

RABBIT: No.

LANX: A chair? Would you like a chair? It's my job to offer things. To make offers.

RABBIT: Yeah, I wouldn't mind a chair.

LANX: (*bellowing off left*) MISS SCOONS! COULD WE HAVE A CHAIR IN HERE RIGHT AWAY! (*to* RABBIT, *confidentially*) What are these items you have tied to yourself?

(MISS SCOONS *enters from left. Very sexy. Short dress, high heels, typical secretary type. She carries a chair on her back, sets it downstage left and exits left again.*)

RABBIT: (*to* LANX *but watching* MISS SCOONS) Oh, these are different bundles. Some of them are medicine bundles and some are just practical bundles.

LANX: Well, which is which? I'm not a mind reader.

RABBIT: (*picking up one of the bundles which looks like a weasel carcass*) Well, you see this one? This one's particularly magical. It's a power bundle. Extremely dangerous. It was stolen from a museum.

(RABBIT *sits in the chair which* MISS SCOONS *brought.* LANX *moves down right, puffing clouds of smoke, clicking his pen, snapping his cuffs, etc.*)

LANX: I see. Well, let's get down to brass tacks shall we? I mean, in my book a bundle's a bundle. To cut it short, my partner, Wheeler, and I are in kind of a jam. A little bit of a fix. We've got ourselves in over our heads in this one particular project and uh—we're looking for an ace in the hole.

RABBIT: (*dropping the weasel bundle to the floor*) How far in have you got yourselves?

LANX: Well, in round figures let's call it eight million. But that's neither here nor there. The point is we need a slight miracle to boost us out, and we heard through the grapevine that you were the doctor.

RABBIT: That's right.

LANX: Of course, I myself, personally, have never even heard of you, but your reputation seems to be widespread in the areas where we're dependent. If you catch my drift?

RABBIT: I do.

LANX: Very sharp. Now try to stick close to my next line of reasoning.

RABBIT: Uh—I think I would like something to drink.

LANX: (*pausing, staring hard at* RABBIT, *then yelling for* MISS SCOONS) MISS SCOONS! A GLASS OF WATER PLEASE!

RABBIT: Thanks.

LANX: That's quite all right. Basically, you'll find that it's better to be direct around here. If you want something you say so. If you don't want something you don't say so. Simple as that.

RABBIT: Right.

(MISS SCOONS *enters again slowly from left balancing a glass of water on the back of her hand. She gives it to* RABBIT, *who takes it off her hand, then she exits.* LANX *continues talking through this.*)

LANX: Now, essentially, what's missing at the heart of the material is a meaningful character.

RABBIT: That's pretty basic, isn't it?

LANX: Well, yes. But that's why we're considering this a state of emergency. I mean, after all we wouldn't have called someone in of your particular ilk if all we needed was a scriptwriter.

RABBIT: Oh.

LANX: I mean you're not just that are you? You're not just another ordinary hack. You're supposed to be an artist, right?

RABBIT: Right.

LANX: A kind of magician or something.

RABBIT: Something like that.

LANX: You dream things up.

RABBIT: Right.

LANX: Right. So what we need in this case is a three-dimensional invention. Something altogether unheard of before. We have the story, the plot, the stars, the situation, but what's missing is this uh—this development. Something awesome and totally new.

RABBIT: I see.

LANX: It has to somehow transcend the very idea of "character" as we know it today.

RABBIT: Well, that's a big order.

LANX: Exactly! We're prepared to pay through the teeth, of course. I mean we're already over the budget, so what the hell. (*short laugh*)

RABBIT: Have you tried holographs or whatever they're called?

LANX: No, no! You don't get the picture. We're looking for an actual miracle. Nothing technological. The real thing.

RABBIT: A miracle.

LANX: That's right! Right here in Culver City.

RABBIT: Well, I've never exactly worked on a case like this before. I mean you want some "thing" to make an actual appearance in the middle of your movie?

LANX: SHHHH! Not so goddamn loud! The air has ears around here. There's spies all over the place.

RABBIT: (*whispering*) But that's the general idea, right?

LANX: (*whispering*) Exactly.

RABBIT: (*whisper*) A kind of an apparition?

LANX: Well, I don't want to explain your business to you. I mean you could call it whatever you want. All I know is that in order to pull this budget out of the hole we've got to have something happen that's never ever happened before. Something unearthly.

RABBIT: Well, I don't know. I mean I'll have to have a lot more information before I can take something like this on. I mean I'll have to know the story, who the other characters are, the plot. All that kinda' stuff.

LANX: Sure, sure. I'll get Wheeler in here right away. He's the backbone of the whole project. You just take it easy for a second. I'll be right back. He'll fill you in on all the details.

(LANX *exits quickly off right leaving* RABBIT *alone. Slow lurking music from the saxophone is heard from offstage. Stage lights dim slightly. Scrim turns pale green. Rectangle lights up blue.* RABBIT *stands and gathers the bundles around him. He starts arranging them in a large circle around him as he talks directly to the audience. Sax continues underneath.*)

RABBIT: (*to audience*) I make an adjustment. I'm basically geared in the old forms. Pre-bop, Lester Young, Roscoe Holcombe. I could run a list of hip references to make your tail swim. I've connived in the deepest cracks of the underground. Rubbed knuckles with the nastiest poets. Done the "Rocky Mountain Back Step" in places where they've outlawed bubble gum. But that's neither here nor there.

(*The* SAXOPHONE PLAYER *enters from up left on the platform playing his horn. He crosses slowly into the space behind the rectangle so that he's framed in the blue neon light with the green scrim behind him. The stage lighting continues to dim. Sax plays slow and mournful.*)

RABBIT: (*continuing*) The point is I've smelled something down here. Something sending its sweet claws way up North. Interrupting my campfires. Making me daydream at night. Causing me to wonder at the life of a recluse. The vision of a celluloid tape with a series of moving images telling a story to millions. Millions anywhere. Millions seen and unseen. Millions seeing the same story without ever knowing each other. Without even having to be together. Effecting their dreams and actions. Replacing their books. Replacing their families. Replacing religion, politics, art, conversation. Replacing their minds. And I ask myself, how can I stay immune? How can I keep my distance from a machine like that? So I wind up here, in the city of the South. Not knowing a thing but convincing them through mysterious gestures that I'm their main man. (*he hears* LANX *coming; secretly to audience*) I'm ravenous for power but I have to conceal it.

(LANX *enters fast from right with* WHEELER. *The lights go out behind scrim and rectangle goes out. Stage lights back up.* LANX *chases the* SAXOPHONE PLAYER, *who exits at a run off left.* LANX *is yelling at him as* WHEELER *stands sheepishly to stage right.* WHEELER *wears a bow tie, glasses, short-sleeved shirt, white and brown brogans, and holds a golf club which he's constantly turning in his hand. His whole manner is shy and intimidated.*)

LANX: (*to* SAXOPHONE) GET OUTA' HERE YOU CREEP! GET AWAY FROM THE WINDOW! I'VE TOLD YOU A HUNDRED TIMES I CAN'T STAND THAT SOUND! YOU'RE GONNA' CRACK MY WINDOW! (*turning back to* RABBIT *after* SAX *exits*) Continuously trying to reverberate us into the past with that solo crap. When will these guys wake up? Oh, uh—this is Wheeler, my partner. Rabbit Brown.

WHEELER: (*stepping toward* RABBIT *shyly, offering his hand*) How do you do.

(RABBIT *just stares at his hand but doesn't shake.*)

WHEELER: I'm afraid this is all my fault in a way. I'm very sorry for having to bring you down all this way.

LANX: (*to* WHEELER) Now don't start apologizing right off the bat. We haven't even made a deal yet. (*laughs nervously to* RABBIT)

WHEELER: (*to* LANX) I'm sorry.

LANX: (*to* RABBIT) He's new to the business even though he is a genius. Wishy-washy. Spineless. Came up through the cutting rooms. We gotta' just work around him. Take it as a necessary handicap.

RABBIT: I'm a little confused.

LANX: You look confused. But don't worry. Looks are deceiving. That's one a' the first things you learn around here. Nothing is the way it appears to be. In fact, very often, it's the opposite.

RABBIT: I see.

LANX: No you don't. But don't worry.

RABBIT: What is it exactly that you're looking for?

WHEELER: Well, we don't know exactly. We have a hunch. We have a feeling. But we don't know for sure.

LANX: Exactly. I thought I made that clear before. We have an idea that this town is ripe for another disaster.

RABBIT: (*pause*) Disaster?

WHEELER: Cinematically speaking. (*nervous laugh*)

LANX: In the profit sense of the word of course. A disaster on the screen, not in the box office. (*laughs*)

WHEELER: Yes. You see, all of the really major box-office smashes have dealt with disaster to one degree or another. Either a disaster is about to happen, it's already happened, or it's actually taking place right now.

RABBIT: Right now?

WHEELER: In the movie. Right now in the movie.

RABBIT: Oh.

WHEELER: We have come to believe that it's only through a major disaster being interjected into this picture that we'll be able to save ourselves from total annihilation.

RABBIT: You mean financial?

WHEELER: (*suddenly serious*) And otherwise. Have you taken a look out the window? (*gestures toward rectangle*)

(RABBIT *looks toward the rectangle then back to* WHEELER *without understanding his point.*)

RABBIT: I don't get ya'.

WHEELER: (*to* LANX, *amazed*) Hasn't he looked out the window yet?

LANX: Well, he's just traveled the full length of California by buckboard, stopping off at all the missions on the way down. I assumed that he knows.

RABBIT: What's going on anyway? There's nothing but a city out there.

WHEELER: The city is eating us alive. Can't you see my skin? Look at my skin.

(WHEELER *steps close to* RABBIT, *holding out his arm.* RABBIT *inspects the skin on* WHEELER'S *arm.* LANX *stands by, puffing and clicking his pen.*)

WHEELER: It's turning us into snakes or lizards or something. Can't you feel that? We need protection.

RABBIT: Oh. (*steps back away from* WHEELER)

LANX: What we're getting at here, Brown, is that we're desperate for a device. We need something which is the next step forward. A step beyond the usual, if you get my meaning.

WHEELER: (*sudden intense secrecy*) That's right. Not simply an act of terror but something which will in fact drive people right off the deep end. Leave them blithering in the aisles. Create mass hypnosis. Suicide. Autodestruction. Something which will open entirely new fads in sadomasochism. Penetrating every layer of their dark subconscious and leaving them totally unrecognizable to themselves. Something which not only mirrors their own sense of doom but actually creates the possibility of it right there in front of them. That's what the people are crying out for and that's what we must give them. It's our duty. We owe it to the public. For without the public we are nothing but a part of that public. We must stand apart, on another plane. We must rise to the challenge. We must help them devour themselves or be devoured by them. The time is ripe for this obliteration. We must rise to the occasion or be lost forever in a tidal wave of oblivion!

RABBIT: Now hold on a second, man. This sounds like something totally out of my ball park. I mean, I'm a stunt man. I fall off horses. I've done some sleight of hand. I've conjured a little bit. I collect a few myths, but this sounds like you need a chemical expert or something.

LANX: Exactly! A chemical expert. Very well put. Now we've prepared this room especially for your needs. You'll have two assistants and, of course, Miss Scoons will be at your complete disposal.

RABBIT: Wait a second!

WHEELER: We'll be checking in from time to time to see how you're coming along. Of course we don't want to interfere with the creative process but we do need to protect our investment.

RABBIT: What investment! I haven't cost you a thing yet!

LANX: There is, of course, a time element involved.

WHEELER: Yes. (*coldly*) If, by the end of the week you haven't come up with anything useful your entire motor functioning will cease to be a private concern. You can see what it's like outside, Brown. You can see what it's doing to us. You can help stop it. It's up to all of us to stop it before it's too late.

(*They both exit left, leaving* RABBIT *alone. He stares around the space numbly. Lights dim slightly.* TYMPANI *enters abruptly from left with his drumsticks and stands behind the drums. He looks at* RABBIT. *They are silent for a while.*)

RABBIT: (*to* TYMPANI) Are you in on this?

TYMPANI: (*facing front*) "It's a great office. A great window. A great life."

RABBIT: Aw, knock it off!

TYMPANI: (*blankly*) "The city thunders with the hollow moan of despair."

RABBIT: Have they got you working on something too? (*no answer from* TYMPANI) What's your position, if you don't mind my asking?

TYMPANI: I play drums.

RABBIT: I get it. I thought it might be more complicated than that.

TYMPANI: They have a theory about rhythm.

RABBIT: I was right.

TYMPANI: I'm experimenting with various rhythm structures in the hope of discovering one which will be guaranteed to produce certain trance states in masses of people.

RABBIT: Have you found it?

TYMPANI: Not yet. I've been here several months now. They take care of me though. I get everything I need here. It's not a bad life.

RABBIT: So we're in the same boat.

TYMPANI: (*matter of factly*) No. I'm above you. You're below me.

(RABBIT *studies* TYMPANI *for a second.*)

RABBIT: Who else have they got here?

TYMPANI: All kinds. I'm not allowed to talk about it. They all like it here, though. We're well paid. Nobody complains.

RABBIT: What about the saxophone player?

TYMPANI: Lanx hates him. The guy wants in on the action, but Lanx can't stand him. Says he belongs in the wax museum.

RABBIT: Have you tried to escape?

TYMPANI: What for? You know what it's like out there. In here we're well protected. Nothing can touch us. Besides, I love the movies. I'm proud to be a part of the industry.

RABBIT: You're a sap.

TYMPANI: (*coldly*) Don't talk nasty or I'll break your back. Nobody talks nasty in here. We all get along. We eat Louis B. Mayer's chicken soup every day. It's a tradition. Louis is dead but his soup lives on.

RABBIT: I'm gettin' outa' here! (*starts to leave, then stops*)

TYMPANI: You won't go far. They've already busted up your buckboard and sold your horses. On foot you're as good as dead in this town. They'll swallow you whole and spit you out as a tax deduction.

RABBIT: Listen, I didn't ask for this! They called me in for consultation! That's all! That's as far as it went!

TYMPANI: Well, things happen fast down here. You gotta' be prepared. One day you're raising chickens, the next day you're buying up half of Mexico. (*he clucks like a chicken*)

RABBIT: I don't want half of Mexico!

TYMPANI: Then you'll want something else. Sooner or later you'll want something, and they'll find out what it is.

RABBIT: What do you mean?

TYMPANI: Some little fantasy. Some dream. Some tiny little delusion that you've got tucked away. They'll pry it out of you.

RABBIT: What do they care?

TYMPANI: Because then they've got you. They'll feed off your hunger. They'll keep you jumping at carrots. And you'll keep jumping. And you'll keep thinking you're not jumping all the time you're jumping.

RABBIT: Is that what's happened to you?

TYMPANI: What does it look like?

RABBIT: Well, how can you know it and still keep doing it?

TYMPANI: What else is there to do?

RABBIT: Are you crazy? They've got you kidnapped in here and you like it.

TYMPANI: So will you. You'd be surprised how fast it happens.

RABBIT: Listen, Mack, no matter how many greasy skinbags think the city's turning them into snakes it's still better out there than it is in here!

TYMPANI: Then why don't you leave? You can walk out easy enough.

(RABBIT *considers a second. Suddenly stage lights dim sharply. Rectangle lights. Scrim turns deep blue. Saxophone comes in slow, heard offstage.* MISS SCOONS *appears from up left on the platform reading from a notepaper and crosses slowly behind the rectangle so that she's framed by it.* TYMPANI *fills in on the drums as* RABBIT *watches her.*)

MISS SCOONS: (*overly dramatic*) "No more pain, she cried, as they lowered half the bleeding city into a deep dark hole and covered it over with smoking rubber tires. She slowly became aware of the truth behind the power of money. The very thing she had desperately tried to avoid all these long months as she shuffled aimlessly up and down the length and breadth of the City of Angels with a toothpick in her hand. Now it stood before her. Glaring down like some awesome demented saint. Its teeth chattering through rusted-out alleyways. Its breath blowing lasciviously at her gingham skirt. All innocence was now behind her. All dreams of the life of man free and unfettered as she once knew it was on the plains of Nebraska. Here was the hard-core cement. The concrete reality of the dreaming-machine. The terrifying destruction which faced her head-on was now met by her own indivisible courage which she felt welling up from some deep primeval source which she knew not of. Suddenly the solution was clear. In her mind's eye was a simple equation. It appeared like a flashlight in a hooker's nightmare. 'Money equals power, equals protection, equals eternal life.' And with that she collapsed at the foot of La Cienaga."

(*Sax stops, drums stop, stage lights back up. Special lights out.* MISS SCOONS *stands on the platform smiling down at* RABBIT, *who stares at her in disbelief.*)

RABBIT: What was that?

MISS SCOONS: (*jumping down from platform*) Something I cooked up at the commissary during my lunch break. What do ya' think?

RABBIT: Great stuff. Really great.

MISS SCOONS: Really? You think it'll sell?

RABBIT: Positive.

MISS SCOONS: What did you think of it, Tympani?

TYMPANI: It's all right. A little wordy maybe.

MISS SCOONS: That's what I was thinking. Sort of too much showing off. Too many big words maybe.

RABBIT: No, I don't think so. In fact, on the whole I think it showed a remarkable economy of language.

MISS SCOONS: Gee, thanks.

TYMPANI: You mean like, ". . . some deep primeval source which she knew not of"?

RABBIT: Well, that was a little sticky in that area, but otherwise I thought it was surprisingly original.

MISS SCOONS: Well, it is based on my own experience.

RABBIT: I could tell. It had that kind of a ring.

MISS SCOONS: Do you think I oughta' present it at the next tribunal?

RABBIT: Sure, why not.

TYMPANI: Are you kidding?

MISS SCOONS: No, I'm not kidding, as a matter of fact. I wanna' advance my position. I can't remain a secretary forever.

TYMPANI: You show up with that kinda' crap they're gonna' cut you right back to part-time lab duty. That stuff is strictly third rate.

MISS SCOONS: What do you know, beef sticks! You can't even come up with a simple thing like an original rhythm.

TYMPANI: All I know is that you'll never get to third base with that kinda' drivel. That went out with Raymond Chandler.

RABBIT: Yeah, he's right. Ayn Rand sorta' did it to death too.

MISS SCOONS: That's the trouble, ya' know.

RABBIT: What?

MISS SCOONS: Nobody knows what's good. Everybody's too easily swayed. One minute it's great, the next minute it's garbage. You have to just go on your own intuition. (*suddenly noticing* RABBIT'S *bundles*) What are these things you have tied to yourself anyway? Nobody's ever showed up here with things tied to them like that before.

RABBIT: I'm working on something for the big fellas. Special project.

(RABBIT *and* TYMPANI *exchange looks*.)

MISS SCOONS: Really? You need any help?

RABBIT: Well, yeah. Sure. I mean I don't know exactly what it is I'm doing yet, but I sure could use some help.

TYMPANI: Nobody helped me when I was in a jam.

MISS SCOONS: When were you in a jam?

TYMPANI: The day I arrived. I was just like him when I first got here, and nobody helped me.

RABBIT: Well, I'll help ya'. We can all help each other.

TYMPANI: Too late.

MISS SCOONS: That's for sure in your case.

TYMPANI: (*to* MISS SCOONS) At least I have a firm position. A title.

MISS SCOONS: Yeah, "Frozen in the Act of Creation."

RABBIT: Listen, I'm not sure if I can accurately assess the danger that we're in here, but I have a feeling we oughta' come up with something fast. I mean these guys are desperate. One of 'em's skin is crawling.

(TYMPANI *smiles at* RABBIT, *satisfied that he's swallowed the bait.*)

MISS SCOONS: Yeah, that's what I been saying all along. We should try to put our heads together and work as a team.

RABBIT: I mean they even threatened me. Did they ever threaten you?

MISS SCOONS: Oh yeah, every once in a while. It's sort of part of their whole approach.

RABBIT: I mean, didn't you uh—get scared or anything?

MISS SCOONS: Scared? What for? They're just crazy, that's all. Nothin' to worry about.

RABBIT: But aren't you being held here against your will?

(MISS SCOONS *looks to* TYMPANI *for an explanation.* TYMPANI *shrugs.*)

MISS SCOONS: What's got into this guy? (*back to* RABBIT) Do I look like a prisoner to you?

RABBIT: No, I guess not. Well, look, maybe we can fool them.

TYMPANI: Hah! You must have a screw loose or something. Lanx and Wheeler have been through every trick in the book.

RABBIT: Yeah, but what if we could come up with a character that nobody's ever seen before. Something in flesh and blood. Not just an idea but something so incredible that as soon as they came in contact with it they'd pass out or go into convulsions or something. That's what they're looking for.

TYMPANI: How could you do that?

RABBIT: We'd have to invent it. Right here. Between the three of us.

MISS SCOONS: That's fantastic! What an idea! A real live experiment!

TYMPANI: It'll never work.

RABBIT: How come?

MISS SCOONS: Like a monster or something!

TYMPANI: First of all, because they're looking for something beyond the imagination. Something impossible.

RABBIT: Well, if they can imagine the possibility of it maybe we can imagine the thing itself.

MISS SCOONS: Yeah, it'd be a great challenge, Tympani. You could get that diner that you're always talking about.

RABBIT: What diner?

MISS SCOONS: (*to* RABBIT) He's always wanted a diner, ever since he was a little boy.

TYMPANI: SHUT UP!

MISS SCOONS: Well, it's true isn't it? You're always talking about it.

TYMPANI: I'm not always talking about it! I mentioned it once!

RABBIT: Take it easy. It's nothing to be ashamed of.

TYMPANI: I'M NOT ASHAMED!!

RABBIT: All right, all right. Jesus, I could care less if you've always wanted to have a diner. I happen to like diners.

TYMPANI: I HAVEN'T ALWAYS WANTED TO HAVE A DINER!

RABBIT: Oh, brother.

MISS SCOONS: He'll be okay in a minute. Shall I get us all some coffee?

RABBIT: Sure.

(MISS SCOONS *turns toward the rectangle as though to leave but stops suddenly. She seems to go into a hypnotic state and just stares at the rectangle.*)

RABBIT: What's the matter, Miss Scoons?

(*She speaks in a kind of flattened monotone, almost as if another voice is speaking through her.*)

MISS SCOONS: I look at the screen and I am the screen. I'm not me. I don't know who I am. I look at the movie and I am the movie. I am the star. I am the star in the movie. For days I am the star and I'm not me. I'm me being the star. I look at my life when I come down. I look and I hate my life when I come down. I hate my life not being a movie. I hate my life not being a star. I hate being myself in my life which isn't a movie and never will be. I hate having to eat. Having to work. Having to sleep. Having to go to the bathroom. Having to get from one place to another with no potential. Having to live in this body which isn't a star's body and all the time knowing that stars exist. That there are people doing nothing all their life except being in movies. Doing nothing but swimming and drinking and laughing and being driven to places full of potential. People never having to feel hot pavement or having to look at weeds growing through cracks in the city. People never having to look the city square in the eyes. People living in dreams which are the same dreams I'm dreaming but never living.

(*She suddenly snaps out of it and exits left.* RABBIT *watches her go. He looks at* TYMPANI.)

RABBIT: Is she all right?

TYMPANI: I don't know.

RABBIT: What's going on around here anyway? Doesn't anybody know each other?

TYMPANI: What's to know?

RABBIT: Well, I mean, you see each other every day, don't you?

TYMPANI: Look, don't go gettin' humanitarian on me, mister. The environment can't take it.

RABBIT: What environment?

TYMPANI: This is a city.

RABBIT: So what?

TYMPANI: We're the brain of the city. The brain's demented. It's a demented brain. You understand? If we disturb that demented condition, the city will collapse around us. Now you don't want that to happen, do you?

RABBIT: Is that what Wheeler's afraid of?

TYMPANI: (*menacing*) Don't poke too deep, you're still on the guest list.

(RABBIT *stops short. Pause.*)

RABBIT: Don't you ever sit down?

TYMPANI: No.

RABBIT: You won't mind if I sit down?

TYMPANI: No.

(RABBIT *sits upstage in the black swivel chair, facing front.* TYMPANI *stays behind the drums facing front.*)

RABBIT: You're always standing?

TYMPANI: Always. Waiting for it to happen.

RABBIT: What "it"?

TYMPANI: "It."

RABBIT: Oh. "It."

TYMPANI: The rhythm. The one, special, never-before-heard-before rhythm which will drive men crazy.

RABBIT: That's a tough one.

TYMPANI: It's possible.

RABBIT: Sure. I guess.

TYMPANI: (*facing front*) One time I could almost taste it. I was standing here just like this. I was playing a standard four-four cross pattern. I'd been into it for maybe half an hour when I began to feel something taking over my left wrist. I was curious at first because I'd never had quite that kind of a feeling enter into a simple four-four pattern before. It was like I could hear a whole other shape and sound to the basic structure. Something behind what I was playing. Then I looked straight down at my hands and I saw somebody else playing the pattern. It wasn't me. It was a different body. Then I got scared. I panicked when I saw that, and right away I lost it. It just vanished like that, and I never have come across it again.

RABBIT: It'll come back.

TYMPANI: What do you know? Your optimism isn't reassuring; it's stupid. You can't make me feel better about it, because I already know what it is. I know it's lost and I'll never find my way back to it. It was the chance of a lifetime.

RABBIT: So now you're just taking up space?

TYMPANI: I'm facing my death.

(*Loud screech from the saxophone offstage.* RABBIT *suddenly whirls the swivel chair around so it's facing upstage. At the same time the lights go black and the rectangle is lit. The scrim turns dark red.* TYMPANI *pulls the other chair downstage center, facing front, and sits in it like a little boy, eating popcorn and watching the movies.* RABBIT'S *voice is heard but he is unseen.*)

RABBIT: (*little kid voice*) I love the newsreels! I could watch the newsreels forever!

TYMPANI: (*little kid voice*) Not me. News is stupid. It has a stupid voice. Sounds like a grown-up. Grown-ups sounding important and not knowing they're stupid.

RABBIT: (*adult newscaster voice*) A two-headed St. Bernard was born to normal parents in Grand Rapids, Michigan. The pup was the only one in the litter, which is unusual for St. Bernards.

(LANX *enters on the platform up left in boxer shorts, black boxing shoes, towel around his neck and swollen eyes, his nose bleeding profusely. He is raising his arms to a distant cheering audience, in victory. He crosses into the rectangle and keeps acknowledging his audience silently.*)

TYMPANI: I wanna' see the one where they find the guy's face in the vacant lot full of shotgun holes.

RABBIT: (*newscaster voice*) The mother died in birth and the baby died shortly thereafter. Medical experts are still uncertain as to the exact cause of death; however, they believe the unusual size of the double-headed baby may be at the root of it.

TYMPANI: That could never happen in this town. Too many cops.

RABBIT: (*newscaster*) Tom Mix got caught stealing towels from the Beverly Wilshire and refused to make a comment.

TYMPANI: I wish it would happen in this town. Wouldn't that be neat? A real murder right here. Where they can't find who did it and everybody's scared to go to bed at night!

RABBIT: The *Howdy Doody Show* will not be seen on television this season due to a contractual disagreement between the producers. The *Sheriff John Show* will fill in the missing slot.

(*Sax backup. Suddenly* LANX *starts talking from the rectangle as though he were being interviewed. Sax builds through this.*)

LANX: Yeah, I love fightin' in this town. There's somethin' about the atmosphere here. The people. The people love me here. They go bananas. This town is crazy. That's why I love it. I go back to Jersey City and I'm just another mug, ya' know what I mean? But out here in the West they can appreciate a real boxer, ya' know? I mean I give the people what they want. They like to see some action when they come to the fights. They don't wanna' see a couple of GIs up there doin' the fox-trot all over the canvas. They wanna' see some boxin'. And that's what I'm here for. And the fans know that. They know when they come to a Jimmy Muldoon fight that they're gonna' see the real stuff. They're gonna' see some leather thumpin'!

(*Sax fades to low backup.* LANX *continues talking to his audience in mime as* RABBIT *and* TYMPANI *go on.* LANX *shadowboxes in the rectangle.*)

RABBIT: (*newscaster*) The kidnapping has stirred the emotions of millions. Everywhere the voice of outrage is on the people's lips.

TYMPANI: (*like an old lady*) Such a sweet little boy too. All alone in the bedroom with the wind blowing the curtains. Only a monster could have dreamed of such a thing.

(LANX *cuts back in with his voice.*)

LANX: Well, I figure I got maybe two or three good years left. You know how it is in this profession. Here today, gone tomorrow. (*laughs*) Anyway, I figure there's a future for me right here in Hollywood. I mean, I still got my looks and my muscle to get me through. I've already been talkin' to a major studio about doin' my life story. Soon's a good offer comes along I just might take it. Who knows? Anyhow, I just wanna' wish all my fans in

L.A. the best of luck and thanks for supportin' me and helpin' me to become a challenger for the title. Thanks a million.

(LANX *raises his arms in victory and waves to the fans. Suddenly* TYMPANI *stands on the chair facing front and shouts like a little kid to his mother upstairs.*)

TYMPANI: I just wanna' go to the movies, Ma! I don't care about anything else! Just the movies! I don't care about school or homework or college or jobs or marriage or kids or insurance or front lawns or mortgage or even the light of day! I don't care if I never see the sun again, Ma! Just send me to the dark, dark movies!

(*Rising sax. Sound of mass applause.* LANX *exits right, shadowboxing as he goes. Rectangle goes unlit. Scrim out. Stage lights back up.* RABBIT *whirls the chair around facing front again.* RABBIT *and* TYMPANI *freeze a second. Sudden silence as* MISS SCOONS *enters slowly trying not to spill two Dixie cups full of coffee. She crosses to center stage and sets the cups down extremely slowly on the floor, so as not to spill them. This sequence should be almost in slow motion. Once she has the cups safely on the floor she breaks back into her normal tempo.*)

MISS SCOONS: All I could find was Dixie cups. Wheeler smashed all the real cups the other day. Went totally crazy. Better drink these fast before the wax melts. Makes the coffee taste really weird.

TYMPANI: (*leaving chair and crossing back to drums*) I don't want any coffee. Makes my teeth itch. Bad enough with smog choking you, making your eyes run, cops giving you walking tickets. Everything's bad enough without coffee to make things worse.

MISS SCOONS: Well, that's just perfect because I only brought two cups anyway!

TYMPANI: What is coffee anyway! Some goddamn bean they invented to make you stay up late.

(RABBIT *gets up from the chair and picks up a cup of coffee.* MISS SCOONS *sits in the other chair.*)

RABBIT: I've got an idea.

MISS SCOONS: Great.

RABBIT: What if we start with ourselves. One of us.

TYMPANI: What do you mean, one of us?

RABBIT: One of us volunteers to be worked on by the other two. To be transformed into this character they're looking for.

TYMPANI: Back to that again. It's not just a character. Why can't you get that straight? If they were just looking for a character they'd be going through the casting agencies. They want a phenomenon.

RABBIT: Why're you in such a bad mood all of a sudden?

TYMPANI: I have no good moods! Every mood I have is a variation on a bad mood. Good moods don't fit into the scheme of things. Good moods are stupid! GOOD MOODS ARE WORSE THAN DIXIE CUPS!

MISS SCOONS: (*to* RABBIT) I'll volunteer.

RABBIT: Great, Miss Scoons will be the guinea pig.

TYMPANI: (*to audience*) And suddenly they were all transported to the world of magic.

RABBIT: This coffee tastes really weird.

MISS SCOONS: It's the wax melting.

RABBIT: Oh.

MISS SCOONS: Come on, Tymp, you can sit in the director's chair. It'll be fun.

TYMPANI: Fun? What is this supposed to be? Mickey Rooney and Judy Garland get their big break and move to Philadelphia with the Dorsey brothers? What is this? We're in the middle of a dung heap here. Where do you think we are anyway? You don't work your way up from the bottom anymore. You rip flesh! You tear your eyeballs out and watch them get kicked down the street.

MISS SCOONS: (*to* RABBIT) He's had some bad breaks.

TYMPANI: It doesn't work that way anymore! Nobody gets breaks! You get broken in half!

MISS SCOONS: Just relax for a while. Let's just try this idea he has. You got nothing to lose. Just pretend everything's all right. Pretend you've had so many successes that now you're retired and living in the East. Boston or Maine or someplace cozy. You can afford to relax. You have a golden retriever at your feet, *The New York Times Review of Books* in your lap, an after-dinner mint in your mouth. You've created more disasters in your time than the whole of Hollywood put together. You're known as "The Master of Disaster."

(TYMPANI's *mood begins to change as* RABBIT *crosses to him and escorts him upstage to the black swivel chair and sits him down in it. He coaxes him along with his voice.*)

RABBIT: That's right. Pretend you've been called from a faraway place by the head chiefs of the whole city. You're the only one who can solve the mystery. Millions and millions are riding solely on your powers of imagination. There's nobody quite like you on the entire planet. You've been called in on similar cases and solved every one of them. But this is something special. This is the case to end all cases. Even you, with all your powers, with all your stature and reputation, are left somewhat puzzled and dumbfounded. Even you, the High Prophet of Disaster. The Master himself.

(TYMPANI *begins to take on the characteristics which* RABBIT *attributes to him. He seats himself in the swivel chair with his hands folded in his lap. He speaks with an air of authority.*)

TYMPANI: (*to* RABBIT) So tell me—this particular entity, I assume it's evil?

RABBIT: (*deep voice*) Can any fear be construed as good?

TYMPANI: That is not my question! I'm not here to dillydally in quasi-philosophical meanderings! I'm here to solve a problem.

RABBIT: But you see, the consistent product of this being is paralyzing fear. Even in its dormant state it can produce severe nausea and depression.

TYMPANI: Would we be safe in assuming then, at the outset at least, that this "thing" is more a kind of force than anything resembling a character?

RABBIT: We could assume, yes.

TYMPANI: Good. Then let's begin.

(*Low lurking sax music bleeds in from offstage. Lights shift.* MISS SCOONS *becomes very still in her chair as* RABBIT *moves steadily around the space.* TYMPANI *remains in the swivel chair with hands folded. Green light on his face. The scrim turns orange.*)

RABBIT: We find it, somehow, at the present, inhabiting the body of a woman.

TYMPANI: What is her age?

RABBIT: The age of the body or the "thing"?

TYMPANI: THE BODY, OF COURSE!

RABBIT: In its twenties, roughly.

TYMPANI: Roughly? How roughly?

RABBIT: Mid-twenties.

TYMPANI: Thank you.

RABBIT: Can you picture it now?

TYMPANI: DON'T RUSH ME!

RABBIT: Sorry.

TYMPANI: I'm having difficulty with the form.

RABBIT: We could change it to a man.

TYMPANI: DON'T BE STUPID! That's not the form I mean. I can't go from drums to this just like a duck to water.

RABBIT: Oh.

TYMPANI: I need some time to work into it.

RABBIT: Well, take your time then.

TYMPANI: Could you stand her up for me?

RABBIT: Yeah, sure.

(RABBIT *goes to* MISS SCOONS *and stands her up. She stands very still, staring straight ahead as though hypnotized.* TYMPANI *faces out and doesn't look at her directly.*)

TYMPANI: She doesn't seem grotesque at all.

RABBIT: Well, she's not. Not now.

TYMPANI: She seems abnormally normal in fact. What's the matter with her?

RABBIT: Nothing's the matter with her! We have to cook up something that's the matter with her! That's the whole point. We have to transform her.

TYMPANI: But maybe that's where the terror lies.

RABBIT: Where?

TYMPANI: In her very normalness. She's terrifyingly normal.

RABBIT: Are you kidding! That won't sell.

TYMPANI: No. She passes herself off as one of us, but then these weird events take place. She demolishes entire populations with her normalness. She enters an advanced civilization where deranged citizens rule the planets. Her normalness destroys them utterly.

RABBIT: That won't scare anybody!

TYMPANI: So, the only alternative is to make her grotesque, then. It's either one or the other.

RABBIT: We have to go beyond that! This is a challenge!

TYMPANI: It's either an Angel or a Devil. Which one's it going to be?

RABBIT: There must be something in between.

TYMPANI: But that's totally boring.

RABBIT: How do you know?

TYMPANI: (*getting up from chair, quits the game*) Because that's where we are right now! IN BETWEEN!

(*Lights come up again. Sax stops.* MISS SCOONS *keeps swaying hypnotically back and forth.*)

RABBIT: (*to* TYMPANI) What's the matter?

TYMPANI: The matter is that you're trying to approach this whole thing in an ordinary way. Like an amateur séance or something. I mean we're just fishing around in the dark for some kind of vague creepiness. This is an eight-million-dollar project you're talking about!

RABBIT: Well, what's your idea then?

TYMPANI: I DON'T HAVE AN IDEA! I already told you. It's impossible. I don't want any part of this thing.

RABBIT: Great.

TYMPANI: (*returning to drums*) It's your predicament, not mine. I'm already sidetracked enough as it is.

(TYMPANI *picks up the drumsticks and begins to play softly on the drums.* MISS SCOONS *starts to sway more intensely. Pause. She slowly starts moving around the stage in a trance. Sax comes in underneath.*)

RABBIT: (*to* TYMPANI *who continues drumming softly*) I don't see it that way.

TYMPANI: What way?

RABBIT: Yours or mine. If one of us escapes, we all escape.

TYMPANI: I'm not looking to escape! This is my job! I like it here. Stop trying to squeeze me out of a good thing.

MISS SCOONS: (*to herself, still moving; drum continues*) In those days God had no need to create anything apart from himself. He was self-contained.

RABBIT: (*to* MISS SCOONS) God?

MISS SCOONS: (*dancing slowly, speaking in trance*) There was such an overflow of divine love that the angels came bursting forth of their own accord. Circle upon circle of spirit lights radiantly dashing the heavens, whirling about the sun in clouds of crystal fragments.

RABBIT: (*to* SCOONS) We have to go the other direction! Fear! Devils! Serpents, not angels! What's the matter with you people! You should know what's commercial by now.

MISS SCOONS: They were blasted out of eternal sleep by the blinding light of a direct vision of Glory. So devastating was this light that only their flaming wings could offer protection from this fire that also gave them their birth.

RABBIT: (*to* SCOONS) We have to work on fear, not glory! Terror! Devastation! That's where the money is! Devastation!

MISS SCOONS: And all at once they began to sing. All nine choirs in descending rank.

(RABBIT *turns to* TYMPANI. MISS SCOONS *whirls around the stage in ecstasy.* TYMPANI'S *rhythm on the drums builds. Sax fills in behind.*)

RABBIT: What is the most frightening thing in the world?

TYMPANI: (*blankly*) A space. (*he continues drums*)

RABBIT: What is the most frightening thing in the whole world?

TYMPANI: A life cut off from all life.

RABBIT: What is the most scary thing in the world!

TYMPANI: Death.

RABBIT: (*pacing*) WHAT IS THE MOST FRIGHTENING THING IN THE WHOLE WIDE WORLD!

TYMPANI: Dying.

RABBIT: WHAT IS MORE FRIGHTENING THAN ANYTHING ELSE?

TYMPANI: Dying alone.

RABBIT: WHAT IS IT THAT EVERYBODY IS SCARED OF!

TYMPANI: The expectation of a death unknown.

RABBIT: What is fear!

TYMPANI: THE IMAGINATION OF DYING!

RABBIT: Now we're getting somewhere!

TYMPANI: Now we're cooking!

RABBIT: THE IMAGINATION OF DYING IS MORE SCARY THAN ACTUALLY DYING!

TYMPANI: How do you know?

RABBIT: I assume.

TYMPANI: You assume, but you don't know.

RABBIT: Having never died my death, I assume that imagining it is more scary than doing it.

TYMPANI: You don't do it. It does it by itself.

RABBIT: Yes. That's true. That must be true.

TYMPANI: But you don't know.

RABBIT: I don't know.

(*Through this the rhythm from* TYMPANI'S *drumming is getting more frenetic.* MISS SCOONS *dances with more and more abandon.* RABBIT *paces.*)

TYMPANI: He doesn't know.

RABBIT: NOT KNOWING IS MORE SCARY THAN KNOWING.

TYMPANI: But since you don't know you can only assume.

RABBIT: NOT KNOWING WHEN OR HOW OR WHY OR WHERE!

TYMPANI: But only that you will.

RABBIT: I will. I WILL DIE!

TYMPANI: HE WILL!

RABBIT: We all will.

TYMPANI: You will.

RABBIT: So will you.

TYMPANI: WE ALL WILL DIE AND NOT KNOW HOW OR WHY OR WHERE!

RABBIT: AND THAT IS WHAT'S FRIGHTENING BEYOND ALL REASON!

TYMPANI: AND THAT'S WHAT MAKES A BOX OFFICE SMASH!

RABBIT: AND THAT'S WHAT MAKES AN INDUSTRY!

TYMPANI: AND THAT'S WHAT MAKES A MILLION BUCKS!

RABBIT: WE'VE GOT IT! WE'VE GOT IT! MISS SCOONS! WE'VE GOT IT! Miss Scoons?

(*Sax stops. Drums stop.* MISS SCOONS *is frozen in place, center stage. She speaks as though in a trance.*)

MISS SCOONS: You haven't got a thing. None of us has got a thing. We're only going in circles. We're only going around and around. We're only getting nowhere. We're going nowhere fast.

RABBIT: No, we've really hit on something! Tympani and me. We both discovered something while you were dancing.

MISS SCOONS: It's nothing. You only got excited by the sound of your own voice. There's nothing in here. The city's dead. The living are replacements for the dead. Nothing moves in this town.

TYMPANI: She'll be all right.

RABBIT: I thought we had something there. (*to* TYMPANI) Didn't you feel like we were onto something?

TYMPANI: I don't know.

RABBIT: Boy, you people are really weird.

TYMPANI: You don't know what weirdness is, chump.

(LANX *enters fast from right, dressed in his suit again, puffing on his cigar. He stops center stage next to* MISS SCOONS *and glares at all of them.*)

LANX: What's going on! I'm not paying you to stand around salivating! Do you realize what's happening! Wheeler's condition is getting worse! He's turning completely green and his top layer is beginning to peel!

RABBIT: We've been trying our damndest to come up with something.

LANX: THAT'S NOT GOOD ENOUGH! THIS IS CULVER

CITY, NOT THE BORSCHT CIRCUIT! WE DEAL IN HARD-CORE PRODUCTS! CASH ON THE LINE!

RABBIT: It's not my fault! I can't work with these people! They don't have any gumption! All the fire's gone out of them.

MISS SCOONS: (*still in trance*) The Cherubim. The Seraphim. The Thrones. The Dominions.

LANX: THEN DO IT ON YOUR OWN!

RABBIT: Where? In this nuthouse? I want a suite of my own with room service. I deserve better than this. I'M AN ARTIST, GODDAMNIT! I CAME ALL THIS WAY BY BUCKBOARD!

MISS SCOONS: The messengers of God.

LANX: (*to* RABBIT) That's very quaint, but that's not the point. The point is that you came. Something drew you down here to us. Isn't that so? Something indescribable?

TYMPANI: I can describe it. Money.

RABBIT: That's right. So what?

LANX: So don't go pulling rank on me with that "Artist" crap! You're no better than any of us.

RABBIT: That's not what I meant.

LANX: You thought you'd come down and whip off a few quick lines, collect a little traveling expenses and a fat contract, and then sashay on outa' here. Right?

MISS SCOONS: (*trance*) The urge to create works of art is essentially one of ambition. The ambition behind the urge to create is no different from any other ambition. To kill. To win. To get on top.

LANX: What's got into her?

RABBIT: Part of our experiment.

MISS SCOONS: Greed is greed.

LANX: Why is she talking like that! She's never talked like that before. I can't even follow it.

TYMPANI: You know what I think? I think it was the rhythm I was playing. THAT MUST BE IT! I MUST'VE FOUND IT ACCIDENTALLY!

RABBIT: I told you we were onto something!

TYMPANI: THAT'S IT, LANX! THAT'S IT! LOOK, SHE'S COMPLETELY ZONKED OUT!

MISS SCOONS: The Angel is against all evil. He appears in the midst of destruction.

LANX: What's going on! Miss Scoons, snap out of it!

TYMPANI: No, you don't understand. I was playing a rhythm on the drums and she was moving to it. I must've hit on the one that I was looking for and didn't even know it.

LANX: So what! If you didn't know it then, you still don't know it.

TYMPANI: But I could find it again! I could trace it down!

LANX: What I want to know is what are we going to do about Wheeler! If he goes under, all of us go with him!

(MISS SCOONS *travels around the space and speaks with a different voice.* TYMPANI *watches her closely.*)

MISS SCOONS: The ambition to transform valleys into cities. To transform the unknown into the known without really knowing. To make things safe. To beat death. To be victorious in the face of absolute desolation.

LANX: Whose script is that? Where did she memorize that?

TYMPANI: It's coming from her!

LANX: Don't give me that! I recognize the style. Sounds like Fritz Lang or early Howard Hawks.

RABBIT: She's going to need some help. Is there a doctor around?

LANX: There are no doctors in this town. They've all been sued to death. What's the matter with you! We're all on the verge of disaster, and you talk about it like it was a simple medical problem. Wheeler's condition can only be solved by you!

RABBIT: But what about Miss Scoons?

LANX: She doesn't count! Only Wheeler counts! His condition is precarious!

RABBIT: But I don't care about Wheeler one way or the other.

LANX: Then you have no business in this business!

RABBIT: Then let me go!

LANX: NO!

RABBIT: This is insane.

MISS SCOONS: The Authorities. The Powers. The Principalities. The Archangels. The Angels.

TYMPANI: (*watching* MISS SCOONS) I think she's going deeper. She's definitely contacting other entities. Listen to her breathing.

LANX: GET HER OUT OF HERE! SHE'S UPSETTING THE WHOLE PROJECT!

MISS SCOONS: El Pueblo de Nuestra Señora la Reina de los Angeles de Porciuncuta. En la ciudad. En todo el mundo. La muerte, ésta es el rey supremo. Viva la muerte!

LANX: PLEASE! I NEED SOME KIND OF ORDER! SOME KIND OF ARRANGEMENT! WHEELER'S SKIN IS TURN-ING GREEN! WE'LL ALL BE EATEN ALIVE!

(*From this point on everyone is in their own world. They speak to themselves.*)

TYMPANI: I have a diner in my dream. One diner.

RABBIT: What's keeping me from leaving? I could leave. Nobody's holding a gun to my head.

LANX: It's not the same for me. My power lies in manipulation. If no one is manipulated, then I'm sunk. I have no purpose!

TYMPANI: One diner. Basically green. Pale green walls. Chrome stools with black leatherette seats. Everyone's face is reflected in those stools.

MISS SCOONS: The Spanish took over. The Spanish Hunger. Spanish stomachs made a sound that rumbled through these canyons. You can still hear it in some parts. The Spanish had no idea they'd ever be in the movies.

LANX: There has to be some form! Even chaos has a form!

TYMPANI: The main dish is chicken gumbo. Served on Saint's Day. The Chef's Special. People go a hundred miles out of their way just to taste it.

RABBIT: It's me! It's me who wants to stay! I could leave but I'm staying.

MISS SCOONS: Absolute greed devoured them whole. Their viciousness was beyond belief. Tearing the gold teeth from half-dead victims. Crushing jade jaguars into green dust. They set the stage with Catholic blood.

LANX: (*looking out through rectangle*) Once there was an industry! A magnificent industry! The studios dominated the scenery. The villages sprang up around them like serfs spawning at the feet of their master. Then there was order! Everyone knew their place!

TYMPANI: In one corner is a chrome jukebox with nothing but Hank Snow records.

RABBIT: (*to audience*) I'm staying and I don't regret it.

MISS SCOONS: Their voraciousness knew no bounds. They were a bottomless pit.

(WHEELER *rushes on from stage right. Everyone stops.* WHEELER'S *skin has turned green, big open sores on his face and arms. He is panting for breath. He screams in desperation.*)

WHEELER: WHERE'S MY DISASTER!!!!!!!!!!!!!!!!

(*Lights black out. Sax rushes into high wailing riff and continues into blackout.*)

ACT 2

SCENE: *Same basic set as Act 1.* LANX *can be heard shadowboxing in the dark. He makes the sharp exhaling sound of a boxer when he throws a punch. The stage lights rise slowly on* TYMPANI, *dressed up in a chef's hat, long white apron, with a spatula in his hand. He is using the two tympani drums as a make-believe griddle.* WHEELER *is seated in the swivel chair, upstage, facing the audience. His skin is a slimy green. He now has two fangs and extra-long fingernails. His posture is slumped over and painful. He seems to be having trouble breathing, and in general his health has depleted considerably. Downstage right, on the floor on hands and knees,* MISS SCOONS *is scrubbing the floor with a big brush and a bucket full of soapy water. She is dressed as a nun and speaks with a light Irish accent. Center stage,* RABBIT *is laying out the bundles to form a large circle on the floor.* WHEELER *watches his every move very closely, as though his life depended on it.* LANX *is dressed in a suit, but his hands are bandaged and bloody. His nose has a wide bandage across it, and his eyes are black and blue. He shadowboxes around the loose space.* MISS SCOONS *sings softly to herself as she scrubs the floor. Lights rise slowly.* LANX *keeps boxing the air.* TYMPANI *cooks and* WHEELER *watches* RABBIT.

MISS SCOONS: (*singing*)
I could've married a thistledown
Or Jesus Christ hisself
Or climbed a holy mountaintop
Or built a ship meself

91

But, no, I cast meself to sea
And sailed for foreign turf
Whereupon I climbed the highest tree
And searched for my sweet home
And searched for my sweet home

(*Lights up full. They are all silent for a while but continue with their actions. The dominant sound is* WHEELER'S *heavy, rasping breathing and* LANX'S *punches.*)

WHEELER: (*to* RABBIT, *having difficulty speaking*) I can't understand the necessity for getting so elaborate with the design.

RABBIT: (*as he works, arranging bundles*) Well, under ordinary circumstances I'd plunge right in and just see what I'd come up with by chance. But this situation seems to call for a more traditional approach.

TYMPANI: (*to* LANX, *cooking imaginary eggs*) Did you say you wanted those over-easy or straight up?

LANX: (*still boxing air*) I want the whites firm. That's the most important. If the whites aren't firm you don't get the full nutrition from the egg. Might as well eat it raw. An athlete has to watch his eggs.

TYMPANI: Right. Don't worry. I'm used to this kind of cooking. Sugar Ray used to stop in here on his way to the Garden. Now there was a finicky eater.

WHEELER: (*to* RABBIT) What do you mean by traditional?

RABBIT: There's a long history to the Medicine Wheel. I'm just learning it myself.

WHEELER: That's what you call this? A Medicine Wheel?

RABBIT: That's what the Indians called it.

WHEELER: Don't get cute. I'm not interested in ethnic origins.

RABBIT: Well, we're taking a risk any way you look at it.

WHEELER: Why's that?

RABBIT: This was always used for prayer, not destruction.

WHEELER: Well, this isn't for destruction. It's for entertainment.

MISS SCOONS: Oh, Mister Wheeler, would you have me clean the entire floor then, or just the alcoves?

WHEELER: Is she talking to me?

MISS SCOONS: Aye, it's you, Mister Wheeler, that I'm addressin'.

WHEELER: (*standing suddenly*) What's happened in here! Something's happened in here since I was last here! I want to know what it is! The air smells different.

(*The rest continue, ignoring* WHEELER. LANX *tries to comfort him.*)

LANX: Don't worry, buddy. It's just the smog. The smog and the Spanish. We're doing something about both problems. We've got our man on it right now. They can't get away with it for long.

WHEELER: I don't understand what's going on. Have I changed as much as you?

LANX: We're exactly the same, old buddy. Everything's exactly the same. I'm in top condition. Look at me pivot!

(LANX *pivots for* WHEELER.)

WHEELER: Show me the window! I WANT TO SEE THE WINDOW!

LANX: Sure thing. Right this way.

TYMPANI: (*to himself*) Cripples and lames. Cripples and lames. All the same as far as I'm concerned. I see all kinds in here. They come and go. All I do is cook and watch.

LANX: (*at window with* WHEELER) There now. Just take a gander out there! Isn't that something. The "City of Angels"! Magnificent! Just like it always was. Palm trees. Duck ponds. Sculptured hedges.

WHEELER: WHAT'S HAPPENED TO THE LEMON ORCHARDS!

LANX: Now take it easy. Those were plowed under to make room for the new lots.

WHEELER: (*backing away from window as if about to faint;* LANX *supports him*) Oh, my God, I feel I'm going to die right here. What's happening to me. The entire scenery's changed!

LANX: It'll be okay. Just sit back down and take a load off. Would ya' like something to eat?

(LANX *escorts him back to the swivel chair.* WHEELER *collapses into it.*)

WHEELER: I couldn't keep it down. Everything's shrunken inside me. I can feel it. All my organs are tiny.

LANX: How 'bout some nice chicken broth?

WHEELER: NO! LEAVE ME ALONE, YOU IDIOT!

LANX: (*backing off*) Yessir.

WHEELER: Are you taking care of me? Is that it? Am I an invalid now?

LANX: Well, someone's got to look after you.

WHEELER: What about these others? What are they doing here?

LANX: Working on the project, sir.

WHEELER: Project? What project!

LANX: The disaster.

WHEELER: Oh, that. Do you still think it's worth it? Aren't we beyond that now?

LANX: Hard to say. Seems like our only choice now.

WHEELER: (*suddenly switching*) YES IT IS! OF COURSE IT IS! You don't have to tell me that. Of course it's our only chance. It always was our only chance. It's our purpose for being here. Right from the start. That's how the town got started, isn't it?

LANX: "Choice," I said, not "chance."

WHEELER: AND I SAID "CHANCE"!!

LANX: Yessir.

WHEELER: Go on boxing, will you. You make me nervous when you talk.

LANX: Yessir.

WHEELER: You're not a good talker. You're dumb, in fact. In fact you never should be allowed to open your yap.

LANX: Yessir.

(LANX *begins to shadowbox again.*)

WHEELER: Box your ass off! It's the only way you'll understand the importance of a dollar.

LANX: You're right, sir.

WHEELER: And wet your lips! Your lips!

LANX: Yessir! (*wets his lips with his tongue as he boxes*)

WHEELER: You're not just another boxer, you're a personality now. You have to look good. Above all else, you have to look good.

LANX: Yessir.

WHEELER: (*to himself*) The whole business has gone to pot.

TYMPANI: (*to himself, referring to* WHEELER) Bananas.

MISS SCOONS: Could you tell me one thing, Mister Wheeler?

WHEELER: (*looking around for the voice*) Who's that talking!

RABBIT: It's Miss Scoons, I think.

WHEELER: Why is she talking like that?

RABBIT: Tympani and I were conducting an experiment, and in the middle of it Miss Scoons fell into a trauma of some kind.

TYMPANI: (*to* RABBIT) Don't explain it. He had his chance already.

LANX: (*still boxing*) "Choice," I said!

WHEELER: I don't understand!

RABBIT: Something to do with rhythm.

TYMPANI: (*to* RABBIT) Don't explain it. I'm cooking now!

WHEELER: Yes, we had a man on that once. A young man. Worked

for several months and then died mysteriously. What happened
to that young man we had, Lanx?

LANX: He's still with us, sir.

WHEELER: YOU JUST KEEP BOXING!

LANX: Yessir.

WHEELER: You've got a press conference in two hours.

MISS SCOONS: Mister Wheeler?

WHEELER: What is it!

MISS SCOONS: Could you tell me one thing?

WHEELER: Maybe and maybe not.

MISS SCOONS: How come the tide has turned? How come now the
people want disasters? I mean what's happened to all those nice
stories they used to have where everyone got along? Jeanette
MacDonald and all that lot?

WHEELER: (*suddenly professorial*) Very simple. No wars. No major
war, that is. No big, major world war. No focus. That's what a
big, major world war does. It brings a focus to the people. They
take sides. Us against them. Simple as that. Now there's no war.
No big, major world war. Just gook wars. Jungle wars. Espionage
wars. Secret little creepy wars in the swamp. So. No war, no
focus. No focus, no structure. No structure spells disaster. And
disaster is our business. Simple.

MISS SCOONS: Thank you, sir. (*goes back to scrubbing*)

WHEELER: You're a very intelligent woman, Miss Scoons.

MISS SCOONS: Thank you, sir.

WHEELER: I'd like to talk to you at length sometime, but you can
see I'm wrapped up at the moment.

MISS SCOONS: Oh, certainly, sir, I was just curious.

WHEELER: No harm in that. Curiosity breeds invention. That's
what we're all here for. To invent! It's incredible. We're here to
invent and there's no invention. Just a dust bowl. What's going
on! We've never spent this much time on a project before! It's
been going on for years now.

LANX: We're not sure of our position, sir.

WHEELER: Our position is to coldly calculate the public mind!

MISS SCOONS: Is there such a thing, sir?

WHEELER: Of course there is, Miss Scoons! Don't be silly. We have
to find that part of our own mind which corresponds to the
masses. We're immune and contaminated at the same time.

MISS SCOONS: A public mind?

WHEELER: Of course! That's what we have to tap into. When you get right down to it, what we are is mind readers. Isn't that right, Mr. Brown?

RABBIT: I don't know.

WHEELER: I don't like your attitude! Lanx, why has Miss Scoons been demoted to scrubbing the floors and this idiot is dancing around making magic circles on the floor?

LANX: (*stops boxing*) Well, she was going off the deep end, Mr. Wheeler. We had to do something.

WHEELER: KEEP BOXING!

(LANX *starts up again.* TYMPANI *begins to speak as though in a world of his own, still cooking, facing audience.*)

TYMPANI: "What dya' say we take in a movie?" What a great sound that has. "What dya' say we go out and take in a movie? What dya' say we get the hell outa' here and go take in a movie? (*he pauses, thinks of another way to say it*) How 'bout let's just drop everything and go to the picture show? (*pause, another approach*) What dya' say, just you and me, we leave the kids, get outa' the house, into the old Studebaker, leave our miserable lives behind, and join the great adventure of a motion picture? (*pause; very simply this time*) What dya' say we just lose ourselves forever in the miracle of film? We nestle down, just the two of us, with a big box of buttered popcorn, a big cup of Seven-Up, a big box of Milk Duds, a giant box of Black Crows, and we just chew ourselves straight into oblivion?"

(*Pause as* WHEELER *seems to have dreamed off into* TYMPANI'S *words.* TYMPANI *goes back to cooking.* RABBIT *interrupts the pause.*)

RABBIT: I'd like to explain this thing to you if you don't mind, Mr. Wheeler.

WHEELER: (*snapping out of dream*) DON'T EXPLAIN IT! MAKE IT WORK!

RABBIT: Well, it's kind of complicated. I mean I'm just a novice at it myself.

WHEELER: Then what are you doing in such fast company! There's no one I can talk to here! That's the trouble. No one! Everyone's off in their own little world. There's no concern for the industry!

RABBIT: I was trying to resolve the problem from a spiritual angle.

WHEELER: (*standing again*) WHAT PROBLEM! WHAT SPIRIT! FOR GOD'S SAKE, ISN'T ANYONE GOING TO TELL ME WHAT'S HAPPENED HERE? DON'T YOU THINK I'VE NOTICED?

TYMPANI: (*still cooking over drums*) I can tell you exactly.

WHEELER: Who's that talking?

TYMPANI: It's me.

WHEELER: (*sitting back down*) Oh.

TYMPANI: We've been locked out of time, and that's all there is to it.

WHEELER: What kind of a statement is that!

LANX: (*still boxing*) Could I stop for a second, Mr. Wheeler? I can explain this whole thing.

WHEELER: NO! YOU KEEP BOXING! There's nothing worse than a lazy boxer. Good men put their money behind you, and what do you do in return? Sluff off! I'm sick of it!

RABBIT: I just wanted to give you some background on the wheel. That's all.

WHEELER: Well, get on with it then!

RABBIT: Yessir. Now, if you'll notice, there's four main bundles in the wheel. One for each point on the compass. To the North is wisdom, and its medicine animal is the buffalo. The color of the North is white.

WHEELER: I hope this isn't going to take too long. I might die any second, you know.

TYMPANI: What's happened is that we're locked into the narrowest part of our dream machine.

WHEELER: WHO'S THAT TALKING OUT LOUD! SHUT HIM UP!

TYMPANI: I was on the verge of discovery. Things were opening up. I could actually see an opening. A rhythm. A whole new pattern.

(LANX *boxes his way over to* TYMPANI *and punches him in the stomach.* TYMPANI *doubles over, but continues cooking from this position.* LANX *goes on shadowboxing.* RABBIT *explains the wheel.*)

WHEELER: (*to* RABBIT) You'll have to excuse me. Go on.

RABBIT: The South is the sign of the mouse, and its medicine color is green. The South is the place of innocence and trust.

WHEELER: Amazing! The Indians dreamed this up?

RABBIT: In the West is the sign of the bear. The West is the "Looks-Within" place, and its color is black—

WHEELER: Hold it! What's that mean? "Looks-Within" place? What does that mean?

RABBIT: Uh—I guess it means the place for looking inside yourself? It's a very dangerous medicine bundle. In fact it's the only authentic bundle I've got. The rest are imitations.

WHEELER: What's so dangerous about it?

RABBIT: There's a warning written on the outside of it saying that if it's ever opened a terrible force will be let loose in the world.

WHEELER: What terrible force? What kind of baloney is that! Go on to the next one. What's the next one?

RABBIT: The East is the sign of the eagle. This is the place of illumination, where we can see things clearly far and wide. Its color is gold.

WHEELER: Very nice. Now, how does it work?

RABBIT: I don't know.

WHEELER: (*standing*) WHAT!

RABBIT: That's what I've been trying to tell you. This is an ancient design. How am I supposed to know. I'm a white man. It took thousands of years to cook this up. I'm just explaining the structure.

TYMPANI: (*still in crouch from* LANX'S *blow*) Two over-easy with bacon!

LANX: (*stops boxing and crosses to* TYMPANI) Right.

(TYMPANI *serves* LANX *the imaginary food, holding his own stomach in pain.* LANX *sits on the floor and eats it. The rest continue.*)

WHEELER: ANCIENT! I'm ancient! We're all ancient! What's ancient got to do with it!

RABBIT: I'm exhausted. I can't keep up with this. I'm just going to look out the window for a while. Maybe something will come to me. Something's got to come sooner or later.

(RABBIT *crosses slowly upstage and stares out the rectangle.* WHEELER *watches him for a second.*)

WHEELER: There's something deadly going on here! I can smell it. It's the smell of my own skin! You've all given up on me, haven't you? That's what it is! That's exactly what it is. Your situation isn't quite so urgent as mine, so you've given up and left me to the dogs. Left me here to rot in my juices! Well, I can tell you one thing! Without leadership you're as good as gone. I know this city inside out! There's nowhere you can go without me! Nowhere!

MISS SCOONS: (*still scrubbing*) I haven't given up on you, sir. I still think you're a smashing gov'nor.

WHEELER: My office used to be swarming with talent, and now it's like a cesspool!

RABBIT: (*looking out rectangle*) You can't see a thing out here. It's all yellow.

WHEELER: It was a gamble right from the start. I gambled on imagination and lost. My dream was to create an industry of imagination! Now look at it! Poisoned! Putrified!

TYMPANI: (*still doubled over*) Would you like some breakfast, sir?

WHEELER: Yes I would. I would like that. That would make things better even though things have never been worse.

TYMPANI: What would you like?

WHEELER: Ham and eggs with the yolks hard. I'll die with the yolk in my chest.

TYMPANI: Right. (*starts cooking*)

RABBIT: You're expecting too much.

WHEELER: I'm expecting to survive! That's all. To live! To be alive! To stay in my skin!

RABBIT: But you haven't even told me who the other characters are, what the story is, or anything. How am I supposed to do anything without information? Even a second-rate hack gets to know what the picture's about!

WHEELER: That's top secret!

RABBIT: Great.

WHEELER: I can see now that I've been abandoned. I should've known.

RABBIT: What is it that's eating you anyway? I mean what is this skin condition that you've developed?

WHEELER: Don't press me, Brown. You're on thin ice.

RABBIT: I mean you've got all of us turning ourselves inside out for you, but nobody really knows what it is you're suffering from.

WHEELER: That's my business!

RABBIT: It's no business! It's a disease!

WHEELER: So what! Something's eating me, and that's all that counts!

RABBIT: You're the disaster, Wheeler. You don't have to look any further. You're it!

WHEELER: You're in no position to be putting the finger on me! I'm the cause for your being here. It turns out you're worthless anyway. All you've brought is a bag of cheap Indian tricks! And only one of those is authentic.

RABBIT: I don't believe there even is a movie. That's it, isn't it? You don't even have a scrap of footage.

WHEELER: Don't be ridiculous!

LANX: I could fix up a cement bathing suit for him real easy, boss.

WHEELER: SHUT UP!

RABBIT: There is no movie! All you've got is a disaster!

WHEELER: I HAVE A MILLION MOVIES! AND DO YOU KNOW WHERE THEY ARE! THEY'RE IN MY BLOOD! THEY'RE CHURNING AROUND IN MY BLOOD! THEY'RE INSIDE THERE WITHOUT ANY FORM OR REASON AND THEY CAN'T GET OUT! EVERY ONE OF THEM IS TEARING ME APART! CHEWING AT THE WALLS! TRYING TO ESCAPE! TRYING TO BECOME SOMETHING! TRYING TO OOZE OUT AND TAKE ON A SHAPE THAT WE ALL CAN SEE! AND EVERY ONE OF THEM IS EATING ME! CHEWING ME APART FROM THE INSIDE OUT! A MILLION DEVILS! MOVIES TO MAKE YOUR HEAD SWIM! DON'T TALK TO ME ABOUT MOVIES!

(WHEELER *starts to shake and tremble violently.* MISS SCOONS *gets up and rushes to him. She escorts him to the swivel chair, where he collapses.*)

MISS SCOONS: Mr. Wheeler, sir! You shouldn't get so wrought up! It's only a movie, for pity sake! You mustn't tax yourself so. You just relax now.

(*She loosens his collar.* WHEELER *gasps for air.*)

TYMPANI: Ham and eggs with the yolks hard!

MISS SCOONS: (*to* TYMPANI) Not now, you bleeding twit!

TYMPANI: But that's what he ordered.

MISS SCOONS: Can't you see he's about to expire, then?

TYMPANI: Well, what am I going to do with this order? He's gotta' pay for it. I can't cook and cook and cook and never get anything in return.

WHEELER: I'll pay for it. I'll pay for everything. All the damages.

MISS SCOONS: Try not to talk, sir.

LANX: (*to* MISS SCOONS) Let him die. What do you care?

WHEELER: (*gasping to* LANX) We'll have to show him the rushes. That's all there is to it.

LANX: (*pause, standing*) Are you crazy?

WHEELER: There's no other way around it. He's got to know what the material is before it's too late.

LANX: What if he's spying for another studio? It's too big a risk.

WHEELER: We'll have to take the chance.

LANX: Listen, my whole future's wrapped up in this. You may die tomorrow, and I'll be left holding the bag.

WHEELER: Makes no difference. Go and load the projectors!

LANX: You can't order me around! You're half dead.

WHEELER: (WHEELER *leaps at* LANX *like a crazed animal*) GO AND LOAD THE PROJECTORS!!

(LANX *runs off stage-left.* WHEELER *is foaming at the mouth and snarling at the others.*)

WHEELER: ALL OF YOU! GET OUT!

(*The rest start to run for cover. He stops* RABBIT *in his tracks.*)

WHEELER: NOT YOU!

(*Everyone has gone now except for* WHEELER *and* RABBIT. *The two of them stare at each other.* WHEELER *breathing heavily and swaying from side to side.* RABBIT *cringes to one side. Through this next section the stage lights slowly dim as the rectangle is lit. The scrim turns pale green. Slowly* WHEELER *stalks* RABBIT *around the stage; his breathing becomes more and more desperate and seems to control the tempo of the scene.* RABBIT *tries to keep his distance as best he can.*)

WHEELER: (*wheezing in half whisper*) What's that black place called again?

RABBIT: What?

WHEELER: The black place? That place on your circle? The dangerous bundle?

RABBIT: Oh, that.

WHEELER: The bear?

RABBIT: The West.

WHEELER: That's right. The West. That's where we are, isn't it? The West? This is the West? We can't get any further West than this.

RABBIT: This?

WHEELER: What's it called again?

RABBIT: What?

WHEELER: (*suddenly unleashing*) WHAT'S THE WEST CALLED!! Don't play stupid with me!

RABBIT: Oh. The "Looks-Within" place.

WHEELER: That's right. "Looks-Within."

RABBIT: I didn't understand you at first.

WHEELER: Of course not. That's because you're full of fear.

RABBIT: What?

WHEELER: FEAR!! YOU'RE FULL OF FEAR! YOU'RE FACING ME AND YOU DON'T KNOW WHAT I AM!

RABBIT: No.

WHEELER: You don't know what's coming next.

RABBIT: No.

WHEELER: That's right. And you're wondering.

RABBIT: Yes.

WHEELER: And your wondering leads you to imagine the worst.

RABBIT: No.

WHEELER: "NO" WON'T HELP!

RABBIT: NO!

WHEELER: Because now, at any moment, what you most fear might actually happen. It might actually crawl out of the walls, and appear.

RABBIT: You don't know what I fear.

WHEELER: There you go again, dreaming you're different. Setting yourself apart.

RABBIT: You can't be inside of me!

WHEELER: WE'RE THE SAME!

RABBIT: NO!

WHEELER: WHAT WE FEAR IS THE SAME! THAT MAKES US EQUAL!

RABBIT: You're crazy, Wheeler! You're a raving maniac!

WHEELER: And you?

RABBIT: What about me?

WHEELER: What are you?

RABBIT: AN ARTIST!

(WHEELER *starts laughing maniacally, doubling himself over.*)

RABBIT: YOU'RE THE PRODUCER, AND I'M THE ARTIST!

(WHEELER *laughs harder.*)

RABBIT: YOU CALLED ME DOWN HERE! I'M IN DEMAND! YOU'RE A DIME A DOZEN!

(WHEELER *stops himself abruptly.*)

WHEELER: That's true. A dime a dozen.

RABBIT: You don't know a thing about creation.

WHEELER: I was created without my knowing. Same as you. Creation's a disease.

RABBIT: What are you talking about?

WHEELER: We're dying here. Right now. In front of each other.

RABBIT: Just stay away from me, Wheeler!

WHEELER: I was turned into this beyond my knowing. I was spawned somehow by a city. I was leaked out. An Angel in disguise.

RABBIT: You're nothing!

WHEELER: I'M SOMETHING AWESOME! I'M FINDING OUT WHAT IT MEANS!

RABBIT: What what means?

WHEELER: The West.

RABBIT: It's just a place.

WHEELER: It's a place of discovery. Things are uncovered here. Gold! Oceans! LOOK INSIDE OF ME!

RABBIT: That's all been discovered.

WHEELER: Only the surface. We're cracking the surface, Brown. We're going into a deep black bear. We're taking the plunge. We're penetrating the flesh and bone.

RABBIT: Get off it, Wheeler. This is a corporation. You're an executive.

WHEELER: We're going straight through all the paraphernalia. All the ponytails, all the jargon, all the Indian lore, all the magic mumbo jumbo. Deeper than California! We're going down, Brown! We're coming face to face with something deadly.

RABBIT: Not me.

WHEELER: You can't get out of it!

RABBIT: I'M NOT IN IT!

WHEELER: What was the sign for the East again?

RABBIT: I'm not playing, Wheeler!

WHEELER: "The place of illumination, where we can see clearly far and wide. The place of the eagle."

RABBIT: So what!

WHEELER: Where's your faith, Rabbit? I thought you prayed regularly? What happened to your missions? Your sense of mission? Your hero?

RABBIT: That's got nothing to do with it. You're twisting things up.

WHEELER: Things are twisted! Monsters are being hatched by the dozens and turned into saints! We can do anything here! Anything is possible here! We can recreate the world and make you swallow it whole! We can make a nightmare out of a molehill! We can tear you to shreds and make you like it.

RABBIT: You can't mix real life with the movies!

(WHEELER *goes into convulsive laughter and starts to have a slight seizure.*)

WHEELER: THE MOVIES! THIS IS THE MOVIES!!

RABBIT: (*suddenly covering his head as though afraid to be photographed*) No camera! No camera!

(WHEELER *chases him, miming a movie camera, trying to photograph him.*)

WHEELER: (*talking to* RABBIT *as though he were a primitive child*) You don't understand. It won't hurt you. It's just a machine. All it does is capture light in a certain pattern. It shows you moving.

RABBIT: (*running away*) No! No camera! No capture!

WHEELER: Don't be silly. It's fun. Look. I'll do it on myself. Look! (*he turns imaginary camera on himself*) See? No pain. It's fun.

RABBIT: It's Devil!

WHEELER: It's not. It's beautiful. It makes us see ourselves. It brings things back to life. It makes us happy.

RABBIT: No happy!

WHEELER: Happy! Everybody loves pictures. It's just like magic. Look, I'll show you.

(WHEELER *goes to swivel chair and pulls it down left for* RABBIT. RABBIT *runs.*)

RABBIT: No capture! No light!

WHEELER: No. I'll show you the footage. You'll love it. You're the only one outside our crew who's even seen it. It's top-secret footage. Absolutely private.

RABBIT: No secret! Devil!

WHEELER: (*trying to coax* RABBIT *into swivel chair*) But we'd love to get your reactions to it. It's so nerve-racking editing a film. Everyone giving you criticism and opinions, but someone like you would give a raw, gut-level reaction which could prove invaluable to us.

RABBIT: (*settling down a little*) No light.

WHEELER: (*escorting him to chair and sitting him down*) Please. Just as a favor. I promise that no one will photograph you. Just sit down and enjoy yourself. Relax. Everything's beautiful. Everything's going to be just fine. The lights will slowly fade. (*lights follow to dark*) The crowd will grow silent. The screen will light up with beautiful colors. (*scrim turns red slowly*) Your body will go limp and your mind will drift off into a wonderful world of adventure.

(RABBIT *is seated downstage in swivel chair facing rectangle upstage, his back to audience.* WHEELER *backs away from him carefully.*)

WHEELER: Now just try to relax and watch the movie like a good boy.

(*Sudden crash of cymbals, bells, and pulsing percussion offstage.* SAX PLAYER *enters down-right corner playing low, lurking melody. He faces upstage to platform.* TYMPANI *enters down left and accompanies on drums. He stands on downstage side of drums facing up to platform. He could bring on another percussion instrument too.* WHEELER *pulls out a long black flashlight and clicks it on in the dark. The only lights now are the neon rectangle, backlighting on scrim, and* WHEELER's *flashlight.* WHEELER *begins to narrate, using the flashlight like a schoolmaster's stick.* RABBIT *stays seated and unseen.*)

WHEELER: (*amplified, documentary voice*) Our story opens with the city in a state of siege. A deadlock between two powers so intent upon destroying each other that even the vanishing of their own existence in that struggle means nothing to them. They would sooner die than attempt to coexist.

(LANX *and* MISS SCOONS *enter from opposite sides of the platform very slowly. They are covered from head to foot in very long, silken robes with Oriental designs in bright colors, intricately woven dragons on their chests and backs. The robes cover their heads, which seem to be extended somewhat. Around their waists are wide black sashes with long tassels, and several long black sticks about the size of broom handles are held in by the sashes. They are both barefoot. Their shoulders are huge under the robes. In general they give the impression of menacing Samurai warriors.*)

WHEELER: By this time the city has long been in the hands of roving bands of outlaw-warriors. At one time content to work under the shackles of the Lords and Bosses, one after the other they have broken away and taken the law into their own hands, preferring the America of their distant frontier past.

(*The two warrior figures inch their way slowly forward toward each other, walking on the balls of their feet and releasing low guttural noises from inside the robes. When they reach a certain point, with some distance between them, they slowly move into a crouched position, knees bending slowly, keeping their backs straight, and come down so that they're sitting on their heels with their hands resting on their thighs. They face each other in this position for a while. Their sounds continue as* WHEELER *shines the flashlight on them and goes on with his narration.*)

WHEELER: The siege, however, has become so bloody and so awesome that even the head chieftains of these two deadly powers have agreed to meet in a remote area of the city to see if they can come to some understanding of the future of their predicament. There has never been a summit conference of this

kind as long as can be remembered. Every battle in their recorded history was fought to the bitter end out of their strange
sense of honor. Even suicides are a thing of the past.

(*Drums and sax fill slowly as the two chiefs slowly withdraw the sticks
from their belts and hold them in front of each other at eye level. This
should seem more like an acknowledgment of battle than a threat.*)

WHEELER: The meeting goes on in silence with the city burning
brightly in the distance. There is no talk of peace. Peace would
only serve to wipe them out slowly. Their only concern is how to
come to a speedy annihilation. They agree to leave their future
in the hands of their two generals and to retire themselves to a
deep system of caves where they will enact their final duel in
solitude.

(*Slowly the two chieftains rise and take off their long robes, revealing
the generals underneath. The robes fall to the ground. Underneath they
are dressed in red crash helmets with long black visors covering their
faces. They each wear heavy football shoulder pads without shirts,
kidney pads tied to their waists, and padded football pants. They have
elbow pads and white tape around their wrists. They slowly bend down
and pick up a stick from the floor. They square off to each other like
Samurai warriors.*)

WHEELER: The generals see each other eye to eye. There's a
meeting in their eyes. They recognize themselves. There's no
way out for them. Their roles are well defined. Their armies are
in position. There's nothing holding back.

(*The generals suddenly come crashing down on each other with the sticks.
Loud clang of percussion, sax, and high shrieking voices of* LANX *and*
MISS SCOONS! *They back off and again face each other with the sticks.
They charge again. High screams, crash of sticks. Percussion, sax, then
back to attack positions. Each return to this position after an attack is
marked by stillness and concentration. Music softens.*)

WHEELER: The battle lasted days, with the armies agreeing finally
to become the audience to their two generals. They watched the
sun rise and fall on them with neither one growing any weaker
than the other. Gambling grew so rampant between the two
armies that soon there grew a bond between them so strong that
they were joined together as one vast army. But the generals
went on.

(*Crash of generals again. Percussion, etc. Back to attack positions.*)

WHEELER: Again and again they crashed into each other with the heavy swords. The cold steel flashed across the City of Angels and cut the stillness of the ruins. No bird sang, no dog barked, no man moved.

(LANX *and* MISS SCOONS *continue with their parries and attacks throughout, with the musical accompaniment along with their voices.* WHEELER *continues, sweeping the scene with his flashlight.*)

WHEELER: The mood of the armies changed from camaraderie to one of fear, for they could all sense the impending doom of this last battle. The generals were exactly matched in strength, endurance, and intelligence. In fact they were so exactly the same in every respect that one couldn't be told from the other. The only possible outcome was death to them both. On and on they fought into the night until slowly the armies began to thin out and wander away into the desert. Finally the generals were left all alone. Their sounds were lonely and distant like two wild bucks on an empty prairie. They couldn't remember a city at all. Civilization had come and gone without them knowing. They were battling into another time. They were crossing continents as they fought. They were passing history by.

(*The clashes between the generals go on with the accompanied sax and percussion. Voices from* LANX *and* MISS SCOONS. *They continue to reposition and attack. The stage is very dark still, except for the glowing rectangle. The scrim has faded to a pale red in the background.*)

WHEELER: As far as they knew, they were the only living things. The moon raced across the sky. The planets howled in space. Their primitive weapons performed a conversation in empty space.

(*Battle goes on. Music rises and falls.*)

WHEELER: Finally, after days of constant combat, one of the generals revealed himself as a woman.

(MISS SCOONS *takes off her helmet and visor and sets it on the floor.* LANX *freezes and stares at her, still keeping his helmet on. Music stops.*)

WHEELER: In that moment, the opposing general was caught off guard, and the female plunged her weapon home.

(MISS SCOONS *lets out a shattering scream and plunges her stick inside the upstage arm of* LANX, *who drops his stick with a groan. He stands there facing her. She keeps hold of the stick without pulling it out of him.*)

WHEELER: At last the generals saw their situation. They were one being with two opposing parts. Everything was clear to them. At last they were connected. In that split second they gained and lost their entire lives.

(*Very slowly* LANX *begins to pull himself along the stick toward* MISS SCOONS, *impaling himself more and more with each step. She holds her ground and waits for him. The saxophone and drums enter in here and gather force.* LANX *finally reaches her. They embrace and stand there in each other's arms. Music reaches a peak, then suddenly stops. Stage lights bang up to bright yellow.* MISS SCOONS *and* LANX *release each other and drop right back into their old characters, as they were in Act 1.* LANX *takes off his helmet and they both rest on the platform. (One of them could even go off and get them both some water and then come back on.) This all should be very relaxed and as though they were two athletes just finishing an event.* RABBIT *is still hidden in the swivel chair.* WHEELER *talks to him as he strides nervously around the stage.* TYMPANI *and the* SAX PLAYER *leave the stage.*)

WHEELER: (*to* RABBIT) So, what do you think?

RABBIT: (*unseen*) Terrible. Corniest stuff I ever saw.

WHEELER: (*pounding the flashlight with his fist and striding angrily*) What's wrong with it! WHAT THE HELL'S WRONG WITH IT!

RABBIT: (*still unseen*) Everything.

WHEELER: What do you mean! It's got a story, a plot, good meaty characters, tremendous language, colorful locations. It has motion, adventure, conflict, excitement, rhythm, poetry. It's got everything!

(*Suddenly* RABBIT *whips the swivel chair around so it's facing* WHEELER. RABBIT*'s skin has turned slimy green; he has fangs, long black fingernails, and a long, thick mane of black hair. He remains seated.* WHEELER *is the only one who notices the change in* RABBIT*'s appearance.* LANX *and* MISS SCOONS *remain indifferent.* MISS SCOONS *starts massaging* LANX*'S shoulders as they sit on the platform upstage.*)

RABBIT: There's no disaster! We're not interested in hanky-panky love stories, romantically depicting the end of the world. We're after hard-core disaster. I thought you understood that.

WHEELER: (*moving backwards slightly*) Wait a minute. Wait a minute!

(WHEELER *looks for reassurance to* LANX *and* MISS SCOONS *but they only smile back at him.*)

RABBIT: (*rising out of chair*) No, you wait a minute, mister.

WHEELER: Don't come any closer! I'm not well! I'm not supposed to have any severe shocks! I might have a heart attack! (*turning to* LANX, *who ignores him*) LANX, WHAT ARE YOU DOING! I'M BEING THREATENED!

RABBIT: They can't hear you. They can't even see you.

WHEELER: What do you mean! Of course they can see me! I can see them! They smiled at me before!

RABBIT: You're in trouble, mister.

WHEELER: I'M NOT IN TROUBLE! HOW COULD I BE IN TROUBLE! I'M PROTECTED HERE!

RABBIT: What'd you think, you could come down here in your provincial gear and pull the wool over our eyes? We've had experience, ya' know.

WHEELER: WAIT A MINUTE! I'M NOT YOU, GODDAMMIT! I'M ME!

RABBIT: You might as well burn that footage up and go back to making campfires. You're washed up in this town, buddy.

WHEELER: I'M ESTABLISHED! I'M FIRMLY ESTABLISHED! I'm in the business. I'm in pictures. I plant pictures in people's heads. I plant them and they grow. They grow more pictures. And the pictures grow like wildfire. People see them in front of their eyes. While they're shopping. While they're driving. While they're making love. Wherever they go I go with them. I spread their disease. I'm that powerful.

RABBIT: Look, if you don't mind, I've got several appointments, and you're burning my time.

WHEELER: LANX! DO SOMETHING ABOUT THIS!

(LANX *and* MISS SCOONS *are now sitting on the edge of the platform, swinging their legs back and forth and eating imaginary popcorn as they watch* RABBIT *and* WHEELER *like two teenagers watching a movie.* LANX *makes no acknowledgment of* WHEELER'S *presence other than that he's an image on a movie screen.*)

RABBIT: We've arranged your bus fare back to wherever it is you came from.

WHEELER: LANX! WHAT'S THE MATTER WITH YOU!

RABBIT: You're on the silver screen, buddy. You've been captured in celluloid and you'll never get out. All they're looking at is a moving picture show.

WHEELER: I'M A PERSON! THEY CAN SEE ME! THEY KNOW WHO I AM! MISS SCOONS! MISS SCOONS! IT'S ME! YOUR

BOSS! MISS SCOONS! LOOK AT ME! LOOK AT ME! I'M
OVER HERE!

(WHEELER *starts waving frantically at* MISS SCOONS *and* LANX *but they
only smile and chew their popcorn.*)

RABBIT: You better get outa' here before you disintegrate right here
on the spot.

WHEELER: (*turning on* RABBIT) I won't disintegrate! I'M IMMORTAL!
I'LL ALWAYS BE REMEMBERED! Right now there's people
watching! Right this very minute! There's people all around me!
Watching and remembering! As long as they're watching I'll be
remembered!

RABBIT: You're dead, Wheeler. You're dead and gone.

(WHEELER *stops and stares at* RABBIT. *Pause. He turns and stares at*
LANX *and* MISS SCOONS *still eating their popcorn. He turns and looks at
the audience. He turns back to* RABBIT.)

WHEELER: (*to* RABBIT) I'll show you who's dead.

(WHEELER *crosses slowly to the medicine bundle depicting the West and
picks it up.* RABBIT *watches him, undisturbed.* WHEELER *turns to* RABBIT,
holding the bundle out in front of him.)

RABBIT: Ah, back to your old tricks, huh? What do you think that's
going to do?

(WHEELER *crosses to* RABBIT *slowly, holding out the bundle.*)

WHEELER: (*quietly to himself*) It's going to open up the world. It's going
to get me out of here. It's going to reveal something. It's going
to change everything from the way it is now to something else.

RABBIT: Can't you stand the way it is?

WHEELER: Can you?

RABBIT: Well, go ahead then. See what happens.

WHEELER: Would you hold my hand while I do it?

RABBIT: Well, how're you going to open it up then?

WHEELER: I never thought of that.

RABBIT: You want me to do it?

WHEELER: No.

RABBIT: You want me to help you?

WHEELER: No.

RABBIT: Well, go ahead then.

WHEELER: (*pauses, staring at bundle*) What if it's worse than we can
imagine?

RABBIT: It couldn't be.

WHEELER: No. I guess not.

(WHEELER *slowly unties the bundle. As the bundle opens up, a slow, steady stream of green liquid, the color of their faces, oozes from it onto the stage.* RABBIT *and* WHEELER *watch it as they stand there.* LANX *and* MISS SCOONS *are still watching them, as though in the movies. They speak as the lights are slowly dimming.* RABBIT *and* WHEELER *remain still while the liquid drips.*)

MISS SCOONS: (*to* LANX) I'm not supposed to stay for the second one, ya' know, Jimmy.

LANX: Yeah, yeah.

MISS SCOONS: Well, I'm not. I'm supposed to be back before eleven.

LANX: I just wanna' stay for the titles.

MISS SCOONS: Last time you said that we never got back until three in the morning.

LANX: That was last time.

MISS SCOONS: I almost got sent to Juvie. I don't wanna' get sent to Juvie again.

LANX: Relax, will ya'. You're not gonna get sent to Juvie, for Christ's sake. I just wanna' see the titles.

MISS SCOONS: Why, do you know somebody in this movie or somethin'?

LANX: Just shut up, will ya'.

(*Lights slowly fade to black with sax filling in softly over the scene.*)

MELODRAMA
PLAY

A Melodrama with Music

Characters

DUKE
DANA
FLOYD
DRAKE
PETER
CISCO

Notes on Melodrama Play

Melodrama Play is unproduced.* A production of this play should not be aimed toward making it strictly satirical but more toward discovering how it changes from the mechanism of melodrama to something more sincere. This change does not just occur slowly from one thing into the other in the course of the play but rapidly as well and very frequently, especially in the case of Dana. There are no stage directions indicating when these changes should take place because some of them appear obvious to me and many of them do not. So I would rather leave their selection up to a director in any case. The selections themselves can also range from the most elaborate down to the most subtle. The band should behave like an additional audience, with dictated reactions to the play instead of spontaneous ones. When they sing, it should be as though they were performing in a discothèque and likewise when the actors dance. This also should be the case when Cisco sings his song but not necessarily when Duke sings. It might be helpful if a musician were cast as Cisco instead of an actor. It seems to me that everything about the play should be abrupt and flashy, except toward the end when Peter gets into his history. It might also be nice to have the band suspended from the ceiling in a cage over the audience's head.

Sam Shepard

*Editor's note: Since the above was written *Melodrama Play* has been produced by the La Mama Repertory and several other companies. The original score was composed by Tom O'Horgan. Mr. O'Horgan also directed the La Mama production.

SCENE: *A room. In the center of the upstage wall is a door. Stage right of the door on the wall is a huge black-and-white photograph of Bob Dylan without eyes. Stage left of the door is an equally large photo of Robert Goulet without eyes. A sofa against the stage-left wall. A small table at the downstage end of the sofa with a radio on it. A piano against the stage-right wall. An electric guitar lies on the floor down-center with a speaker and amplifier facing the audience. There is a four-piece rock-and-roll band seated in a cage on top of a platform at the back of the audience all dressed exactly like* DUKE. *They stand to sing their songs, then sit back down when they're finished. The lights come up fast.* DUKE DURGENS *enters very fast through the door wearing extra long hair, shades, jeans, boots, vest, etc. He crosses directly downstage center, bows to the audience, and begins to improvise the following song without accompaniment.*

DUKE: Everybody knows that everybody grows
  And everybody starts out fast
  And everybody knows that anybody knows
  How to make it last and last
  And everybody says that you shouldn't snoop around
  You shouldn't put your nose down to the ground
  You shouldn't say out loud what we already know
  You should say it to yourself
  You should play it by yourself
  You should keep it in your mouth
  You should hold it in your throat
  Even if you bloat
  Even if you get to the point where you burst.

(*He stomps his foot on the ground and stops the song; he paces up and down, mumbling to himself and hitting his fist into his hand; he does this for a while, then stops and bows again to the audience.* DANA, *a girl with long hair, boots, jeans, leather jacket, shades, etc., enters fast with an envelope in her hand and sits on the sofa; she opens the envelope and pulls out a letter which she reads to herself while* DUKE *starts singing again to the audience.*)

DUKE: Nobody knows where the pain got started
It's still the same as it always was
Nobody sees how the pain gets started
So it just goes on like it always does
But if you'll come around to the back of my shack
If you'll come around when your legs start sagging
Then I know a way to stop you from gagging
I know a way to rest your head
But if you go on like you always do
If you go on thinking you're so true
Then the day will come when we'll all be dead
Without ever knowing what we could have done instead
So if you'll come around to the back of my shack . . .

(*He stomps his foot again and paces up and down as before.*)

DANA: How's it going?

DUKE: You heard. Shit. Garbage. Stuff I could have done in school behind everyone's back. Boy. It's terrible. Just terrible. I don't know what to do.

DANA: You got a letter.

DUKE: Good. (*continuing to pace*)

DANA: I'll read it out loud.

DUKE: Thank you.

DANA: (*reading the letter*) "Dear Mr. Durgens: I am a sociologist at Corning University and am currently engaged in a study of contemporary American musicians. I would like to ask you to participate in this study. My main interest is in discovering what changes occur in the life of a singer when one of his songs is received and acclaimed by the public at large. For example, how did you go about getting your first song, 'Prisoners, Get Up out of Your Homemade Beds,' recorded and once it became a hit how did this affect your life?"

(DUKE *starts singing as he continues to pace,* DANA *stops reading.*)

DUKE: Won't you pretty please move a little to the left
Won't you pretty please move a little to the right
Won't you shake your ass
Won't you shake your tits
Won't you please shake, baby, before I have fits
Wow!

DANA: Could I continue, please.

DUKE: Please do! Please continue on. There's more coming and if that's true I certainly would not want to be the one to block it from coming. Not me! Not I! After all, who am I to say stop! Stop coming, my dear? Not me.

DANA: Thanks.

(*She continues with the letter as* DUKE *paces.*)

DANA: "After the public response to 'Prisoners, Get Up out of Your Homemade Beds,' did your relations with friends, colleagues, and others in the music business change? Did you begin work on a new song or go back to work you had done previously? Did new opportunities become available in other media, etc.?"

DUKE: Yes! Oh yes. Mr.—Mr.—who?

DANA: Mr. Damon.

DUKE: Yes, Mr. Damon. Certainly. Vistas opened out and up and all around me. I saw things that I'd never seen before. I saw dogs burying their own shit as soon as they'd shat and what's more wiping themselves afterwards. I saw waiters tipping bankers and—

DANA: Shall I go on with this?

DUKE: As you wish. (*he continues to pace and hit his hand*)

DANA: (*reading*) "I mention these few questions to give you a more definite idea of the content of the study. No previous studies have been done concerning the singer and how his personal relationships are affected by the response to his work. The usual question that the historian or academician asks is how a singer's life affects the content of his work. Here I am concerned with how the reception of his work affects the singer's social environment. I realize how busy you must be but I hope you will consent to being interviewed. The interview should take about one hour. I can assure you of complete anonymity. I do hope you will participate and I'm looking forward to your reply. Sincerely yours, Daniel Damon."

DUKE: Good, good. Give it here. Let me see. (*he crosses to her and takes the letter; he pulls out a pen and writes on the back of the letter*) "Dear Daniel Damon . . ."

DANA: Oh Duke. Don't be silly. Honestly.

DUKE: "In reply to your letter I would like to say thank you very much. Sincerely, Duke Durgens."

(*He begins folding the letter into a paper airplane.*)

DANA: You should just turn it in to your manager, that's all. You don't have to reply personally like that. Turn it in to Floyd.

DUKE: Floyd's got work to do.

DANA: Well so do you.

DUKE: So do I. I have work and Floyd has work and there's no gaps in between for anything like replies to Danny Damon. But it must be done. We can't leave old Dan hanging. Not a sociologist, at any rate. Sociologists are movers. They don't hang around waiting for replies. They make up their own if they don't get them on time. And I'd hate to see him do that. To create a lie out of my negligence.

(*He rushes downstage and throws the letter out into the audience.* DANA *jumps to her feet.*)

DUKE: Here it comes, Danny! Watch it come! Don't let it get away! Yoo hoo!

DANA: Duke! What have you done! You ridiculous idiot! You've thrown the letter into the audience. Do you know what that means? That means anyone can pick that letter up and read it! And that means that anyone can pretend to be Duke Durgens and walk right up to Danny Damon and say hello I'm Duke and Danny will say well I'm glad to meet you at last Mr. Durgens and then he'll sit down with Mr. Damon and then they'll just proceed with the interview as though he were you and he'll tell Danny Damon whatever he wants and Mr. Damon will believe him and write it all down and pay him a great deal of money thinking it's you and he'll just leave and go spend it somewhere and there's no way to trace him because they don't know his real name or anything and meanwhile all this fake personal life that he's conjured up and slandered you with will be written down and printed by Daniel Damon and held forever in the private vaults of Corning University forever and ever with no way of our ever getting to read it. You stupid, stupid boy.

(FLOYD, DUKE'S *manager, enters wearing shades and a suit; he crosses to the piano, sits, and starts to play "Chopsticks."* DANA *crosses over to him but* FLOYD *keeps playing,* DUKE *just stares at the audience.*)

DANA: Floyd, I'm glad you arrived but Duke is really getting entirely out of hand here recently. He made an airplane out of a letter and threw it away. Can you imagine that?

FLOYD: (*still playing*) How did you manage that, Dukie?

DUKE: I made the wings and weighted it just right and gave it a little snap with my wrist and away she flew.

DANA: Bad news, Floyd, if that letter ever gets into the hands of a stranger. Anybody could pick that letter up. Anybody at any time. They might even go all the way. With a letter like that you've got a free ticket into almost anything you'd like. Who knows, someone could even start cutting records in Duke's name and get away with it even. Or charge free meals at Duke's expense or—

(FLOYD *stops playing and stands slowly, then crosses over to* DUKE *and puts his arm around his shoulders.*)

FLOYD: There's something bigger going on than that, Dana. We can handle that without too much sweat or pain. Right now the thing that bothers us more and more, my colleagues and I, is when will Duke produce for us his next hit tune. When is it that Duke will come to us with a shiny new tune that we can sell. Duke knows of course about his date in Phoenix coming up within the week. And he also knows that that date can be easily filled with his one original, million-dollar, gold-label, award-winning song, "Prisoners, Get Up out of Your Homemade Beds," and the rest of the evening can be spent with Duke singing songs from other artists' repertoires, but when is it that Dukie will come to us and say look Floyd I've done it, I've come through, here's my next hit?

DUKE: I don't know, Floyd. I'm stuck.

FLOYD: But he will. It just takes time. And before you know it there it is staring you in the face. It was there all along but he just couldn't see but now he sees with his own two eyes and his eyes light up like never before because he knows he's got it now. He knows he can show it to Floyd and then Floyd can show it to the world and the world will see it for the very first time and the world will say we were just stuck before but now Dukie's come through and shown us the way.

DANA: He's been trying, Floyd.

(FLOYD *digs his fingers into the back of* DUKE'S *neck.*)

FLOYD: Then everything just falls off Dukie's back. There's a general relief for Dukie and the pressure he felt in the back of his neck is gone forever and ever. And he doesn't know how to thank himself for that. (*he breaks away from* DUKE *and heads toward the door*) There'll be two guitarists here at two o'clock sharp and I've told them to be at your complete disposal. They'll give you all the time you need but you'd better use it because they cost twenty-five an hour plus tips so I don't want any clowning around. Dana, you get Duke whatever he needs, coffee or anything, and see that he stays up here until something gets done. And don't bother him about trivia because that's for me and my men to deal with and no one else. Is that clear? I'll be back here at six to see how things are shaping up. Good luck.

(*He exits. As soon as he closes the door the band stands and begins this song and* DANA *and* DUKE *do the frug onstage; this song should be loud and fast.*)

#1 BAND SONG

Well ya' grew up small
Then ya' grew up big
And the folks in town
Ask ya' what ya' dig
And ya' said to them
Well I hadn't thought
And they said to you
Don't let yourself get caught
Just jerkin' off behind some dark tree
'Cause the neighbor's kid got caught doin' that
And a' course ya' know where he wound up at
He's now in either

Sing Sing or Alcatraz or either
Sing Sing or Alcatraz or
The county zoo
It's no good for you, boy
It's no good for you.

Then ya' said that sounds pretty scary to me
That's not really the place where I'd like to be
So ya' walked alone for four days straight
Ya' walked alone and ya' grew to hate
All the people in your hometown
All the people who brought you down
And ya' walked alone for eight days straight

Till ya' couldn't remember when it was ya' last ate
And ya' still didn't know how to seal your fate
Against the sounds of

Sing Sing or Alcatraz or either
Sing Sing or Alcatraz or
The county zoo
It's no good for you, boy
It's no good for you.

So ya' buried your face in some dark tree
And ya' sighed and gasped what's to become of me
But a man sat smokin' behind his desk
Right above the tree where you lay down to rest
And his voice echoed out right through the trunk
Boy, take my advice and don't believe in that junk
And ya' said okay but what can I do
And he said there's a' lot a' songs that I got for you
And ya' said boy oh boy I can hardly wait
And he said I already got you a date at either

Sing Sing or Alcatraz or either
Sing Sing or Alcatraz or
The county zoo
Just take your pick, boy
It'll be good for you.

Then ya' jumped right up off a' the ground
And you yelled wow when can I start
And he said well first we gotta' look around
For somebody who can accompany you
And ya' said I already know just who could do that
It's the neighbor's kid and ya' know where he's at
And he asked where and ya' told him true
Just like the folks in town had once told you
You said he's in either

Sing Sing or Alcatraz or either
Sing Sing or Alcatraz or
The county zoo
Either one I'm sure
Will be fine with you
Either one I'm sure
Will be fine with you.

(DANA *and* DUKE *finish dancing and applaud the band, the band bows and the play continues.*)

DUKE: Dana.

DANA: What?

DUKE: Do you have some scissors around?

DANA: No. Why?

(DUKE *reaches into his pocket and pulls out a roll of bills.*)

DUKE: Take this and go downstairs somewhere to a scissors shop and buy a pair and then come right back up.

DANA: What for? (*she takes the money*)

DUKE: Do as I say! You're supposed to get me what I want.

DANA: All right but you'd better get down to work or it'll be bad news all the way around.

DUKE: Take off, chick!

DANA: Scissors.

(*She exits,* DUKE *crosses down and bows to the audience, then sings.*)

DUKE: My baby's gone
Where did she go
I loved her so
Why did she go
She left me by myself
She left me in a trance
And I couldn't even dance for
Days and days.

My baby left
She left me all alone
She didn't leave a bone
For me to chew
I'm so very blue . . .

(*He stomps his foot, the band boos him,* DUKE *gives them the finger,* DANA *enters with scissors.*)

DANA: Scissors.

DUKE: Beautiful. Now cut my hair.

DANA: What!

(DUKE *crosses to the sofa and sits.*)

DUKE: I want you to cut off all my hair and then I have a surprise for you.

DANA: Duke, you can't do that. You have a date to do. You can't! You can't! You can't do that.

DUKE: Dana, I'm stuck. You know I'm stuck and I know it. But I have a surprise for everyone. I have a love song to sing but it has to correspond with the way I look or it just won't work. Now please cut my hair or I'll be stuck forever.

DANA: But Duke—

(*There is a loud knock at the door.*)

DANA: Who is it?

(*Another knock.*)

DUKE: Go see.

(DANA *crosses to the door.*)

DANA: Who is it, please?

(*A voice comes from the other side.*)

DRAKE'S VOICE: It's Drake, baby. Open up.

DANA: Duke, it's your brother. What shall I do? Oh what shall I do, Duke? Oh what can I do?

DUKE: Let him in.

(DANA *opens the door and* DRAKE DURGENS *enters with his friend* CISCO; *they both have long hair, shades, and are dressed exactly like* DUKE.)

DANA: Hello, Drake.

(CISCO *goes to the piano and starts playing "Chopsticks."*)

DRAKE: Howdy. Nothing going on here, eh? That's funny, Dukie. Every time we come around here there's nothing going on. How do you account for that?

DUKE: Must be the time of year.

DRAKE: Couldn't be that, baby, since we been here at all seasons and hours and the same nothing keeps going on. Don't you write or something? Don't you sing a little now and then to fill in the gaps?

DANA: Duke works all the time. There aren't any gaps to fill.

DRAKE: Can't expect one song to last you forever, Duke. What's the average duration of a hit like yours? What would you say offhand? Just candidly?

DUKE: I couldn't say. I'm not a sociologist.

DRAKE: I'd make a rough guess of about eight months, maybe nine. No more than that.

DUKE: Could be.

DRAKE: 'Course with a swinging head like yours you should have no trouble. You should have the mothers rolling out as fast as they come in. You know, a song a day at the very least. Maybe two if the climate's right. You know, if you're really tuned in to what's going on out in the streets. And given of course if the streets are tuned in to what's going on in the jukebox. It's like a circle, Dukie. You got to keep turning. Right?

DANA: Listen, Drake, Duke has to have his hair cut now so if you could go away for a while—

(CISCO *stops playing the piano and stands*, DUKE *stands*.)

DUKE: Dana, shut up!

DRAKE: Dukie's cutting his hair? No.

CISCO: You're cutting your hair?

DUKE: Look, Drake, I have some new songs that Floyd needs. I mean I've written a new love song and I need to change my hair for it. You know what I mean?

DRAKE: Sure, baby. I understand.

DUKE: It's not so drastic as all that. It'll grow back again. I'm sure of it.

DRAKE: Sure. Here, Dana, let's have those. (*he takes the scissors from* DANA *and crosses up to* DUKE) It's not so bad, Dukie. It'll just be like it was before you decided to let it grow. It'll just be shorter, that's all. (*he backs* DUKE *up until* DUKE *sits back down on the sofa with* DRAKE *standing over him holding the scissors*) So just relax. Try to think of something else if this bothers you at all. It won't be painful, in any case. And like you say, it'll all grow back in case you change your mind.

DUKE: I know, Drake, but I'm—

DRAKE: Shhhh. Cisco might even sing us a song if we just relax. If we take it easy and don't worry about anything at all. Cisco, what do you say? You sing our song, baby. Our own original song. And I'll cut Dukie's hair and Dukie will just relax and maybe Dana will hum or something. How does that sound, Dana?

DANA: I suppose. But be careful. He has a date to do.

CISCO: What song, Drake?

DRAKE: Sing the song we wrote last year in the bar across the street. The song we wrote at the table where Dukie was with us drinking wine and smiling.

DANA: What song was that?

DRAKE: You weren't there, Dana, but Dukie remembers. Go ahead, Cisco.

(CISCO *crosses downstage and picks up the guitar, bows to the audience and starts to play and sing while* DRAKE *cuts* DUKE'S *hair very short.*)

CISCO: Well early one day you got out a' bed
And then you decided to go to sleep instead
So early one day you got back in the sack
And fell fast asleep in your homemade rack.

Well you don't know how you decided this,
All that you know is there's somethin' you missed
But you don't know what and you don't know where
So you just stay put and ya' go nowhere.

Oh prisoners, won't you get up out a' your homemade beds,
Oh prisoners, won't you get up out a' your homemade beds.

Well early one night you got so very uptight
And you said this sleepin' it just ain't right
But there was nothin' at all that you could do
'Cause your eyes stayed shut with your homemade glue.

(DANA *starts yelling but* DUKE *just sits and lets* DRAKE *cut his hair as* CISCO *continues the song.*)

DANA: Stop it! Stop it! That's Duke's song! Stop singing! Stop it! I'll call the police!

CISCO: But you couldn't hear your own voice speak
And ya' couldn't walk 'cause your legs was too weak
So ya' lay in bed cryin' to yourself
And your life just sat there hanging on the shelf.

Oh prisoners, get up out a' your homemade beds,
Oh prisoners, get up out a' your homemade beds.

And now the day and night are just the same
And now the light and dark don't have no name
And you just lay in bed without no game
And you just lay there sleepin' without no fame.

But when you do awaken from your deep sleep
The bed will disappear and you won't even weep,
You'll walk right outside without no name,
You'll walk right outside from where you came.

So prisoners, get up out a' your homemade beds,
Oh prisoners, get up out a' your homemade heads.

(*The band applauds*, CISCO *bows*.)

DANA: You lousy bastards! Duke, they stole your song! Duke wrote that song, not you!

DRAKE: (*still cutting* DUKE'S *hair while* DUKE *just sits passively*) Duke *sold* the song. Didn't you, Dukie?

DANA: He wrote it, too! I remember the night he came home with it in his head. He came right through that door and he said darling I have a song! I have a beautiful, beautiful song with a protest message and poetry and everything. And I said I'm so happy and we both sat down right here and went to work on it. It took us four and a half hours because I timed it. And when it was done we played it on the piano and sang it and ran around here laughing and singing. And we called up this guy named Floyd and sang it to him over the phone and Floyd said we'll cut it tomorrow morning early and we did and within a week it was number ten on the hit parade, then nine, then eight, then it jumped to number two and at last by the end of the month it was number one and the biggest smash hit this country had ever heard or seen before. Isn't that right, Duke! Ask Duke, he'll tell you. Go ahead and ask him! Ask him. Ask him. Go ahead and ask him.

CISCO: Shall I play another song?

DRAKE: What did you have in mind, Cisco?

CISCO: Something simple.

DANA: No more songs! You both have to go now. Go on! Get out of here! We're expecting a couple a' musicians to come and help Duke. Now go on!

(CISCO *sets down the guitar and goes to the piano and starts playing* "Chopsticks" *again*.)

DUKE: It's all right, Dana.

DANA: What do you mean! They've accused you, Duke. They've accused you of stealing. Your own brother! Your own brother and your brother's friend.

(DUKE *stands with his hair all cut and crosses to her while* CISCO *continues to play* "Chopsticks.")

DUKE: Dana, I want you to do me a favor. I want you to throw everything you heard out of your head and go downstairs and buy me a black suit and tie and some black shoes and a white shirt. I want you to do that now and come back as fast as you can. Please. It's very important. (*he pulls out another roll of bills and hands it to her*)

DANA: You really did steal that song, didn't you! (*she takes the money*)

DUKE: Now go on, Dana.

DANA: You did! You stole it from your very own brother. I remember now because when you came in that night you said your brother was singing this groovy song but you had a better one. It was the same one, though! It was! How could you, Duke!

DUKE: No, Dana. That night I was talking with Floyd. Now go get my suit!

DANA: I'm not your flunky! Go buy your own suit!

(*She throws the money at* DUKE *and turns to go out the door as* FLOYD *enters.*)

FLOYD: Great! Do I have to get a special guardian to guard you people and watch you to make sure you do your work? Is that what I have to do? All right! I'll do it.

(*He opens the door and whistles,* CISCO *continues to play "Chopsticks."*)

FLOYD: Peter! On the double!

(PETER, *a bodyguard, enters wearing a guard's uniform complete with pistol and badge and holding a billy club; he also wears shades.*)

DANA: Floyd, Duke's an impostor. He stole that song that's made you rich. It isn't even his.

FLOYD: This is Peter. He's completely trained and attuned to— stop that silly music!

(CISCO *stops.*)

FLOYD: I hired you clowns to accompany Duke, not to piddle around on the piano.

DUKE: You hired my brother! You hired my brother to accompany me!

(*He lunges at* FLOYD *but* PETER *steps in and hits him on the head with the club,* DUKE *falls to the ground,* DANA *screams.*)

DANA: Duke! You've killed him! You've killed him! You've killed my Duke. (*she kneels at his side, sobbing*)

FLOYD: Shut up, broad. He'll come to in a second and then you can

all get down to business. I said I wanted a new song and I'm
going to get one.

DANA: Not out of Duke! He'll never sing again!

FLOYD: Then somebody else. How about you? (*he crosses to* DRAKE)

DRAKE: I accompany, I don't sing.

(DANA *rises.*)

DANA: Don't believe him, Floyd. He sings. In fact he sings very
well. He even writes his own tunes. Original ones.

FLOYD: Original, eh? Well, let's hear some. What's your name,
boy?

DRAKE: Cisco.

FLOYD: Well, Cisco, who knows, we may even have a date for you
in Phoenix if you have what it takes.

DANA: He's Duke's brother, Floyd. His name is Drake Durgens.

DRAKE: Actually Drake writes all the songs and I just accompany.

(FLOYD *turns to* CISCO.)

FLOYD: Is that right? Well Drake, could you sing a few for us?

CISCO: I just did.

DANA: It's the other way around. He's Cisco, not Drake. They're
lying to you, Floyd!

FLOYD: What difference? He has a song that he'd like to sing and
we'd like to hear it. Right, Drake?

CISCO: I just sang it.

FLOYD: Well, sing it again, boy.

DANA: No! If you sing that song, Cisco, I'll kill you! That's not
your song! You have no right to sing that song.

FLOYD: Peter! Take this girl and hold her and then take out your
pistol and put it to her head and if these guys don't sing by the
time I count to five, then pull the trigger.

(PETER *follows his instructions.*)

DANA: No! You can't sing that song! That's not your song! They
stole Duke's song, Floyd!

(PETER *covers her mouth and holds the pistol to her head.*)

FLOYD: One! Two! Three! Four! Five!

(PETER *fires the pistol, it makes a tremendous boom,* DANA *falls to the
floor.*)

FLOYD: What did you do! What in the hell did you do!

PETER: I pulled the trigger.

FLOYD: You pulled the trigger! Do you realize what you've done! Look at what you've done!

PETER: I know.

FLOYD: Are you two going to play ball now or not? Look what's happened on account of your negligence.

(DUKE *starts to groan and slowly gets up, rubbing his head;* FLOYD *rushes to him and helps him up.*)

FLOYD: Dukie! Oh Dukie baby, they've killed your girl. They've killed your sweet little girl by just plain old not cooperating. Look what they've done to Dana, Dukie. Just look at that. Isn't that a shame?

DUKE: She's dead. Oh my God.

FLOYD: Yes, Duke, I'm afraid so.

DUKE: Did she get my suit?

FLOYD: Your suit?

(CISCO *crosses to the piano again and starts to play "Chopsticks";* DRAKE *crosses up to* DANA *and kneels down beside her as* DUKE *walks around the stage in a daze, followed by* FLOYD.)

DUKE: She was going to get a suit. Black with a tie and white shirt with black shining shoes and buttons.

FLOYD: Duke! What has happened to your hair! Oh my God!

(DUKE *feels his hair.*)

DUKE: It's there. It's always there. In the summer it's short and grows long in the winter on account of the changing climate. I never have to do a thing. It just corresponds itself to the climate and that's that. I never knew anything like it before. But it's been going on for as long as I can remember.

FLOYD: Phoenix, Duke! What will they say in Phoenix? They won't even know who you are. They'll laugh you right off the stage!

DUKE: I tell them look, I've been around for a century with changing hair on my head. My pubic hair remains constant but the head manages by itself. It comes and goes. Long and short. Thick and thin. And there's nothing to do about that. If you lose your hair it's gone and you just realize one day that it's thinner than before. That's all.

FLOYD: Stop playing that music!

(CISCO *stops, the band stands and begins this song which should be slower and somewhat softer than the first; all the actors dance individually around the stage except* DANA, *who remains dead on the floor.*)

#2 BAND SONG

Well now that you're older than ya' was before
And ya' can tell that you're older
'Cause everything is a bore
Well now that you're clumsy instead of so quick
And now that your head
Seems to make your stomach sick

Who'll open the door
While you lay on the floor,
Who'll brush your long hair
While you just sit and stare
At the friends all around you
Who pump you and pound you
For the truth you can't see
For either them or either me
'Cause we're sunk on the ground
And your heart don't even pound
While you lay on the floor
And they just ask you for more
Of the same that ya' gave,
Of the same that they took,
But they all want a look
At the black secret book
That ya' lost from your hand
When your hand hit the page
And the page turned to fire
And the fire burned your arm
And your arm burned your chest
And all of your lovin' friends they all know the rest

So now that you're down flat on the ground
All of your friends create the sound,
All of your pals create the pound
Of the sound of the song that they all want you to hear
But your ears can't begin
'Cause they're all jammed up with tears
From your eyes that both watch the years
And the years that watch your eyes disguise your fears
So please tell me now when they ask you for more
Who'll open the door
While you lay on your back,
Who'll destroy your pride

While ya' lay on your side,
Who'll ease you with grace
While ya' lay on your face,
Who'll coax your short hair
So it doesn't stay bare,
Who'll give you the sign to resign from your sleep,
Who'll give you some sleep to resign from the test
Of your arm and your chest
That got burned with the rest
When your zest turned to jelly
Inside your belly
But don't worry now, whatever you do,
Just do your dance and forget about who

So now that you're younger
Than ya' was before
And ya' can tell that you're younger
'Cause ya' don't mind the floor
Where you crawl up and down
With your nose to the ground
And ya' don't mind the smell
'Cause you can't even tell
The difference 'tween heaven and hell anymore
And the floor and the sky
Shine right through your eye
And ya' sigh and ya' groan
But ya' can't pick the bone
Of the dead that won't die
And their sigh and their groan
Match right with the tone of your own
But don't worry now, whatever you do,
Just do your dance and forget about who,
Just say your prayers and go softly upstairs,
Just eat your food 'cause nobody cares,
And nobody dares to say prayers in the street
And the street doesn't care if ya' just sit and eat
So eat while ya' can and it all might come true
'Cause who is around who can tell what to do
And who is around who can save you from you,
Who is around who can save you from you?

(*They finish dancing and applaud the band, then continue the play.*)

FLOYD: All right! You asked for it and now you're going to get it. You two guys were hired by me. Right? I paid you money in advance to accompany my boy here. But now my boy has lost his hair and he's in no shape to cope with Phoenix. So seeing as how you both are paid in advance for a job you haven't done, you're both going to Phoenix in place of my boy. From now on your name is Duke Durgens. You got that?

CISCO: Roger. (*he salutes*)

FLOYD: And your name is whatever it already is.

DRAKE: Cisco.

FLOYD: Right. So you'd both better just accept that right now. Now Peter will get you whatever you want but I'm leaving specific instructions with Peter not to let either of you out of this room without my okay.

DRAKE: What about her?

FLOYD: I'll have some men sent by to take the body away somewhere. Peter, don't let either of them out and don't let anyone in unless it's me or my men. Do you understand? Do I make myself clear?

PETER: Roger. (*he salutes*)

FLOYD: And don't use that gun again or it'll be the end of your job. In fact, give it to me now and I'll keep it for you in a safe place.

PETER: I don't know. We're not supposed to let unauthorized personnel touch or handle any of our—

FLOYD: Give me the gun, Peter!

(PETER *takes the pistol out and hands it to* FLOYD.)

FLOYD: That's a boy. And you two had better come up with some new songs or it'll be bad news for you both. Good luck.

(*He exits,* PETER *starts hitting the club against the palm of his hand.*)

PETER: Stand back away from the body, Cisco.

(DRAKE *moves away.*)

DRAKE: My name is Drake, if you don't mind. Drake Durgens.

PETER: Let me tell you all something to start things off with. First of all, I'm thoroughly trained and attuned to every possible kind of devious methods and trickery that you could possibly pull as a means of escape and/or assault. (*he begins moving around the stage, slapping the club into his palm more firmly*) I have no doubts that you know more than me either collectively or individually. It may even be possible that singly or collectively you may be even smarter than me in certain areas or even in most areas but not in the most important one for this precise time and place and situation. In this particularly unique circumstance I have everything in my control simply because I was once in a position exactly like yourselves. Given that one simple little historical fact, I now have indisputably the upper hand. Not simply because I have a weapon but because I exhausted every possible avenue of escape once myself when I was exactly like you are now. And I tried every one. I tried possibility after possibility over a period of ten years until at last one of them worked. The very last one. And I was free for the very first time. So you see, here I am. The one and only person here who knows what that possibility is and the one and only person who won't tell. And the one and only person to stop any one of you if you happen to accidentally come across it, either singly or collectively. And God help you if you do.

DUKE: Look, Peter, my name's Duke and I'm a singer and—

PETER: I know your names. There's no need for introductions here.

DUKE: I'm not introducing. I'm telling you my actual life. I was a singer, a very popular singer with very long hair, a girl friend, and a song that I stole from my brother Drake over a bottle of wine across the street. But nobody knew that and the song became a fantastic hit, a beautiful smashing hit. I was admired from coast to coast by the people dearest to me and closest to my heart. By the people of my generation. I was admired and cherished because the song was true and good and reflected accurately the emotions, thoughts and feelings of our time and place.

(*The band cheers.*)

DUKE: Thank you. But it was the only song I had. The only one. And I became stuck, Peter. I got stuck somewhere in the middle between— (*he crosses up to the photographs and points first to Bob Dylan and then to Robert Goulet*) Between him and him. Somewhere almost right in the middle and everyone was crying for a brand-new song. For a song like the one I'd sung before or even just for any song. So I made up a love song and cut my hair so I'd look like a lover.

(*The band boos.*)

DUKE: And then the theft of my unoriginal song was revealed and my girl was killed and my brother was hired to accompany me and Floyd said I couldn't go to Phoenix looking like this, without any hair and without a song. So you see, I have no business here anymore. I'm only in your way so I'd like permission to leave, please. I'm not stuck anymore, Peter, and I'd just like to leave before Floyd gets back. (*he breaks down in tears*)

PETER: I suppose you figure the simplicity of your plea would give the impression to anyone of absolute sincerity but I can see right through that to the real truth of the matter and it turns out to be a lie.

DUKE: Peter, there's no reason to keep me here! I have no business here!

DRAKE: He's right, Peter. He's my brother and I can vouch for that. He's telling you the truth.

CISCO: Me too. Even though he's a thief, he's telling the truth.

PETER: Oh well, all right. Step right up, Dukie old boy. Just step right out the door there. You're free to go now. I mean, you have all these vouchers and everything so help yourself.

DUKE: Really?

PETER: Of course. Be my guest. Right this way.

DUKE: Thanks a lot. Thanks, Drake. Cisco. I hope things turn out all right in Phoenix. Say good-bye to Floyd for me, will you? And I'm sorry about the song and everything.

DRAKE: Sure thing, Duke. Good luck.

CISCO: So long.

(DUKE *makes for the door and* PETER *slugs him on the back of the head with the club,* DUKE *falls to the ground.*)

DRAKE: That was pretty shitty, Peter.

PETER: I've decided you two should sit together on the couch and also that you should put your hands on top of your heads as an added precaution.

(*They do so and cross to the sofa and sit.*)

CISCO: We're supposed to be working, Peter. We have a date in Phoenix coming up soon. We can't just clown around.

PETER: Don't worry about that. As soon as we're clear on where we stand, then we'll start thinking about work.

DRAKE: Floyd's coming back pretty soon and it'll be bad news all the way around if we don't have something new for him to hear.

PETER: We'll have something. Just sit tight. But first of all I have a personal question I'd like to ask you boys before we do anything else.

DRAKE: What do you mean?

(PETER *walks up and down in front of them, slapping the club into his palm.*)

PETER: I'd like to redirect the attention for just a moment and turn it off of you and onto me. Just for a change. I'd like to ask you both what you think of me as a person. Just frankly. Don't be afraid of hurting my feelings or anything like that. Just tell me what you think.

CISCO: Well—

PETER: I'd like Cisco to answer first, please.

CISCO: I'm Cisco.

PETER: Now don't start that shit, goddam it! I'm giving you both a chance to relax and feel more comfortable in this already slightly uncomfortable situation and what do you do! You start pulling shit with me! All right. Now then. Give yourself a moment to catch your breath, Cisco, and answer my question as best as you can.

DRAKE: Well I think—

PETER: Just relax for a second and then start in. Don't start in right off the bat. Now are you ready?

DRAKE: Yes.

PETER: Then answer me!

DRAKE: I think you're a fairly nice guy, Peter, but—

PETER: Now don't give me bullshit generalities. "Nice guy," that fits anyone. Anyone's a nice guy.

DRAKE: I know but you're a specific kind.

PETER: What kind?

DRAKE: Well—

CISCO: Peter, maybe if you told us a little about your past life, then maybe we could be more accurate. You could fill in the gaps, so to speak.

PETER: Didn't I just say I wanted Cisco's answer and not yours.

CISCO: I guess.

PETER: But you answered, didn't you! Didn't you! Answer me!

CISCO: Yes.

PETER: You can go now. I want to be alone with Cisco. I said you could go!

CISCO: All right. You're not going to hit me?

PETER: Drake, don't be silly.

CISCO: All right.

(CISCO *gets up and crosses to the door,* PETER *watches him;* CISCO *turns the doorknob but the door won't open, he tries again.*)

CISCO: The door's locked, Peter.

PETER: Don't be silly. (*Peter crosses to the door and opens it wide*) There, you see.

CISCO: Oh. Thanks. So long.

PETER: Have a good time, Drake.

(CISCO *makes to go out the door and* PETER *slugs him with his club,* CISCO *falls to the ground,* DRAKE *stands.*)

PETER: Sit back down, there!

(DRAKE *sits again with his hands on his head;* PETER *pulls* CISCO *into the room and shuts the door, then crosses slowly back up to* DRAKE.)

DRAKE: Look, I really have to get down to work before Floyd gets back.

PETER: We will, Cisco. We'll work all we want just as soon as you answer my question. It's a very simple question really. All it requires is an unbiased opinion of my character. There's no right or wrong answer in this case. It's just a straightforward opinion. That's all. Then you're free to work.

DRAKE: Well, I've known you such a short time, Peter. It seems so—

PETER: I know, Cisco. You're right. In that case I feel somewhat obligated to fill you in on my brief background. Now listen very carefully and see what you can pick up. Anything at all that might be helpful in your answering. One night, several years ago when I was sixteen, I'd just arrived in a very huge city. It doesn't matter which one. (*he begins pacing slowly around the stage, slapping his club*) The point is I'd come out of the hills where I'd lived up until that point with my father and two brothers and several sheep. On this particular night I was walking along very early in the morning by myself with nobody else around. I'd been walking for quite some time, listening to my steps, when I suddenly saw this man about a block ahead of me crawling along the curb and coughing very loud. I didn't change my pace at all but nevertheless gradually caught up to him since he was crawling very slowly and not making much headway at all. When I got alongside of him I just kept my eyes straight ahead and kept at my constant pace but I could hear him coughing and crawling along the curb. Well I'd walked maybe twenty yards when I discovered he was still alongside me but I hadn't looked down this whole time. I could just hear him crawling along and hacking away and it even made me feel slightly good. Like having a dog at your side in the early morning. Do you see what I mean?

DRAKE: Yes.

PETER: Well that comforting feeling lasted for a while but then began to leave me and be substituted by a kind of panic since by this time I'd walked some sixty yards and the man was still with me. I decided to speed up my pace a bit and even got to the point where I was jogging but all the time he was right at my side and his coughing changed to panting and his crawling changed to trotting. So I stopped, thinking he'd go right on by and disappear up the street, but he stopped too and there was a long time while the both of us just stayed in one place, not seeing each other but knowing we were both there. Then I turned my head just slightly over my shoulder and sort of glanced down into his face and his face had no eyes. Mind you, they weren't eyes that had gone bad and closed up or white eyes that were glazed over or eyes like a blind man has. There weren't any eyes there at all. Just a mouth and nose and ears and everything else. Then I asked him what he wanted with me and why he was tagging along and if I could be of any help at all. And he spoke very clearly without any accent at all and no trace of slurred vowels or consonants. He was perfectly sober and he asked me if I'd please bend down and read the address to him off a metal tag he had hanging from his neck on a silver chain. And I said why not and bent down and held the tag in the palm of my hand and read the only word that was on the tag. I read "Arizona" to him very loudly in his left ear for fear he was deaf, but he wasn't since he jumped a little at the sound. Then he asked if I would please point him in the right direction for Arizona and I said of course and turned him around the opposite way and patted him on the back and off he went on all fours. I watched him for quite some time going right up the middle of the street and getting smaller and smaller when suddenly I felt this hand on my right shoulder and jumped slightly and turned and looked right at the face of this very old policeman in a long blue coat and a badge and a hat and boots and a club and a gun and he said to me was that a friend of yours and I said no and then he asked what business I had with him. So I told him what I just told you. Word for word. Exactly, precisely, without leaving one thing out. Without even coloring it to be in my favor. And then he put his hand around the back of my neck and dug his thumb into one side and the rest of his fingers into the other side and he led

me by the neck into the doorway of a building where everyone
was fast asleep. He led me right down this hallway by the back
of my neck and there were only a couple of lights and he took
me way in the back behind this staircase where everything was
damp and dark and told me to take off my pants.

(*There is a loud knock at the door,* PETER *jumps,* DRAKE *stands up.*)

PETER: Sit back down there!

(DRAKE *sits.*)

PETER: Who is it!
VOICE: We come to get the body! Floyd sent us.
PETER: There ain't no body here! You got the wrong door!
VOICE: It's the right number! This is where we're supposed to
come, all right!
PETER: You better get away from here or we'll call a cop!
VOICE: Look, buster. Floyd told us you was a knucklehead and we
might have to break the door down! So open up or we'll do what
he says!
PETER: I have specific instructions not to let anyone in or out! I
don't know you! You could be anyone. How do I know who you
are?
VOICE: Well we'll go get Floyd then and you'll see who we are.
PETER: Go ahead!
VOICE: You'll be sorry, punk!
DRAKE: Peter, we have to do something before he gets back. He's a
desperate man. He needs a new song and he'll stop at nothing to
get it.
PETER: You're probably right. But you haven't answered my question yet and until you do there'll be no chance at all to learn
anything new.

(PETER *unbuttons his pants and takes them off while* DRAKE *stays seated
on the sofa.*)

DRAKE: What can I say? I like you very much.
PETER: That explains nothing to me. I want to know what I'm like,
that's all. Not anything else.
DRAKE: Well that's part of it, though. If you like someone it's
usually because they're nice. I mean, I don't like any bad guys.
PETER: You don't?
DRAKE: Well no. Do you?
PETER: I never met one.

(*As soon as he's taken off his pants he crosses to the piano and starts to play "Chopsticks" while* DRAKE *stays sitting on the sofa.*)

DRAKE: It seems like you could get someone else to tell you what you're like. Someone who knows you better. Someone who's close to you and lived with you for a while. I mean what do you want, Peter? I've never done this kind of thing before. Peter!

(DRAKE *stands but* PETER *keeps playing "Chopsticks."*)

DRAKE: We're in a dangerous situation here! The two of us. They're not going to treat you any different than they are me. When Floyd gets back he's going to be pretty pissed off at you for locking his men out. He's going to knock you down the same as me. In fact he'll probably hire you on to go with me to Phoenix, seeing as how you play the piano so well and also now that Cisco's out of commission. Peter, are you listening to me!

(DRAKE *starts moving slowly toward* PETER *as* PETER *continues to play, ignoring* DRAKE.)

DRAKE: This is no joke! I can't give you what you want because I don't know what it is. I can't just make it up. I could, I guess. Do you want me to make it up, Peter? Peter!

(PETER *stops playing abruptly, there is a loud knock on the door;* PETER *wheels around on the piano stool and grabs* DRAKE; *he puts his hand over* DRAKE'S *mouth and bends one of* DRAKE'S *arms behind his back.*)

FLOYD'S VOICE: Peter! This is Floyd and his men! Now listen, we know you're inside there! And I realize that I gave you specific instructions to let no one in and no one out but now I'm telling you the opposite. I'm telling you to let us in. Do you hear me, Peter! Open this door.

PETER: The problem is I can't be sure if you're Floyd or if you're more likely just some imposter who's trying to mosey in on a good deal.

FLOYD: What good deal! There's nothing in there that could possibly be of any value to anyone but me. Now let me in this door!

(*The door shakes violently.*)

PETER: I'm sorry. I'm thoroughly trained and attuned to every possible—

FLOYD: All right, meathead! You're through! Finished! Washed up! Down the river! I'm going out to get some cops and when I get back your thorough training ain't going to be worth a hill of beans! You'll be blackballed from every guard corporation in the country! You'll never work again and that's a promise! Come on.

(PETER *slowly lets go of* DRAKE, *they face each other.*)

DRAKE: I told you.

(PETER *hits him in the stomach with his club*, DRAKE *doubles over.*)

PETER: You'd better think of something fast, boy. There's no telling what they'll do when they get back. Once they break down that door and come in here with guns.

DRAKE: Just let me sing a song, Peter.

PETER: You haven't answered my question yet.

DRAKE: I can't! Don't you see, I can't! I like you very much! I've told you that. I've told you you're a nice guy!

PETER: Good! (*he slugs* DRAKE *in the back with the club*) Now what am I like when you look in my face!

DRAKE: I can't see you, Peter!

PETER: Come on, boy. They'll be back very soon. You can't beat around the bush at a time like this. In a moment of crisis.

DRAKE: What do you want me to say?

PETER: Say whatever you'd say if you happened to be walking down the street alone, by yourself, and just accidentally ran across me in the dark.

DRAKE: But I didn't.

PETER: Pretend you saw me in a flash and we had a short encounter and then someone came up and asked you what you thought of that man you were just now talking to. What was he like, that man?

DRAKE: Peter, I can't! I'm stuck!

PETER: And then you say whatever just comes into your head in that split second. Whatever happens to be sitting there in your memory of the second before and it just spiels out trippingly off the tongue. It just gushes out in its most accurate way. Word for word, without a moment's hesitation to calculate where it's going or how or why. It just falls out into the air and disappears as soon as it's heard. That's what I want to hear! That's what I want you to say to me. Right now, before it's too late!

DRAKE: Just let me sing a song, Peter. Please. Let me make up a song for Floyd.

PETER: That'll save your skin but how about mine? What do you suggest for me, meathead?

DRAKE: You could open the door. You could leave the door wide open so that when they arrive they won't be so mad at you.

PETER: Why not?

(*He slugs* DRAKE *again across the back,* DRAKE *falls to all fours.*)

DRAKE: Wait! They—when they see the door wide open they're liable to cool down and then they won't be so rough on you, Peter, because they'll think you thought it over and reconsidered. Maybe they will.

PETER: Maybe you're right, Drake. Maybe that's a good idea.

(*He goes to the door and opens it wide,* DRAKE *starts moving slowly around the stage on all fours as* PETER *follows him.*)

PETER: There! Now you'd better get down to work, boy. You'd better think up a new song, now that my skin's saved. By the way, thanks very much. I never would have thought of that possibility. The open-door routine.

DRAKE: That's all right.

(DRAKE *paces faster on all fours as* PETER *crosses slowly to the sofa and sits next to the radio.*)

PETER: I'm not much good on songs, though. Wish I was, though, so I could help you out. I could play a little something on the piano if you want. Just something to help you get started.

DRAKE: No, I'm all right. I'll be okay.

(*He paces faster up and down the apron of the stage while* PETER *just sits on the sofa, slapping the club in his lap.*)

PETER: It wouldn't be anything fancy, Drake. All I know is the simple stuff. But it might be just enough to kick something off for you. To get the wheels turning, so to speak. I'm sure glad I'm not in your shoes.

DRAKE: No, it's all right. It's coming. (DRAKE *starts humming some kind of tune now*)

PETER: Must be really something to have that kind of facility. To be able to make up a song whenever you feel like it. Just on the spur of the moment like that. How about the radio, Drake? That might do the trick. What do you say?

(PETER *turns on the radio as* DRAKE *continues to pace up and down more frantically;* PETER *just sits on the sofa, slapping the club in his lap, as the following comes from the radio.*)

RADIO: DANIEL DAMON'S VOICE: So I do hope we have given all of you somewhat of an indication of just exactly how the personal life of an artist is affected and/or altered by the reception of his work by the public at large. And we would like to thank our special guest tonight, Mr. Duke Durgens, for being so cooperative in this survey of ours and to wish him all the luck in the world. Duke, it's been a pleasure.

DUKE DURGENS' VOICE: Thank you, Danny.

DANNY'S VOICE: And now we would like to close out this evening's session of the Corning Interview Hour with the sensational sound of the number-one hit tune in the world. Thank you for joining us and until next week this is Dan Damon saying—

(*The song should break in extremely loud, over the radio.*)

Well early one day you got out a' bed
And then you decided to go to sleep instead
So early one day you got back in the sack
And fell fast asleep in your homemade rack

Well you don't know how you decided this,
All that you know is there's somethin' you missed
But you don't know what and you don't know where
So you just stay put and ya' go nowhere.

(DUKE *gets up slowly and rubs his head, then exits quietly out the door;* PETER *stays sitting on the sofa, keeping time to the song with his club;* DRAKE *continues pacing up and down; the band joins the radio at this point and sings along with it to the end.*)

Oh prisoners, won't you get up out a' your homemade beds,
Oh prisoners, won't you get up out a' your homemade beds.

Well early one night you got so very uptight
And you said this sleepin' it just ain't right
But there was nothin' at all that you could do
'Cause your eyes stayed shut with your homemade glue.

But you couldn't hear your own voice speak
And ya' couldn't walk 'cause your legs was too weak
So ya' lay in bed cryin' to yourself
And your life just sat there hanging on the shelf.

(CISCO *gets up slowly and rubs his head, then exits quietly out the door; the song continues.*)

Oh prisoners, get up out a' your homemade beds,
Oh prisoners, get up out a' your homemade beds.

And now the day and night are just the same
And now the light and dark don't have no name
And you just lay in bed without no game
And you just lay there sleepin' without no fame

But when you do awaken from your deep sleep
The bed will disappear and you won't even weep,
You'll walk right outside without no name,
You'll walk right outside from where you came.

(DANA *gets up slowly and yawns, then exits quietly.*)

So prisoners, get up out a' your homemade beds,
Oh prisoners, get up out a' your homemade heads.

(*The song finishes, the band stops,* PETER *turns off the radio as* DRAKE *continues pacing,* PETER *gets up slowly and crosses to the door, he slams the door shut and turns to* DRAKE; DRAKE *freezes in place staring at* PETER, *who crosses to* DRAKE *and stands over him for a while, tapping the club in his palm, then suddenly raises the club to hit* DRAKE; *there is a loud knock at the door, the LIGHTS BLACK OUT.*)

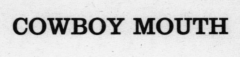

COWBOY MOUTH

Characters

CAVALE: a chick who looks like a crow, dressed in raggedy black.

SLIM: a cat who looks like a coyote, dressed in scruffy red. They are both beat to shit.

LOBSTER MAN

Cowboy Mouth was first performed at the Traverse Theatre, Edinburgh, on April 12, 1971. It was directed by Gordon Stewart, with the following cast:

SLIM:	Donald Sumpter
CAVALE:	Brenda Smiley
LOBSTER MAN:	Derek Wilson

It was subsequently given its American premiere in a special performance at the American Place Theatre, New York, on April 29, 1971, as an afterpiece to Mr. Shepard's *Back Bog Beast Bait*. This performance was directed by Robert Glaudini, with the following cast:

SLIM:	Sam Shepard
CAVALE:	Patti Smith
LOBSTER MAN:	Robert Glaudini

SCENE: *A fucked-up bed center stage. Raymond, a dead crow, on the floor. Scattered all around on the floor is miscellaneous debris: hubcaps, an old tire, raggedy costumes, a boxful of ribbons, lots of letters, a pink telephone, a bottle of Nescafé, a hot plate. Seedy wallpaper with pictures of cowboys peeling off the wall. Photographs of Hank Williams and Jimmie Rodgers. Stuffed dolls, crucifixes. License plates from southern states nailed to the wall. Travel poster of Panama. A funky set of drums to one side of the stage. An electric guitar and amplifier on the other side. Rum, beer, white lightning, Sears catalogue.*

CAVALE *has kidnapped* SLIM *off the streets with an old .45. (She wants to make him into a rock-and-roll star, but they fall in love. We find them after one too many mornings. They're both mean as snakes.* SLIM *is charging around screaming words;* CAVALE *is rummaging through junk, yelling with a cracked throat. The lights come up on them in this state.)*

SLIM: Wolves, serpents, lizards, gizzards, bad bladders, typhoons, tarantulas, whipsnakes, bad karma, Rio Bravo, Sister Morphine, go fuck yourself!

CAVALE: Fucking dark in here. Fucking old black dog. You fucking. Where's Raymond? Where's Raymond, goddammit? Shit. Raymond, Raymond, where's my crow, old black tooth?

SLIM: Your Raymond! My wife! My kid! Kidnapped in the twentieth century! Kidnapped off the street! Hot off the press! Don't make no sense! I ain't no star! Not me! Not me, boy! Not me! Not yer old dad! Not yer old scalawag! This is me! Fucked! Fucked up! What a ratpile heap a dogshit situation!

CAVALE: Shit, man . . . Raymond, come on, baby, where are you? Come on, honey, is your beak hurt? Raymond? Raymond, don't be scared, honey, come on, he's an old snake, a water moccasin, a buffalo, an old crow . . . No, I'm jes' fooling. Raymond! Fuck them, fuck you.

(SLIM *goes to the drums and starts beating the shit out of them, yelling at the top of his voice through a microphone.*)

SLIM: (*wailing*)

You cheated, you lied, you said that you loved me.
You cheated, you lied, you said that you need me.
Oh what can I do but just keep on loving you?
Oooooooooooooooooh what can I do but just keep on loving you?*

Fuck it.

(*He stops.* CAVALE *finds Raymond the dead crow and talks to him.*)

CAVALE: Oh, here's my baby. Here's my little crow. He's no crow, I was jes' fooling. We're the crows, me and you, Raymond. (*she sings him something like the theme from* Lilith)

SLIM: Will you stop fucking around with that dead crow? It makes me sick! It's morbid and black and dark and dirty! It makes me sick! Can't you see what's happening here? Here we are stuck in some border town, some El Paso town, and you're fucking around with a dead crow. I should just leave and go back to my family. My little family. My little baby. I should, shouldn't I? Shouldn't I!

CAVALE: Fuck you. Fuck you. Fuck, fuck. Can't you see what's happening here? A dream I'm playing. I love Raymond, I love you, Raymond. You don't talk about yesterday stuff. Yeah, you fucking coyote, Slim, always howling after yesterday. Raymond don't squawk 'bout his ole nests, do you, baby? He sleeps on my belly 'cause my belly's today. Yesterday yesterday, that's you, sulking shitface—Mr. Yesterday.

SLIM: Tell me about Johnny Ace.

CAVALE: I already told you about Johnny Ace.

SLIM: I know, but I want to hear it again. Okay?

CAVALE: Okay. C'mere though.

(SLIM *goes to her and curls up in her lap.*)

CAVALE: Johnny Ace. Johnny Ace. Johnny Ace was cool. He was real cool, baby. Just like you. And he came East from Texas and no black guy had a hit record and no rock-and-roll boy had a hit record. And in rode Johnny Ace, from a moving train, pledging his love. That was his best song, man. What a great fucking song. And all the girls would cry when he sang. He sang all them pretty ballads. And one day when all the girls were waiting, when everybody paid their fare to see Johnny Ace on stage in person singing sad and dressed in black, Johnny Ace took out his revolver, rolled the barrel like his 45 record, played Russian Roulette like his last hit record, and lost. *Johnny Ace blew his brains out*, all the people jump and shout. All the people jump and shout *Johnny Ace blew his brains out*.

SLIM: You think that takes balls, I suppose. Do you?

CAVALE: Oh man. You're always saying that shit. Why don't you just play? Just play, it don't mean nothing, it's just a neat story. Fuck. You always wreck everything. Jus' like when I told ya' about Villon. You never just listen, you always got to place stuff. And hey, fuck you, you asked me to tell you it. I ain't telling you no more stories. (*she gets teary and nervous*)

SLIM: Aw, come on, baby. Baby crow. Don't crow, baby crow. I'm sorry. I love ya'. I love ya' to tell me stories. It's like listenin' to the streets. Ya' know? Like listenin' to summer sounds. Like it could be the dead of winter but some kind of sound like just a bunch of people laughing makes it sound like summer. That's why I love your stories. I'm sorry, baby.

CAVALE: Baby. Baby. Baby. Slim, I hurt my foot. (*she lifts up her foot. It's wrapped in a piece of ragged scarf*) Raymond bit it. Johnny Ace bit it, Villon bit it, a tarantula bit it. Summer bit it. Kiss it, will ya', Slim?

(SLIM *bends down and licks her foot all over. He growls like a coyote and howls.*)

SLIM: It's them damn steel plates they put on yer foot when you was a punk. They called ya' splayfoot, no 'count. I know. I know 'bout them jealous creeps. Lookin' at my crow like a freak. I'll kill 'em! I'll tear out their throats! I kiss your foot. I lick your toes. I suck your pinkie 'cause I love ya'. How's that for openers?

CAVALE: Slim, don't tease me.

(*Pause.*)

SLIM: How's about a little lobster? Could ya' go for a little lobster with drawn butter?

CAVALE: I guess.

SLIM: You don't dig lobster?

CAVALE: Sure.

SLIM: Who do we call for lobster?

CAVALE: Call the lobster man.

(SLIM *goes to the phone and dials. Someone answers.*)

SLIM: Listen, is this the lobster man? Good. Send us up some lobster with drawn butter and two scrambled eggs and four toasted bialys with cream cheese and some Pepsi-Cola and a bottle of tequila with plenty of lemon. You got that? Good. (*he hangs up*)

CAVALE: I'm not that hungry.

SLIM: Tell me about Nerval.

(*He holds her close and they dance while she talks; an old waltz or a fox-trot.*)

CAVALE: Nerval. Hey, Slim, really he's "de" Nerval, but we'll can that "de" stuff 'cause it's too fancy. Hey, Slim, tomorrow can we go into town and you buy me something fancy? I don't got nothing fancy. Oh, Slim, ya' know what I want? Tap dance shoes. Red ones, red ones with pretty ribbons. Could we do that, huh, baby?

SLIM: We'll do that right now. Right now we'll do that!

(*He stands up and pulls her to her feet. They take an imaginary walk to the shoe store.* CAVALE *limps along,* SLIM *helps her. They walk through the room as though it were the city.*)

SLIM: Now ya' gotta look sharp. Ya' know what I mean. No limpin'. Try not to limp.

CAVALE: I can't help it, Slim.

SLIM: I know, I know. Just get it together. It won't be far now. Just a little ways. Up past Ridge Avenue, down through Ashland, we'll slide through Mulberry, and bingo! We'll be there.

CAVALE: It won't take long, will it, Slim?

SLIM: We'll be there before you can spit in a hornet's eye. In fact! In fact! In fact, you know what?

CAVALE: What?

SLIM: We're here.

CAVALE: Already?

SLIM: Yeah. Now just take yer pick. There's all them pretty dancin' shoes in the window there. Just take yer pick.

CAVALE: I want the red ones, Slim. The red ones with the ribbons.

SLIM: Okay, now I'm gonna' break the window, so stand back.

CAVALE: But we got money.

SLIM: A good thief never hesitates.

(*He smashes the window and steals the shoes. They run away to another part of the room and sit down exhausted.* SLIM *puts a beat-to-shit pair of high-topped sneakers on* CAVALE.)

SLIM: Now, madam, if you'll just slip your foot into these, we'll see how they suit you.

(*She tries them on. She takes a walk in them and looks them over.*)

CAVALE: Oh, Slim, they're beautiful.

SLIM: Good. Now will you tell me about Nerval or "de" Nerval or whatever the fuck his name is?

CAVALE: Can the "de," baby. He's Nerval to me. He had a fucked-up foot too. Poor baby. Always banging into walls. Always dreaming when he's walkin'. (*she spins around and tells the story singsong*) It hurts just to think about. Singing, I try to sing it out. Dead in winter. Two calico shirts. They cut the rope, that rope that cut him down. It hurts just to think about or how I'll do without him.

SLIM: Cut the shit, baby. You never knew that guy; he's a million years old. Just tell the story.

CAVALE: I do so, I do know him, Slim. He hung himself on my birthday. *My birthday.* And some lady tole my mom I was made from a hanged man. Poor bastard. And, Slim, he had a crow too. Just like Raymond. I read this dream book Baudelaire writ, and he said Nerval came to him half-crow, half—half—half-ass. Nah. I'm just teasing. I'm sorry, Nerval. Slim, I don't wanna' tell this story. It's stupid. I'm sick of telling about people killing themselves, it makes me jealous.

SLIM: Okay! Okay! Then don't tell me a story! Don't never tell me a story! Don't never tell me another fucking story! See if I care! Nobody gives a rat's ass anyway! I'm gonna' play rock-and-roll! I'm gonna' play some mean, shitkickin' rock-and-roll!

(*He goes to the electric guitar and starts playing loud rock with a lot of feedback. He sings "Have No Fear."*)

SLIM: Have no fear
The worst is here
The worst has come
So don't run
Let it come
Let it go
Let it rock and roll
The worst has come.

Have no fear
The best is here
The best has come
So don't run
Let it come
Let it go
Let it rock and roll
The best has come

Every night I sit by my window
Watchin' all the dump trucks go by
Have no fear
The worst is here
The worst has come
So don't run
Let it come
Let it go
Let it rock and roll
The worst has come

(CAVALE *plays dead on the floor with Raymond on her stomach. After a while* SLIM *stops.* CAVALE *stays "dead.")*

SLIM: Hey! Is that the lobster man? Hey! Cavale, did somebody knock? Cavale!

(CAVALE *stays "dead" on the floor.*)

SLIM: Stupid broad.

(SLIM *goes to the door and opens it. The* LOBSTER MAN *enters. He's dressed like a lobster and carries all the food they ordered.*)

SLIM: Oh, you must be the lobster man. Just drop everything in the middle of the floor.

(*The* LOBSTER MAN *grunts, then goes center stage and drops all the food in a heap.*)

SLIM: Great. Thanks a lot. Just charge that to my office number. Gramercy 6–5489. Here's a little something for yourself.

(*He tips the* LOBSTER MAN. *The* LOBSTER MAN *grunts and exits.* CAVALE'S *still playing dead.*)

SLIM: The lobster man came. Cavale? You can stop playing dead now. We can eat. Cavale? Well, I'm going to eat, I don't know about you but I'm going to eat. (*he sits on the floor and digs into the food*)

CAVALE: I'm dead, baby. Dead as dogshit. Dead and never baptized. Dead. Slaughtered. Without the Christian aid of water. Water makes me cringe.

SLIM: Cut the mystical horseshit and come eat.

CAVALE: (*runs to the food and starts overacting disgustingly*) Oh, man, look at all this neat shit. Have some cream pie, Raymond honey. Slosh up that shit, blackie baby. Shove a little sausage in that ole cracked beak. Here's tuna in yer eye.

SLIM: I'm gonna' roast that fucking crow.

(*She tells the story of Raymond as they slop around in the food.*)

CAVALE: Hey, man. Watch that shit. Raymond's real sensitive. It's bad enough you don't let him in bed with us anymore.

SLIM: Gimme that sausage. Well, goddammit, it's sick. Fucking dead crow sucking me off in the morning. You went too far with that one, baby. There's nothing in my contract says I gotta have a rotting stuffed blackbird for a groupie.

CAVALE: Hey, shut up, will ya'? Raymond's been a real chum. All them nights in that fuckin' hospital, all them electric shocks. All those hours they stole my dreams, all those people in white face masks saying I was crazy. Only ole Raymond stuck by me. Never gave me any shit. And the dirty fuckers broke his beak. Poor beak.

(CAVALE *bandages Raymond's beak with an old piece of lace.*)

SLIM: Poor beak, poor beak, poor beak. All I ever had was a dog. A dog. Like any good American boy. I had a dog. A live dog. A cattle dog. The reason I got him was 'cause he was a fuckup. He used to chase the cows out of the pasture instead a' bringin' 'em for milking. He was a fuckup.

CAVALE: What was his name?

SLIM: Blaze. Blaze Storm. Named after the stripper.

(CAVALE *sings something like "Put the Blame on Mame" in stripper style and picks up the Sears catalogue.*)

CAVALE: Hey, Slim, I wanna electric dishwasher.

SLIM: We don't have any dishes.

CAVALE: But I want one. I don't have any housewife shit. I want some stuff ladies have.

SLIM: You don't want that shit, you're not the type. Look, tomorrow I'll take you into town and buy you a nice calico shirt. Just like your pal Nerval. How's that, my little rabbit?

CAVALE: Fuck Nerval. I wanna dishwasher. I wanna stovepipe and a scrambled-egg maker. Here, Slim, we can get it all in the catalogue. All the stuff you always miss when you get like Mr. Yesterday. Then you'd be gladder, Slim. We could even get Raymond a little cradle. And a rattle. And booties. And a black baby lamb with a bell in its tail.

SLIM: I don't need no black baby lamb with a bell in its tail and I ain't gettin' no cradle for no dead crow. I have a baby! My own baby! With its own cradle! You've stolen me away from my baby's cradle! You've put a curse on me! I have a wife and a life of my own! Why don't you let me go! I ain't no rock-and-roll star! That's your fantasy. You've kept me cooped up here for how long has it been now? I've lost track of the time. A long time. A long fucking time. And I'm still not a star! How do you account for that?

CAVALE: I don't know. I never promised nothin'.

SLIM: But you led me on. You tempted me into sin.

CAVALE: Oh, fuck off.

SLIM: Well, it's true. What am I doing here? I don't know who I am anymore. My wife's left me. She's gone to Brooklyn with the kid and left me. And here I am stuck with you.

CAVALE: You can go if you want.

SLIM: I don't want! I do want! I don't want! I want you!

CAVALE: Then stay.

SLIM: I want her too.

CAVALE: Then go.

SLIM: Good-bye!

(SLIM *gets up and stomps over to the drums. He starts bashing them violently.* CAVALE *goes through a million changes. Plays dead. Rebels. Puts on a bunch of feathers and shit to look alluring. Rebels. Motions like she's gonna bash the amps with a hammer. Hides in a corner.*

Then, shaping up, she grabs her .45. SLIM *is still slamming. She yells over the drums.*)

CAVALE: Look, you jive motherfucker, I'm still packing this pistol. I'm still the criminal. I'll fill you with—I'll—Hey, listen to me. I'm threatening your life. You're supposed to be scared. Look, baby, kidnapping is a federal affense. It means I'm a desperate . . .

SLIM: (*still slamming the drums*) It's "offense," not "affense."

CAVALE: What? Hey, what do ya' mean?

SLIM: (*stops drumming and sorta slumps over*) I mean your grammar stinks. I mean you talk funny. I mean—

CAVALE: Shit. Goddammit. How could you? How can you bust up my being a hard bitch with that shit? What a lousy thing. You know I'm sensitive about my talking. Shit. Just when I was really getting mean and violent. Murderous. Just like François Villon. You fuck it up. You wreck everything.

SLIM: Cavale?

CAVALE: Yeah?

SLIM: How come we're so unhappy?

CAVALE: Must be the time of year.

SLIM: Yeah. It's that time of year, all right. That must be it. Maybe we could change it.

CAVALE: What?

SLIM: The time of year. Let's change the time of year to Indian summer. That's my favorite time of year. What's your favorite time of year?

CAVALE: Fall.

SLIM: Okay, we'll change the time of year to fall. Okay?

CAVALE: Okay.

SLIM: Okay, now it's fall. Are you happy?

CAVALE: Yeah.

SLIM: Good. Now tell me a story.

CAVALE: Stop asking me that. I can't tell no stories unless I'm inspired. Who wants to listen to something uninspired?

SLIM: Okay, then tell me what it means to be a rock-and-roll star. Tell me that. I'm supposed to be a rock-and-roll star. You're going to make me into a rock-and-roll star, right?

CAVALE: Right.

SLIM: So tell me what it means, so I'll have something to go by.

CAVALE: Well, it's hard, Slim. I'll try to tell you but you gotta stay quiet. You gotta let me fish around for the right way to tell ya'. I always felt the rhythm of what it means but I never translated it to words. Here, hold Raymond. Come on. It's like, well, the highest form of anything is sainthood. A marvelous thief like Villon or Genet . . . they were saints 'cause they raised thievery to its highest state of grace. Ole George Carter, black and beat to shit on some dock singing "Rising River Blues" . . . he was one. He sang like an ole broke-down music box. Some say Jesse James was one . . . and me . . . I dream of being one. But I can't. I mean I can't be the saint people dream of now. People want a street angel. They want a saint but with a cowboy mouth. Somebody to get off on when they can't get off on themselves. I think that's what Mick Jagger is trying to do . . . what Bob Dylan seemed to be for a while. A sort of god in our image . . . ya' know? Mick Jagger came close but he got too conscious. For a while he gave me hope . . . but he misses. He's not whole. Hey Slim . . . am I losing ya'? I mean, just tell me if I'm getting draggy. It's just hard and it's real important.

SLIM: No, baby, it's beautiful.

CAVALE: Well, I want it to be perfect, 'cause it's the only religion I got. It's like . . . well, in the old days people had Jesus and those guys to embrace . . . they created a god with all their belief energies . . . and when they didn't dig themselves they could lose themselves in the Lord. But it's too hard now. We're earthy people, and the old saints just don't make it, and the old God is just too far away. He don't represent our pain no more. His words don't shake through us no more. Any great motherfucker rock-'n'-roll song can raise me higher than all of Revelations. We created rock-'n'-roll from our own image, it's our child . . . a child that's gotta burst in the mouth of a savior. . . . Mick Jagger would love to be that savior but it ain't him. It's like . . . the rock-'n'-roll star in his highest state of grace will be the new savior . . . rocking to Bethlehem to be born. Ya' know what I mean, Slim?

SLIM: Well, fuck it, man. I ain't no savior.

CAVALE: But you've got it. You've got the magic. You could do it. You could be it.

SLIM: How?

CAVALE: You gotta collect it. You gotta reach out and grab all the little broken, busted-up pieces of people's frustration. That stuff in them that's lookin' for a way out or a way in. You know what I mean? The stuff in them that makes them wanna' see God's face. And then you gotta take all that into yourself and pour it back out. Give it back to them bigger than life. You gotta be unselfish, Slim. Like God was selfish, He kept Himself hid. He wasn't a performer. You're a performer, man. You gotta be like a rock-and-roll Jesus with a cowboy mouth.

SLIM: You fucking cunt!

(*He jumps up and starts tearing the place apart, throwing things against the walls and screaming his head off.*)

SLIM: You stupid fucking cunt! Two years ago or one year ago! If it was then! If this was happening to me then, I could've done it! I could've done it! But not now! Not fucking now! I got another life! I can't do it now! It's too late! You can't bring somebody's dream up to the surface like that! It ain't fair! It ain't fucking fair! I know I could do it, but you're not supposed to tempt me! You're twisting me up! You're tearing me inside out! Get out of my house! Get the fuck out of my house!

CAVALE: This ain't your house. This is my house.

SLIM: It's nobody's house. Nobody's house.

(*He collapses, exhausted from his violence.* CAVALE *goes to him as if to soothe him, then realizes it's her dream being busted and not his. She starts yelling at him while he just lies there wiped out.*)

CAVALE: You're fucking right—nobody's house. A little nobody with a big fucking dream. Her only dream. My only dream. I spread my dreams at your feet, everything I believe in, and you tread all over them with your simpy horseshit. Fuck you. Fuck you. Poor, poor baby. I take your world and shake it. Well, you took my fantasy and shit on it. I was doing the streets looking for a man with nothing so I could give him everything. Everything it takes to make the world reel like a drunkard. But you have less than nothing, baby, you have part of a thing. And it's settled. And if it's settled I can't do nothing to alter it. I can't do shit. I can't give you nothing. I can't. I can't. You won't let me.

SLIM: Come here.

(*He pulls her to him. They hug each other. A pause. They lie on the bed.*)

SLIM: Listen to the traffic. It sounds like a river. I love rivers. I love the way they just go wherever they want. If they get too full they just overflow and flow wherever they want. They make up their own paths. New Paths. I tried to make a dam once in a river. It was just a little river. I put a whole bunch a' rocks and sticks and shit in that river. I even put a tree in that river, but I couldn't get it to stop. I kept coming back day after day putting more and more rocks and mud and sticks in to try to stop it. Then one day I stopped it. I dammed it up. Just a little trickle coming out and a big pool started to form. I was really proud. I'd stopped a river. So I went back home and got in bed and thought about what a neat thing I'd done. Then it started to rain. It rained really hard. All night long it rained. The next morning I ran down to the river, and my dam was all busted to shit. That river was raging like a brush fire. Just gushing all over the place. Gushing up over the sides and raging right into the woods. I never built another dam again.

CAVALE: You're so neat. You're such a neat guy. I wish I woulda' known you when I was little. Not real little. But at the age when you start finding out stuff. When I was cracking rocks apart and looking at their sparkles inside. When I first put my finger inside me and felt wonderment. I would've took you to this real neat hideout I had where I made a waterfall with tires and shit, and my own hut. We could've taken all our clothes off, and I'd look at your dinger, and you could show me how far you could piss. I bet you would've protected me. People were always giving me shit. Ya' know what? Once I was in a play. I was real glad I was in a play 'cause I thought they were just for pretty people, and I had my dumb eyepatch and those metal plate shoes to correct my duck foot. It was *The Ugly Duckling,* and I really dug that 'cause of the happy ending and shit. And I got to be the ugly duckling and I had to wear some old tattered black cloth and get shit flung at me, but I didn't mind 'cause at the end I'd be that pretty swan and all. But you know what they did, Slim? At the end of the play I had to kneel on the stage and cover my head with a black shawl and this real pretty blonde-haired girl dressed in a white ballet dress rose up behind me as the swan. It was really shitty, man. I never got to be the fucking swan. I paid all the dues and up rose ballerina Cathy like the North Star. And afterwards all the parents could talk about was how pretty she looked. Boy, I ran to my hideout and cried and cried. The lousy fucks. I wish you were around then. I bet you would've protected me.

SLIM: Poor baby. (*pause*) Well, what're we gonna' do now?

CAVALE: We could howl at the moon.

SLIM: Okay. Ready?

(*They both let out howls, then laugh and fall on the floor. They play the coyote and the crow game on their hands and knees.* SLIM *talks in an old cracked, lecherous voice.*)

SLIM: Now, the coyote is mean. He's lean and low-down. He don't fool around with no scraggly crows. When he sees hisself somethin' he likes, he chomps it down.

(*He growls and goes after* CAVALE. *She scurries away.*)

CAVALE: Little crow didn't do nothin'. Jes' out here peckin' in the desert. Checkin' out the sand for little corn grains. Jes' a little somepin' to nibble.

SLIM: Coyote gettin' hungry 'bout now. He ain't seen a chicken for he don't know how long. Crow look pretty good at this point. He don't care if it be fat and saucy. Just a little somepin' ta tear the wings off of.

CAVALE: Without no wings little crow bait have a hard time singin'. Starts to run all crazy through the night.

SLIM: Coyote he howl and chomp down on that crow now. Tear into that crow now!

(*He jumps on* CAVALE *and tears into her. They roll around on the floor for a while, then stop.*)

SLIM: Now coyote full. He ate up his tidbit. Now he roll on his back and make a big belch and fart and scratch his back against some cactus bush.

CAVALE: Little crow feel pretty good inside coyote belly. Not bad she says for a day on the range. Not bad at all. Though she may never see daylight again. Not bad at all.

(*A pause.*)

SLIM: Now what'll we do?

CAVALE: I don't know.

SLIM: We could call back the lobster man just for laughs.

CAVALE: Okay. Let me do it, okay?

SLIM: Sure.

CAVALE: Goody. (*she runs to the telephone and picks it up*) Hello. Is this the lobster man? It is? Could you come back over here again? We need some cheering up. You would? Oh great! Thanks a lot. Bye. (*she hangs up*) He's coming right over.

SLIM: Good.

CAVALE: Let's play a trick on him when he comes, okay?

SLIM: Like what?

CAVALE: I don't know.

SLIM: What could we do?

CAVALE: Too bad he isn't a tuna fish. We could have a great big giant can and put him in it.

SLIM: Let's just talk to him when he comes.

CAVALE: What about?

SLIM: About what it's like to be a lobster man. It must be pretty weird, you know. Weirder than being us.

CAVALE: We're not weird, man. He's weird, but we're not weird.

SLIM: We could ask what the bottom of the ocean is like.

CAVALE: We could put him in a movie.

SLIM: What movie?

CAVALE: *Three Coins in the Fountain. The Prophet.*

SLIM: *The Swimmer.*

CAVALE: *You're Just My Little Chicken of the Sea.*

SLIM: No, we gotta be nice to him. He's had a hard life.

CAVALE: How do you know?

SLIM: You can tell by his claws. He's got barnacles on his claws.

CAVALE: That means he's a wily old devil. He's outfoxed all the fishermen for years and years. He's never been caught.

SLIM: That's why he's so big. Lobsters never get that big.

CAVALE: He'll never be boiled, that one.

SLIM: We could boil him.

CAVALE: I thought you wanted to be nice to him.

SLIM: Did you ever hear a lobster scream when they hit the boiling water? It's awful. It's like a peacock fucking.

CAVALE: We can't boil him. We don't have any dishes.

SLIM: I could stab him with my switchblade. (*he pulls out a giant switchblade and stabs it into the floor*)

CAVALE: Now, dear, don't get violent. Our company's arriving any minute now.

SLIM: I could cut through that hard shell and tear his heart out. I could eat his heart. You know that's what warriors used to do. Primitive warriors. They'd kill their opponent and then tear his heart out and eat it. Only if they fought bravely, though. Because then they believed they'd captured the opponent's strength.

CAVALE: What kind of strength does a lobster have?

SLIM: Ancient strength. Strength of the ages. Ancient sea-green strength. That's why I love lobster so much. They're very prehistoric.

CAVALE: But this one's a monster.

SLIM: You'd say the same thing about a Tyrannosaurus if he came in the door. I suppose you'd call him a monster too.

(*Loud banging on the door.*)

CAVALE: Jiggers, it's the lobster man! Quick, put away that knife. We don't want to scare him off.

(SLIM *folds up his knife and puts it away.*)

CAVALE: Okay. Ready?
SLIM: Ready.

(*More loud banging.*)

CAVALE: Coming!

(*She goes to the door and opens it.* LOBSTER MAN *enters.*)

CAVALE: Oh, Mr. Lobster Man. We're so happy to see you. We were just talking about you. Won't you come in?

(LOBSTER MAN *saunters to center stage and grunts. He looks ill at ease in the situation.*)

SLIM: Have a seat.

(LOBSTER MAN *sits on the bed and stares out at the audience.* SLIM *and* CAVALE *move around him.*)

CAVALE: How long have you been a lobster?

(LOBSTER MAN *grunts.*)

SLIM: What'd he say?
CAVALE: He doesn't speak too clear. Could you try to speak up so we can understand you?

(LOBSTER MAN *grunts.*)

SLIM: Listen, the little lady here and I were discussing how we'd like to get to know you on a more intimate level. You know what I mean? I mean it's a drag to have servants just bringin' ya' shit up the stairs and throwin' it down in the middle of the floor and then leavin' and you never get a chance to know them on a more intimate level. You know what I mean?

(LOBSTER MAN *grunts.*)

CAVALE: Yeah, you must be a very interesting person, and we don't even know you. That's not fair. We'd like to know your darkest nightmares, your most beautiful dreams, your wildest fantasies, your hopes, your aspirations. Stuff like that.

SLIM: What about it?

(LOBSTER MAN *grunts*.)

CAVALE: I think we oughta try a different tactic.

SLIM: Like what?

CAVALE: Like just ignoring him for a while. Pretend like he's not here. I mean, how would you feel if you walked into a situation like this?

SLIM: I never would.

CAVALE: I know, but just pretend you did. Let's just ignore him for a while.

SLIM: The whole point in bringing him over was so that we'd have something to do.

CAVALE: I know, but it ain't workin' out.

SLIM: So what're we gonna' do then?

CAVALE: Let's go down to the deli and leave him here alone.

SLIM: He might rip us off.

CAVALE: So what? We don't need this shit.

SLIM: What about my drums? My guitar?

CAVALE: What about them? Man, you knock me out. You just gave it to me on the line. And like the Chinese say, sweetie, fuck the dream, you fuck the drum. Let the lobster man be the new Johnny Ace. It's the Aquarian Age. Ya' know it was predicted that when Christ came back he'd come as a monster. And the lobster man ain't no James Dean. . . . Hey, honey, hit some hot licks on the Fender. We're going out for a little shrimp cocktail.

SLIM: "Now what rough beast slouches toward Bethlehem to be born?" So now you want *him* to take *my* place. Is that it? You think this creep is gonna' take me over! Is that it! You're gonna' pour your magic gris-gris into this fool! Well, I'm gonna' cut his ass wide open!

(*He pulls out his switchblade again and starts to threaten the* LOBSTER MAN.)

CAVALE: Slim! Cut the shit! He's only a poor old lobster. Leave him alone.

SLIM: (*to* LOBSTER MAN) Pretty sneaky. Pretty fuckin' sneaky. Squirmin' yer way into our lives. Pretendin' dumb. We know you can talk. We know you understand what's goin' on. You've got the silver. You've got the gold. Out with it! Out with it, Lobster Man, or the sun won't shine on your slimy shell.

CAVALE: No, don't, Slim. Leave him alone. He didn't do nothin'.
Leave my savior alone.

SLIM: Your savior? Your savior! He's supposed to be your savior?
Okay, we'll just see what kinda' stuff he's made of then. We'll
just play him a little music and see what makes him tick. All
right, Lobster Man, this is your big chance.

(SLIM *goes to the guitar and starts playing the old C–A minor–F–G
chords as* CAVALE *soothes the* LOBSTER MAN.)

CAVALE: All right now, this won't hurt. Don't be afraid. I'll be right
back. Okay?

(CAVALE *gets up and goes to the microphone. She begins to talk the song
"Loose Ends" as* SLIM *plays behind her. He comes in on the choruses,
singing. During the song, the* LOBSTER MAN *gets up from the bed and
comes downstage. As the song unfolds he begins to break open and crack,
revealing the rock-and-roll savior inside the shell, dressed in black.*)

CAVALE: I'm at loose ends
I don't know what to do
Always dreaming big dreams
Half dreams
Wanting him and loving you
To tell the truth I don't know which way to turn
Give me something to hold on to
Something I can learn
Oh come right here

*Come right here when you feel alone
And no one speaks for you
You can do it on your own*

Show me the way to it
You know I need a friend
A song to pull me from the hole I'm in
Give me something low-down
Give me something high
Pulling in the power of dark or light
To destroy to the left
Create on the right
Oh come right here

*Come right here it's such a simple song
It'll cure all your misery*

It won't move you wrong
So open up your mouth don't think about a thing
Feel the movement in you and sing

Sing sing sing sing

(CAVALE *sings this part.*)

Oh I was at loose ends
Not knowing what to do
I needed to open up
So I turned to you

(*She talks.*)

Help me to do it
I was always dreaming too high
Help me pull my star down from the sky
Down on the ground
Where I can feel it
Where I can touch it
Where I can be it

Oh I don't want to give up
I believe a light still shines
It shines for everyone
It's yours
It's mine
Oh come right here

(CAVALE *talks the chorus,* SLIM *sings. They alternate lines.*)

Come right here you know you're not alone
If you got no savior you can do it on your own
Open up your heart don't think about a thing
Feel the movement in you and sing

(*By the end of the song the* LOBSTER MAN *is completely out of his shell and stands center stage as the rock-and-roll savior. He stares out at the audience.* SLIM *sets down his guitar and goes to the gun. He picks up the gun and goes to the* LOBSTER MAN. *He holds out the gun for the* LOBSTER MAN *to take. The* LOBSTER MAN *takes the gun very slowly.* SLIM *smiles at the* LOBSTER MAN, *then crosses to the door. He pauses a moment and turns to look at* CAVALE. *They stare at each other for a moment. Then* SLIM *exits through the door.* CAVALE *turns to the* LOBSTER MAN *and gives her speech very simply and softly, sitting on the edge of the stage. As she talks, the* LOBSTER MAN *spins the chamber of the gun, almost in rhythm with the speech. All through this he stares at the audience.*)

CAVALE: Nerval. He had visions. He cried like a coyote. He carried a crow. He walked through the Boulevard Noir inhuman like a triangle. He had a pet lobster on a pink ribbon. He told it his dreams, his visions, all the great secrets to the end of the world. And he hung himself on my birthday. Screaming like a coyote. The moon was cold and full and his visions and the crow and the lobster went on *cavale.* That's where I found my name. Cavale. On my birthday. It means escape.

(*As* CAVALE *finishes, the* LOBSTER MAN *slowly raises the pistol to his head and squeezes the trigger. A loud click as the hammer strikes an empty chamber. The lights slowly fade to black.*)

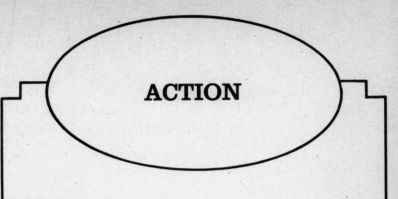

ACTION

Action was first performed at the American Place Theatre, New York, in 1975. It was directed by Nancy Meckler, with the following cast:

SHOOTER:	R. A. Dow
JEEP:	Richard Lynch
LIZA:	Dorothy Lyman
LUPE:	Marcia Gean Kurtz

SCENE: *Upstage center, a small Christmas tree on a small table with tiny blinking lights. Downstage center left, a plain board table with four wooden chairs, one each on the four sides. The table is set very simply for four people. Just plates, forks and knives. Four coffee cups and a pot of hot coffee in the middle. Running across the middle of the stage above is a clothesline attached to a pulley at either side of the stage. The light onstage is divided exactly in half, so that upstage is in complete darkness except for the blinking lights of the Christmas tree. Downstage is lit in pale yellow and white light which pulses brighter and dimmer every ten minutes or so, as though the power were very weak.*

The characters are all in their late twenties to early thirties. SHOOTER *and* JEEP, *the two men, are dressed in long dark overcoats, jeans, lumberjack shirts, and heavy boots. They both have their heads shaved.* LUPE *wears a flowered print dress in the 1940s Pearl Harbor style. She wears platform heels.* LIZA *wears a long, full, Mexican type skirt, plain blouse and an apron. She wears sandals.* LUPE *sits upstage of the table facing* LIZA *across from her.* LIZA'S *back is directly to the audience.* JEEP *sits stage right at one end of the table across from* SHOOTER, *who sits at the other end.*

The stage is in darkness for a while with just the tree blinking. The lights come up very slowly downstage. Nothing happens for a while except the slight movements of the actors drinking coffee. JEEP *rocks slightly in his chair.*

All the exits and entrances occur upstage into or out of the darkness.

JEEP: (*leaning back in his chair and rocking gently*) I'm looking forward to my life. I'm looking forward to uh—me. The way I picture me.

SHOOTER: Who're you talking to?

JEEP: Uh— (*pause*) I had this room I lived in. Shall I describe this room? (*pause as the others take a sip of coffee together*) I had a wall with a picture of Walt Whitman in an overcoat. Every time I looked at the picture I thought of Pennsylvania. I had a picture of an antelope on a yellow prairie. Every time I looked at this picture I saw him running. I had a picture of the Golden Gate Bridge. Every time I looked at it I saw the water underneath it. I had a picture of me sitting on a Jeep with a gun in one hand.

(*He lets the chair come to rest on the floor again. Pause as they all sip coffee. Suddenly* LIZA *jumps up and makes a big gesture with her hands melodramatically.*)

LIZA: Oh my God! The turkey!

(*She goes running off upstage and disappears into the darkness.*)

LUPE: (*to herself*) It's funny the way the snow is.

SHOOTER: (*pulling a book out from his lap and placing it on the table*) Maybe we should read.

LUPE: We'll have to wait for Liza.

SHOOTER: Yeah. But we could be looking for the place. Do you remember where it was?

LUPE: I thought we marked it.

SHOOTER: I lost the place.

LUPE: (*taking the book and thumbing through it*) Here, let me look.

JEEP: Shooter, can you do a soft shoe?

SHOOTER: Naw. I don't think so.

JEEP: I was wondering if we could both do it sitting down. Without getting up. Just our legs.

SHOOTER: Just like this you mean?

JEEP: Yeah.

LUPE: Was it chapter sixteen?

SHOOTER: Uh—Maybe. (LUPE *continues thumbing*)

JEEP: Just try. Put your hands on the table.

(*They both put their hands on the table.*)

JEEP: One, two, three, quatro!

(*They both break into an attempt at a soft shoe patter as they stare blankly at each other in their seats.* LUPE *keeps looking through the book. This lasts for about thirty seconds and ends with* LIZA *coming back into the light sucking on her fingers and wiping her hands on her apron. She sits back down in her chair.*)

LIZA: (*noticing* LUPE *with the book*) Oh. Are we gonna' read?

LUPE: I can't find the place.

LIZA: Let me take a look.

(LUPE *shoves the book across the table to* LIZA, *who takes it and starts thumbing through it. She keeps sucking on her fingers in between turning the pages.*)

LUPE: Shooter lost the place.

JEEP: Uh—I saw this picture of a dancing bear. Some gypsies had it on a leash. They were all laying by the side of the road and the bear was standing on all fours. Right in the middle of the road. In the background was this fancy house.

(SHOOTER *pulls his overcoat over his head and holds his hands up in front of him like bear paws. Slowly he pushes his chair back and rises. He takes short staggering steps like a bear on his hind legs.* LIZA *keeps looking through the book.*)

JEEP: (*to* SHOOTER) Don't act it out.

(SHOOTER *keeps on.*)

LIZA: (*referring to book*) Were we past the part where the comet exploded?

JEEP: (*to* SHOOTER) You don't have to act it out.

(SHOOTER *pays no attention.*)

LUPE: I never saw a dancing bear. That was before my time. I guess they made it illegal. Too cruel or something.

(SHOOTER *goes back and forth downstage like a trained bear, looking out at the audience.*)

SHOOTER: It doesn't feel cruel. Just humiliating. It's not the rightful position of a bear. You can feel it. It's all off balance.

LUPE: Well, that's what I mean.

JEEP: What?

LUPE: That's cruel. For a bear that's cruel.

SHOOTER: No. It's as though something's expected of me. As though I was human. But it puts me in a different position. A different situation.

JEEP: How?

SHOOTER: Performing. Um— Without realizing it. Um— I mean I realize it but the bear doesn't. He just finds himself doing something unusual for him. Awkward.

JEEP: You're not the bear.

LIZA: I found it! They've returned to earth only to find that things are exactly the same. Nothing's changed.

JEEP: That's not it. Let me try.

(JEEP *takes the book from* LIZA *and goes through it.* SHOOTER *drops his bear routine and pulls his overcoat down on his shoulders. He looks blankly at the audience, then strolls back to his seat and sits. They all sip their coffee. After a long pause.*)

SHOOTER: I think I'll take a bath.

LIZA: The turkey's almost ready.

SHOOTER: I'm too scared to eat. (*not showing it*)

LUPE: (*to* LIZA) Let him take a bath. It'll calm him down.

SHOOTER: Is there any hot water left?

JEEP: (*thumbing through the book*) There was the last time I was up there.

SHOOTER: I don't want to go up there alone.

LUPE: If you could remember the last time when you got scared it might help you this time.

SHOOTER: I know. It's the same. It's the snow. Being inside. Everything's so shocking inside. When I look at my hand I get terrified. The sight of my feet in the bathtub. The skin covering me. That's all that's covering me.

LIZA: (*pulling out a hip flask from her apron*) You want some rum?

(SHOOTER *takes the flask and has a drink.*)

LUPE: I can remember the last time I got scared. I thought I'd poisoned myself. I thought I'd eaten something. I imagined it working its way into me. I went outside in my bare feet and forced myself to throw up. It was that kind of a night.

LIZA: I remember that night. We were watching the stars.

(*The two girls start laughing, covering their mouths, then stop.*)

SHOOTER: I know I'll get over this. It just sorta' came on me.

(*He hands the flask back to* LIZA, *who puts it in her apron.*)

LIZA: (*without giving it back*) You can keep it.

SHOOTER: (*blankly*) I've got this feeling that females are more generous. I've always felt that.

JEEP: (*pushing the book away from him*) OH THIS IS RIDICULOUS!! I CAN'T FIND THE PLACE!!

(*He stands suddenly, picks up his chair and smashes it to the floor. The chair shatters into tiny pieces. Pause. None of the others are shocked.*)

LIZA: (*standing*) I think there's another one out on the back porch.

(LIZA *leaves. She disappears in the darkness upstage.* JEEP *pulls his overcoat up over his head and raises his hands like* SHOOTER *did. He goes through the same bear motions as* SHOOTER *did before.* LUPE *takes the book again and looks through the pages.*)

SHOOTER: (*to himself*) That's what I do. I get this feeling I can't control the situation. Something's getting out of control. Things won't work. And then I smash something. I punch something. I scream. Later I find out that my throat is torn. I've torn something loose. My voice is hoarse. I'm trembling. My breath is short. My heart's thumping. I don't recognize myself.

LUPE: Shooter, weren't you the last one to read?

SHOOTER: Was I?

LUPE: Yeah. It was you.

SHOOTER: It doesn't matter does it?

LUPE: Only if you can remember where you left off.

SHOOTER: Well, let me look. I'll see if I can find it.

(*He takes the book and looks through it.* LUPE *starts into a soft shoe sitting down.* JEEP *has his back to her, but as he hears her feet tapping he stops his bear routine and turns to look at her. She continues with a smile.* JEEP *pulls his overcoat down on his shoulders and just stares at her.*)

JEEP: (*flatly*) There's something to be said for not being able to do something well.

(LUPE *stops. Her smile disappears.*)

JEEP: No, I mean it's all right. It takes a certain amount of courage to bring it out into the open like that.

LUPE: It's no worse than the one you guys did.

JEEP: No, I know. I'm not trying to insult you or anything.

(LUPE *starts up the soft shoe again in defiance.*)

JEEP: I mean we've got this picture in our head of Judy Garland or Gene Kelly or Fred Astaire. Those feet flying all over the place. That fluid motion. How can we do anything for the first time. Even Nijinksy went nuts.

LUPE: (*continuing with her feet*) What about it?

JEEP: It's hard to have a conversation.

(*He sits down on the floor.* LUPE *continues dancing for a while after* JEEP'S *seated. She slowly stops.* SHOOTER *thumbs through the book. They sip their coffee.*)

LUPE: (*to* JEEP) When you're in a position of doing something like that it's hard to talk about it. You know what I mean? I mean while I was doing it—while I was in the middle of actually doing it—I didn't particularly feel like talking about it. I mean it made me feel funny. You know what I mean. It was like somebody was watching me. Judging me. Sort of making an evaluation. Chalking up points. I mean especially the references to all those stars. You know. I mean I know I'm not as good as Judy Garland. But so what? I wasn't trying to be as good as Judy Garland. It started off like it was just for fun you know. And then it turned into murder. It was like being murdered. You know what I mean.

JEEP: Didn't mean to piss you off.

(*Pause.* LIZA *enters from upstage with a new chair in one hand and a broom and dustpan in the other. She sets the chair down.* JEEP *gets up off the floor and sits in the new chair, folding his arms across his chest.* LIZA *starts sweeping up the pieces of the old chair.* JEEP *watches her.*)

JEEP: (*to* LIZA) I'm not going to offer to clean it up because you're already doing it.

(LIZA *continues sweeping in silence.*)

SHOOTER: (*looking up from the book, directed at everyone*) I know that feeling of being out of control. Powerless. You go crazy. In a second you can go crazy. You can almost see it coming. A thunderstorm.

JEEP: (*to* SHOOTER) It's not that.

SHOOTER: Oh.

(SHOOTER *goes back to thumbing through the book.*)

JEEP: I mean sometimes it's like that but this time it wasn't.

LIZA: (*still sweeping*) Did you find the place yet?

SHOOTER: Nope.

LUPE: I'm starving. (*she licks her lips*)

JEEP: This time it came from something else. I had an idea I wanted to be different. I pictured myself being different than how I was. I couldn't stand how I was. The picture grew in me, and the more it grew the more it came up against how I really was. Then I exploded.

SHOOTER: (*without looking up from the book*) That's what I meant.

LUPE: Oh, when are we gonna' EAT! (*hitting the table once with her fist*)

LIZA: It's almost ready.

(LIZA *exits upstage with the pieces of the old chair, leaving the broom onstage.*)

JEEP: I couldn't take it. Just thumbing through the book. Not even looking. Not even seeing the papers. Just turning them. Acting it out. Just pretending.

(*Suddenly* LUPE *starts gnawing ravenously on her own arm.* JEEP *and* SHOOTER *pay no attention.*)

SHOOTER: (*still looking through the book*) I know.

JEEP: Is that what you're doing? Is that what you're doing right now?

SHOOTER: (*without looking up*) I'm looking for the place.

JEEP: I admire your concentration. I couldn't concentrate. I kept thinking of other things. I kept drifting. I kept thinking of the sun. The Gulf of Mexico. Barracuda.

SHOOTER: (*still into the book*) That's okay.

JEEP: (*standing suddenly and yelling*) I KNOW IT'S OKAY!! THAT'S NOT WHAT I'M SAYING!

(*He picks up the new chair and smashes it to the ground just like the other one.* LUPE *stops chewing on her arm and licks it like a cat licking a wound.* SHOOTER *keeps looking for the place in the book.* JEEP *stands there looking at the damage.*)

SHOOTER: (*after a short pause, referring to book*) Was it just after the fall of the Great Continent?

LUPE: Oh my stomach!

(*She clutches her stomach with both hands and holds it like a baby.* LIZA *enters with a huge golden turkey on a silver platter with the steam rising off it. She sets it down on the table in front of* LUPE.)

LUPE: I'll carve.

(LUPE *picks up a knife and begins to slice the turkey in a calm way, very formally, and laying the slices on plates for everyone.* LIZA *walks over to* JEEP, *who is still looking at the broken chair. They look at the chair together as though seeing it as an event outside themselves.*)

LIZA: (*to* JEEP *but looking at the broken chair*) You'll have to stop doing that. We've only got one left.

(LIZA *picks up the broom.* JEEP *grabs it. They both hold it together.*)

JEEP: I'll do it.

LIZA: That's okay.

(*A short pause as they look at each other, then* JEEP *yanks the broom out of* LIZA'S *hand and starts sweeping up the broken chair.* LIZA *goes to the table and sits folding her hands in her lap while* LUPE *continues to carve standing up.* SHOOTER *sticks with the book.*)

LUPE: We're lucky to have a turkey you know.

LIZA: Yes, I know.

LUPE: It was smart thinking to raise our own. To see ahead into the crisis.

LIZA: Whose idea was it anyway?

SHOOTER: (*not looking up*) Mine.

JEEP: (*still sweeping*) I think it was mine.

SHOOTER: (*not looking up*) It was your idea, and then I went and bought it.

JEEP: That's right.

LIZA: That's right.

LUPE: We're sure lucky.

LIZA: Do you know what they say is the best way to prepare a turkey? They say that before you kill it—about two weeks before—you start feeding it a little cornmeal and some sherry. About a teaspoonful of sherry, three times a day. Then in the second week you force a whole walnut down its throat once a day and keep up the sherry dosage. When it comes time for the kill you'll have a turkey with a warm, nutty flavor.

LUPE: Is that what you did?

LIZA: Partly. I started out the first week with the sherry, but by the time the second week rolled around I couldn't bring myself to do it. I mean the walnut thing. I couldn't do that.

JEEP: (*as he exits upstage with the broken pieces of the chair*) It's not cruel.

LUPE: Who killed it anyway?

LIZA: I did.

SHOOTER: I can't find the place.

(SHOOTER *folds the book and puts it on the floor, opens his napkin and tucks it into his shirt, picks up his knife and fork and waits to be served.*)

SHOOTER: Aren't we going to have any vegetables?

LIZA: No. We had a late frost remember?

LUPE: We're lucky to have a turkey.

SHOOTER: I know we are. I was just wondering about the vegetables. The creamed onions and stuff. The candied yams.

LUPE: (*to* SHOOTER) Dark or light?

SHOOTER: White.

(*She hands* SHOOTER *a plate of turkey. He digs in.*)

LIZA: No wine either, I suppose?

LUPE: You were in the kitchen.

(*She hands* LIZA *a plate of turkey.* LIZA *eats.* LUPE *serves herself and sits down to eat.*)

LIZA: Yes. I've never cooked over an open fire before. I mean a big fire blazing like that. It's hard to keep from cooking yourself. Your arms start roasting. You get afraid the kitchen's going to burn down.

LUPE: I can imagine.

LIZA: The heat is tremendous.

SHOOTER: I thought turkeys were supposed to cook slow.

LIZA: Well, you let the flames die down. It's just the embers you're cooking on. But the heat!

SHOOTER: Yeah, it's hot in here for a change.

(JEEP *enters from upstage into the light, shivering and rubbing his arms.* LIZA *stops him.*)

LIZA: Oh Jeep, could you get us all some water?

JEEP: (*standing still, shivering*) Right now?

LIZA: Yeah, if you don't mind.

JEEP: From the well? It's a lot of work you know. We can't just turn on a tap.

LUPE: We're lucky to have a turkey.

(JEEP *turns upstage and exits.*)

SHOOTER: It *is* freezing out there. I don't envy him. Hauling up water. Spilling it on his hands. It's freezing.

LIZA: It's all right.

SHOOTER: In the dark. Feeling your way around. He might fall in.

LIZA: We'll hear him.

LUPE: It's all right, Shooter.

SHOOTER: (*standing suddenly*) I KNOW IT'S ALL RIGHT!

(*The two women continue eating, paying no attention.* SHOOTER *sits down after a while.*)

SHOOTER: (*quietly to himself;* LUPE *and* LIZA *eat quietly*) Just because we're surrounded by four walls and a roof doesn't mean anything. It's still dangerous. The chances of something happening are just as great. Anything could happen. Any move is possible. I've seen it. You go outside. The world's quiet. White. Everything resounding. Not a sound of a motor. Not a light. You see into the house. You see the candles. You watch the people. You can see what it's like inside. The candles draw you. You get a cold feeling being outside. Separated. You have an idea that being inside it's cosier. Friendlier. Warmth. People. Conversation. Everyone using a language. Then you go inside. It's a shock. It's not like how you expected. You lose what you had outside. You forget that there even is an outside. The inside is all you know. You hunt for a way of being with everyone. A way of finding how to behave. You find out what's expected of you. You act yourself out.

(JEEP *enters from upstage with a bucketful of water and four cups in the other hand. Each cup dangling from one of his fingers by the handle. He sets the bucket down on the table with the cups. He picks up a cup and dips it into the bucket. He does the same with each cup and serves everyone at the table with a cup of water. Then he sits down on the floor. This all happens in silence, except for the sounds of the others eating and the water.*)

LIZA: (*standing*) There's one chair left.
SHOOTER: (*standing and moving upstage*) I'll get it.

(SHOOTER *exits.* LIZA *sits again.*)

LUPE: Dark or light, Jeep?
JEEP: White.

(LUPE *serves him a plate of turkey.* JEEP *eats, sitting on the floor.*)

JEEP: I was thinking. If things get worse we should get a cow.
LIZA: Nobody's selling.
JEEP: You've asked around?
LIZA: Nobody's selling.
LUPE: I was thinking chickens would be better.
LIZA: Nobody's selling.
JEEP: That's all right.

LUPE: A goat might be good.

LIZA: There's no way of actually preparing. We'll have to do the best with what we've got. We're all eating now. At least we're eating. We'll have to gauge our hunger. Find out if we actually need food when we think we need it. Find out how much it takes to stay alive. Find out what it does to us. Find out what's happening to us. Sometimes I think I know, but it's only an idea. Sometimes I have the idea I know what's happening to us. Sometimes I can't see it. I go blind. Other times I don't have any idea. I'm just eating.

(SHOOTER *comes back on from upstage empty-handed. They all stop eating and look at him.*)

SHOOTER: I forgot what it was I went for. I got out there and forgot.

JEEP: (*still on the floor*) The chair.

SHOOTER: Oh yeah.

(SHOOTER *turns upstage and exits again. They go back to eating.*)

JEEP: (*to himself*) It doesn't really matter. I'm okay on the floor.

LIZA: I made a move to go get it, and then he beat me to it.

JEEP: It doesn't matter.

LUPE: Was he being polite?

LIZA: I guess.

LUPE: (*to* LIZA) Just to keep you from going out there?

LIZA: I guess so.

LUPE: But he's getting the chair for Jeep, and Jeep doesn't even care.

LIZA: It's all right.

JEEP: (*suddenly, to himself*) Walt Whitman was a great man. He kissed soldiers. He held their hands. He saw mounds of amputated limbs.

LUPE: I don't know anything about him.

(SHOOTER *comes on from upstage pulling a very heavy, stuffed red armchair. He huffs and puffs with it, pulling it by inches downstage as the others stay sitting and eat their turkey.*)

JEEP: He expected something from America. He had this great expectation.

LUPE: I don't know. I never heard about it.

JEEP: He was like what Tolstoy was to Russia.

LIZA: I don't know much about it either.

JEEP: A father. A passionate father bleeding for his country.

LIZA: (*staying seated*) Do you want some help, Shooter?

SHOOTER: (*between heavy breaths*) No— I'm uh— okay. It's— not much— further. I'll be all right.

JEEP: Almost a hundred years ago to the day. The same thing happened. Everybody at each other's throats. Walt was there. He could tell you.

LIZA: I thought he was dead.

JEEP: (*conversationally*) "Manahatta," it was called then. Indian. They had big, open tents on the Bowery with sawdust on the floor. German beer. Juggling acts. Dancing bears. The Civil War was just beginning.

LUPE: When was this?

JEEP: He'd tip his hat to Abe, and Abe would tip his hat back.

LIZA: They liked each other.

JEEP: (*in a Walter Cronkite newscaster voice*) The poet and the President. The poet all gray and white standing on his feet. The President all dark and somber, glooming down from his horse. The face of war in his eyes. The two of them seeing each other from their respective positions. The entire nation in a jackknife. This all happened on Vermont Avenue near L Street. The street itself was raining. Blue soldiers were lying wounded in every doorway; some having slept there all night with gaping wounds. Soaked through to the bone. Walt was a witness to it.

(SHOOTER *finally gets the chair downstage right and stands by it trying to catch his breath. He looks at* JEEP, *who stays seated on the floor.* SHOOTER *makes a motion toward the chair with his hand. He tries to speak, but he's out of breath. He tries again.*)

SHOOTER: (*motioning to chair*) There it is.

JEEP: I'm okay here.

(SHOOTER *looks at him for a while.*)

SHOOTER: You don't want it? (*no answer from* JEEP, *who keeps eating*) Don't you want it?

(*Still no answer from* JEEP. SHOOTER *moves in front of the armchair and collapses into it, staring out at the audience.*)

SHOOTER: Aaaaaaaah! This is the life. Now I'm glad I went through all that.

LIZA: (*to* SHOOTER) Aren't you hungry?

SHOOTER: No. I'm glad.

(*He folds his arms behind his head and smiles.*)

LIZA: (*standing*) Well, time to wash up.

(*She starts gathering all the dishes together very quickly, whipping the plates out from under everyone.* JEEP *and* LUPE *pick their teeth and smack their lips loudly.*)

JEEP: (*with his back to* SHOOTER) Do you want some water, Shooter? There's plenty of water.

SHOOTER: Nope. This is it for me. I'm never leaving this chair. I've finally found it.

JEEP: (*standing and moving to the bucket on the table*) I'm gonna' have some water. I'd be glad to get you a cup if you want.

LUPE: He just said he doesn't want any.

(JEEP *stands by the bucket with a cup in one hand. He dips the cup into the bucket, raises the cup slowly, and tips the water back into the bucket, watching the trickle of water as he does it. He keeps doing this over and over as though hypnotized by his own action. When* LIZA *has all the dishes she exits upstage leaving the remains of the turkey on the table.*)

LUPE: Does anyone want to read? (*pause*)

SHOOTER: I'm never leaving again.

LUPE: I don't mind looking for the place.

(*She goes and picks up the book on the floor and sits back down in her chair. She looks through it.*)

SHOOTER: I could conduct all my business from here. I'll need a bedpan and some magazines.

JEEP: (*looking at the remains of the turkey*) We should save the bones for soup.

SHOOTER: This is more like it. This is more in line with how I see myself. I picture myself as a father. Very much at home. The world can't touch me.

JEEP: Shooter? You remember when you were scared? Shooter? You remember? Oh, Shooter?

SHOOTER: Naw. I don't remember that. Better to leave that. People are washing dishes now. Lupe's looking for the place again. Things are rolling right along. Why bring that up?

LUPE: (*in the book*) Wasn't it around where the spaceship had collided with the neutron?

JEEP: Shooter, I remember. I remember you were so scared you couldn't go up to take a bath.

SHOOTER: Naw. That's not me at all. That's entirely the wrong image. That must've been an accident.

JEEP: Oh.

(JEEP *keeps pouring the water over his hand.*)

SHOOTER: I've never been afraid of baths. I've always been brave in those situations. I've plunged right in.

JEEP: Oh, I thought it was you.

SHOOTER: I knew a guy once who was afraid to take a bath. Something about the water. Stank to high heaven. "High Heaven." That's a good one. He stank, boy. Boy, how he stank. Boy, did he ever stink.

JEEP: Was it the water?

SHOOTER: Yeah. Something about how it distorted his body when he looked down into it.

JEEP: Then, it wasn't the water.

SHOOTER: Yeah. The water. The way it warped his body.

JEEP: But that's just the way he saw it. That was him, not the water.

SHOOTER: Then, he began to fear his own body.

JEEP: From that? From seeing it in the water?

SHOOTER: He began to feel like a foreign spy. Spying on his body. He'd lie awake. Afraid to sleep for fear his body might do something without him knowing. He'd keep watch on it.

JEEP: Was he a close friend?

SHOOTER: I knew him for a while.

JEEP: What happened to him?

SHOOTER: His body killed him. One day it just had enough and killed him.

JEEP: What happened to the body?

SHOOTER: It's still walking around I guess. (*pause*) Would somebody tell Liza to bring me the flask?

LUPE: (*not looking up from the book*) She's washing the dishes.

JEEP: (*still pouring*) That's an interesting story, Shooter.

SHOOTER: Thank you.

JEEP: How did it get started?

SHOOTER: What?

JEEP: I mean how did he get into this relationship?

SHOOTER: Who knows. It developed. One day he found himself like that.

LUPE: (*without looking up*) Remember the days of mass entertainment?

JEEP: No.

LUPE: (*not looking up*) This could never have happened then. Something to do every minute. Always something to do. I once was very active in the community.

JEEP: What's a community?

LUPE: (*looking up*) A sense of— A sense um— What's a community, Shooter?

SHOOTER: Oh uh— You know. You were on the right track.

LUPE: Something uh—

JEEP: I know.

LUPE: Yeah. You know. It doesn't need words.

(*She goes back into the book.*)

JEEP: I know what you mean.

LUPE: Just a kind of feeling.

JEEP: Yeah, I know what you mean.

SHOOTER: I think we're beginning to get it a little. To get it back. I mean you can feel it even in the dead of winter. Sort of everybody helping each other out.

JEEP: Did he suspect his body of treason? Was that it?

SHOOTER: I'm not sure. It was a touchy situation.

(SHOOTER *rolls both his pants legs up above his knees and starts scratching his legs as he talks.*)

JEEP: He must've had a hard time. I mean he couldn't reach out. I mean he wouldn't expect anyone else to be in the same boat probably.

SHOOTER: Probably not.

LUPE: (*without looking up*) Well it *is* rare.

JEEP: Was it in a particular time of hardship?

SHOOTER: I can't rightly say.

JEEP: I mean were things crumbling?

SHOOTER: I suspect he couldn't see it. I mean I suspect he had his ideas. His opinions. Certain stiff attitudes.

LUPE: (*not looking up*) When was this?

JEEP: And his body's still walking around?

SHOOTER: That's right. A walking stiff.

JEEP: Can anyone tell? I mean if we ran into this body could we tell it was vacant?

SHOOTER: I'm not sure.

LUPE: (*still thumbing through the book*) Well, how *could* you tell?

JEEP: (*to* LUPE) There must be a way. I mean something must be missing. You could tell if he wasn't all there.

SHOOTER: I don't know.

LUPE: (*still in book*) How? How could you tell?

JEEP: You'd know. I'd know. I mean with us, we know. We know. We hear each other. We hear our voices. We know each other's voice. We can see. We recognize each other. We have a certain— We can tell who's who. We know our names. We respond. We call each other. We sort of— We— We're not completely stranded like that. I mean— It's not— It's not like that. How that would be.

(*Pause as* JEEP *slowly pours the water over his hand.* SHOOTER *scratches his legs.* LUPE *thumbs through the book. After a short while* SHOOTER *sits back in the armchair with a jerk and holds his stomach.*)

SHOOTER: I'm starving. Did we eat already?

LUPE: (*still in book*) You weren't here.

SHOOTER: I was here. I was here all along.

LUPE: (*in book*) Not at the right time.

(SHOOTER *stands suddenly in the chair with his pants legs still rolled up.* LUPE *and* JEEP *pay no attention.*)

SHOOTER: You mean you ate without me!

(*Pause as* SHOOTER *looks around the space slowly.*)

SHOOTER: (*to himself*) Now I'm beginning to regret my decision.

LUPE: What.

SHOOTER: (*gazing around him in amazement*) To stay in the chair.

LUPE: Oh.

SHOOTER: It was shortsighted. I'd give anything just to travel around this space. Just to lick the corners. To get my nose in the dust. To feel my body moving.

LUPE: (*referring to book*) Was it near the place where the sky rained fire?

SHOOTER: I can picture it. I give in to it. I let my body go. It moves out. It sniffs the board. My head imagines forests! Chain saws! Hammers and nails in my ears! A whole house is being built!

LUPE: (*in book*) Keep it to yourself.

SHOOTER: My nose finds things. Everything's churning with new pictures. Then suddenly it all ends again, and I'm back in the chair. But now I've ruined it. Now I've had my cake. Now neither one is any good. The chair doesn't get it on, and neither does the adventure. I'm nowhere.

LUPE: I'm trying to concentrate.

SHOOTER: Shall I tell a story?

LUPE: (*looking up from book*) Oh God! If I could find the place we could *read* a story!

SHOOTER: (*still standing*) I'll tell a story. I feel like a story. Jeep? How 'bout it?

JEEP: (*still pouring water, blankly*) You bet.

LUPE: (*back into book*) Oh Jesus!

(*Through the story which* SHOOTER *tells standing on the armchair,* JEEP *keeps pouring the water slowly over his hand into the bucket, and* LUPE *keeps looking through the book.* SHOOTER *tells it directly to the audience.*)

SHOOTER: One night there was some moths. A bunch of moths. In the distance they could see a candle. Just one candle in a window of a big house. The moths were tormented by this candle. They longed to be with this candle but none of them understood it or knew what it was. The leader of the moths sent one of them off to the house to bring back some information about this light. The moth returned and reported what he had seen, but the leader told him that he hadn't understood anything about the candle. So another moth went to the house. He touched the flame with the tip of his wings but the heat drove him off. When he came back and reported, the leader still wasn't satisfied. So he sent a third moth out. This moth approached the house and saw the candle flickering inside the window. He became filled with love for this candle. He crashed against the glass and finally found a way inside. He threw himself on the flame. With his forelegs he took hold of the flame and united himself joyously with her. He embraced her completely, and his whole body became red as fire. The leader of the moths, who was watching from far off with the other moths, saw that the flame and the moth appeared to be one. He turned to the other moths and said: "He's learned what he wanted to know, but he's the only one who understands it."

(JEEP *suddenly slaps the water in the bucket with his free hand and pulls a large dead fish out of the bucket and throws it on the floor.* SHOOTER *looks down on it from the chair.* LUPE *sticks with the book.*)

JEEP: I've about had it with this bucket! I can't figure out what I've been doing here all this time.

SHOOTER: (*still standing and looking down at the fish*) How deep is our well anyway?

JEEP: (*to* LUPE) What's happened to Liza?

LUPE: Washing dishes.

JEEP: (*to* LUPE) Have I been standing here all this time?

LUPE: (*looking up*) I don't know! I've been looking for the place! I wish people would just leave me alone!

SHOOTER: I'm not standing up here because I'm afraid of fish, I'll tell you that much. I was standing up here before the fish ever arrived. It's just a coincidence. It's not the way it looks.

JEEP: Shooter, could you create some reason for me to move? Some justification for me to find myself somewhere else?

SHOOTER: Only if you promise that you're not thinking that I'm afraid of fish just because I'm standing up here on the chair and there happens to be a fish in the house.

JEEP: I'm not thinking about you!

(*Suddenly* LUPE *gives an exasperated exhale of air, slams the book shut, glares at the two men, stands and exits upstage.* SHOOTER *and* JEEP *are stuck in their respective positions. Short pause as they look at each other.*)

SHOOTER: Go and pick up the fish.

(JEEP *goes to the fish and picks it up.*)

SHOOTER: Go and put the fish on the table.

(JEEP *goes upstage of the table, facing audience, moves the turkey carcass to one side and lays the fish down on the table.*)

SHOOTER: (*still standing*) Take your jackknife out of your pocket.

(JEEP *does it.*)

SHOOTER: Open your jackknife. The big blade.

(JEEP *does it.*)

SHOOTER: Cut open the belly of the fish, starting from the pee-hole and slicing toward the head.

(JEEP *cuts open the fish.*)

SHOOTER: Now clean it like you would any other fish.

(JEEP *goes about cleaning the fish in silence.* SHOOTER *sits back down slowly in the chair. He looks at his bare legs.*)

SHOOTER: What's been going on in here? (*to* JEEP) Was there a party?

(JEEP *keeps cleaning the fish.* SHOOTER *looks at his legs again.*)

SHOOTER: Was someone taking liberties?

(*He leans back in the chair with a sigh.*)

SHOOTER: It's agonizing. All this time I could've swore I was getting something done. I can't even remember eating. (*back to* JEEP) Did we eat already? Wasn't there a turkey? (*turns front again and leans back*) Somebody's gonna' have to bring me some food, you know. I've made this decision not to leave the chair and I'm gonna' stick with it. Come hell or high water. It's not my fault. (*back to* JEEP) I could have the fish. When you're finished with it, could you fry it up and bring it to me? If it's not too much trouble? (*no response from* JEEP, SHOOTER *turns front again and leans back in the chair*) This isn't the worst. It's just that my stomach is growling. I COULDN'T STAY HERE FOREVER! I don't know what possessed me. (*back to* JEEP) Didn't I say that I'll never leave the chair? (*back front again*) If I get up, it would be a sign of my weakness. Jeep? If I got up would you think I was weak? (*no answer*) This isn't the worst thing that could happen. (*short pause*)

JEEP: The table's littered with carcasses. Guts. Bones. The insides. I'm in the middle of all this.

SHOOTER: Who are you talking to?

JEEP: I'm swimming in it.

SHOOTER: (*still front*) It's nobody's fault, you know.

JEEP: I can't help eating. I'll eat to my dying day.

SHOOTER: Oh, brother!

(SHOOTER *gives a heave and a groan and pushes with his feet so that the armchair tips over backwards with him in it. The bottom of the chair conceals* SHOOTER *from the audience. Only his voice is heard.* JEEP *continues with the fish methodically.*)

JEEP: (*looking at the fish*) If you were alone would you have done that?

SHOOTER: I'm still in the chair. I'm sticking to my promise.

JEEP: You wouldn't call it showing off?

SHOOTER: I'm at my wit's end. The whole world could disappear.

(*The two women enter from upstage. Each one holds a handle on either end of a large wicker basket full of wet laundry.* LUPE *is now wearing* LIZA'S *apron with the pockets full of clothespins. They haul the basket down left center where the clothesline is. They set the basket down on the floor, and* LUPE *grabs one of the chairs and stands up on it to reach the clothesline* LIZA *starts handing her the wet clothes, one piece at a time, from the basket, while* LUPE *pins them onto the line and pulls the line out, making room for the next piece. Gradually the clothes are strung clear across the stage but high enough so as not to block too much of the action.* JEEP *keeps working on the fish, cutting the head off, scaling it, fileting it, cleaning it off in the bucket of water, etc. He is very meticulous about it and gets more involved as he goes along.* SHOOTER *remains hidden behind the armchair. The two girls remain closed off in their activity.*)

JEEP: I'm starting to feel better already. You remember before when I was getting the fears?

SHOOTER: No. When was that?

JEEP: When I was asking you if you remembered when you were scared to go up and take a bath.

SHOOTER: That was a long time ago.

JEEP: I'm getting better now. Even in the middle of all this violence.

SHOOTER: You should've told me you were scared. I would've done something about it. I didn't realize you were scared.

JEEP: I'm in a better position now. Now I've got something to do.

(SHOOTER *pulls the armchair over on top of himself so that his arms stick out the sides like a headless turtle. He moves the chair slightly from side to side with his back. The women continue in silence with the laundry.*)

JEEP: I can even imagine how horrifying it could be to be doing all this, and it doesn't touch me. It's like I'm dismissed.

SHOOTER: Am I completely hidden?

JEEP: More or less.

SHOOTER: Maybe I'm gone.

JEEP: Maybe.

SHOOTER: That's what it's like.

JEEP: Maybe that's it, then. Gone.

(SHOOTER *starts moving the armchair slowly around like a giant tortoise. The girls pay no attention.*)

SHOOTER: That's it all right. Flown the coop. Is there anyone to verify? To check it out?

JEEP: (*looking at the girls*) Are you sure you want to?

SHOOTER: Maybe it's better like this. We can keep it a secret.

JEEP: Are you sure you're not there?

SHOOTER: More or less. Something creeps back, now that you mention it.

JEEP: Oh.

SHOOTER: What's the matter?

JEEP: I don't know. I got no references for this. Suddenly it's shifted.

SHOOTER: What's the matter? You have to clue me in.

JEEP: Once I was in a family. I had no choice about it. I lived in different houses. I had no choice. I couldn't even choose the wallpaper.

SHOOTER: Are you getting to the point?

JEEP: I found myself in schools. In cars. I got arrested. That was when it changed. The second I got arrested.

SHOOTER: Have you forgotten about me?

JEEP: The second I got arrested I understood something. I remember the phrase "getting in trouble." I remember the word "trouble." I remember the feeling of being in trouble. It wasn't until I got in trouble that I found out my true position.

SHOOTER: What was that?

JEEP: I was in the world. I was up for grabs. I was being taken away by something bigger.

SHOOTER: The cops?

JEEP: Something bigger. Bigger than family. Bigger than school. Bigger than the 4-H Club. Bigger than Little League Baseball. This was Big Time. My frame of reference changed.

SHOOTER: Did you go to jail?

JEEP: I went everywhere. Cop car, court, jail, cop car, jail, court, cop car, home, cop car, jail. And everywhere I noticed this new interest in my existence. These new details. Every scar was noted down. Every mark. The lines in my fingers. Hair. Eyes. Change in the pocket. Knives. Race. Age. Every detail.

SHOOTER: Who was interested?

JEEP: A vast network. A chain of events. I entered a new world.

SHOOTER: Weren't you scared?

JEEP: I used to have this dream that would come to me while I was on my feet. I'd be on my feet just standing there in these walls, and I'd have this dream come to me that the walls were moving in. It was like a sweeping kind of terror that struck me. Then something in me would panic. I wouldn't make a move. I'd just be standing there very still, but inside something would leap like it was trying to escape. And then the leap would come up against something. It was like an absolutely helpless leap. There was no possible way of getting out. I couldn't believe it. It was like nothing in the whole wide world could get me out of there.

I'd relax for a second. I'd be forced to relax because if I didn't, if I followed through with this inward leap, if I let my body do it I'd just crash against the wall. I'd just smash my head in or something. I had to relax. For a second I could accept it. That I was there. In jail. That I wasn't getting out. No escape. For a second. Then these thoughts would come. "How long? How long was I there for? A day. Maybe I could last a day. A week. A month? I'd never last a month! FOREVER!" That's the thought that did it. FOREVER! And the whole thing would start up again. Except worse this time. As though it wasn't just a thought. As though it really was. And then I'd start to move. I couldn't help myself. My body was shaking.

(JEEP *begins to move around the stage. The words animate him as though the space is the cell he's talking about but not as though he's recalling a past experience but rather that he's attempting his own escape from the space he's playing in. The other actions continue in their own rhythm.*)

I'd start to make sounds. It just came out of me. A low moan. An animal noise. I was moving now. I was stalking myself. I couldn't stop. Everything disappeared. I had no idea what the world was. I had no idea how I got there or why or who did it. I had no references for this.

(JEEP *just stands there. The others continue their actions. Lights fade slowly to black. The Christmas tree keeps blinking.*)

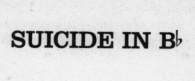

SUICIDE IN B♭

A Mysterious Overture

Suicide was first produced at the Yale Repertory Theater in New Haven, Connecticut, on October 15, 1976. It was directed by Walt Jones in association with Denise A. Gordon with the following cast:

PIANIST:	Lawrence Wolf
PABLO:	Clifford David
LOUIS:	Joe Grifasi
PETRONE:	William Hickey
LAUREEN:	Alma Cuervo
NILES:	Paul Schierhorn
PAULLETTE:	Joyce Fideor
Music composed by:	Lawrence Wolf

SCENE: *Slightly raked stage. A plain white muslin flat represents the upstage wall. It does not run the full width of the stage but leaves empty space on either side of it. It should be made obvious that it's a flat to the audience. There are no side walls. Dead center upstage, almost flush with the flat, is a black upright piano. Not a grand piano. Downstage left is a blue stuffed armchair with a brass floor lamp set to the upstage side of it. The lamp has a pale yellow shade with small green palm trees painted all around it in a circle. These are the only objects onstage. The floor of the stage is not painted but left bare. The entire set is visible to the audience as they come in. In the center of the floor, the outline of a man's body sprawled out in an awkward position of death is painted in white. The lights begin to dim very slowly. At their halfway point, the* PIANO PLAYER *rushes on from stage right, hiding his face from the audience with his coat, as though afraid to be photographed. He is wearing a shabby black suit. He sits quickly on the piano stool, back to audience, and faces the piano. As the lights continue to dim, he raises both arms very slowly with the fingers of both hands interlaced until they are straight above his head. When he gets to the top of his stretch he cracks his knuckles loudly. The lights go to black. A loud gunshot is heard offstage, in the dark. Sound of a body falling hard to the floor. Lamp is switched on. Lights bank back up fast.* PIANO PLAYER *is still sitting at the bench with both arms still raised high, fingers together. Lights begin to slowly dim again. As they do,* PIANO PLAYER *lowers his arms slowly and sets them on the keys of the piano. He begins to play.* PABLO *and* LOUIS, *the two detectives, enter from right accompanied by the music.* LOUIS *is playing dead and being dragged across the floor by his heels by* PABLO. PABLO *is dressed in a long overcoat, baggy pants, shiny black shoes and a detective's hat.* LOUIS *wears striped pants, brown and white brogans, striped shirt and tie, black vest, black garters on his arms and a black detective's hat which he holds on his stomach while he's being dragged. The piano music continues as* PABLO *pulls him into center stage with some effort then drops both heels to the floor. Piano stops.* LOUIS *stays on the floor on his back.* PABLO *looks down at him.* PIANO PLAYER *just sits with back to audience. Lights stop at ½ level.*

PABLO: (*catching his breath*) Trying to reconstruct the imagination of it.

LOUIS: (*still on his back*) What?

PABLO: The imagination. (*between breaths*) The imagination of it. How we suppose it might have been. It's useless. All we come up with is "supposes."

LOUIS: Where's your briefcase?

PABLO: (*suddenly hysterical, slapping his pockets as though he's lost something, going in circles*) Oh my God! What's happening to me!

LOUIS: You left it by the fire hydrant.

PABLO: Oh my God!

(PABLO *rushes back off stage right.* LOUIS *slowly gets to his feet. He pauses a moment, standing there, looks down at the outline of the body on the floor. He pretends to be shot by a silent bullet and tries to fall into the shape of the outline. On the floor he checks out his position in relationship to the outline and adjusts his body accordingly.* PABLO *enters again from right with a big black briefcase. He crosses straight to the armchair down left, sits quickly, opens the briefcase on his lap and worriedly checks through reams of typewritten papers.* LOUIS *stays on the floor.*)

LOUIS: These positions remind me of hieroglyphs.

PABLO: It's lucky the whole thing wasn't ripped off. There it was, sitting there plain as day. Just sitting on the cement.

LOUIS: The similarity between positions of death and the positions of birth are too awesome to be ignored.

PABLO: Will you get up off the floor and help me with this!

LOUIS: (*sitting up*) What's to help? It's all there isn't it?

PABLO: How should I know! That's why I'm checking!

LOUIS: Well, what if it wasn't all there? So what?

PABLO: Why are you so casual? Why are you always so goddamn casual!

LOUIS: (*lies back down in position of outline*) The guy's dead, right?

PABLO: (*still going through papers*) That's right. That's right. The guy's dead. Very brilliant.

LOUIS: This is all after the fact.

PABLO: Not if there's extenuating circumstances!

LOUIS: Don't use big words. It's embarrassing.

PABLO: I'm not afraid of my education! It serves me. It gives me a certain support. Even in the company of goons, it's a comfort. It gives me hope of a certain kind.

LOUIS: (*still on floor*) What kind of hope?

PABLO: I'm not getting into this with you, Louis. Every time you sucker me into this I regret it. I'm not even going to start.

(LOUIS *gets up off the floor quickly and crosses to the lamp beside* PABLO. *He stares at the lampshade and turns it in a circle with his hand.* PABLO *keeps poring through the papers.*)

LOUIS: Beautiful shade. Antique probably.

PABLO: (*not looking up*) I doubt it on his salary.

LOUIS: (*still turning shade*) Do composers get a salary?

PABLO: Commissions. Whatever. He didn't make much.

LOUIS: How come?

PABLO: Nobody bought it, that's how come! Nobody bought the music.

(LOUIS *starts pulling the chain switch on the lamp, turning it off and on as he stares at the shade.* PABLO *keeps on with the papers.*)

LOUIS: Nobody bought the music?

PABLO: That's right.

LOUIS: So he blew his brains out.

PABLO: That's a little oversimplified.

LOUIS: So he got depressed.

PABLO: We don't know that for sure.

LOUIS: Down in the dumps.

PABLO: We don't know.

LOUIS: That's no reason to blow your brains out. I mean, love is a better reason isn't it?

PABLO: I don't know! And stop switching that lamp on and off!

(LOUIS *stops. Pause.*)

PABLO: Why don't you go into the kitchen and make us a b.l.t. while I go through these papers.

LOUIS: (*moving back toward center*) It's not our kitchen.

PABLO: So what?

LOUIS: It's his kitchen.

PABLO: What're you superstitious or something?

LOUIS: I have my doubts.

PABLO: About what?

LOUIS: About being here so soon. I mean it wasn't that long ago he was dragged out of here.

PABLO: (*throwing papers up in the air*) I can't find it anywhere in here! Our one piece of evidence and it's gone!

LOUIS: Don't get yer pants in a bunch. It'll turn up.

PABLO: Listen, Louis! If you don't bottle this bullshit right here and now, I'm calling the Squad and asking them to send me a new man! I mean it, Louis! I've had it!

LOUIS: You certainly have.

PABLO: I've had it up to here with your goddamn casual attitude! It's as though nothing matters. As though nothing's happened. We could be sitting in the governor's mansion for all you give a shit.

LOUIS: I have a theory.

PABLO: There could be big stakes involved in this for us if you had eyeballs to see into the possibilities. If you thought for one second about the implications!

LOUIS: I have a theory.

PABLO: The ramifications. It's chocked full of juicy potential criminal action against some very big steam in some very high places and you can't even see beyond your own nose.

LOUIS: I have a theory. Do you wanna hear it?

PABLO: (*pausing, catches his breath*) What theory?

(PIANO PLAYER *begins to play, accompanying* LOUIS *as he speaks.* PABLO *keeps going through the papers, half listening to* LOUIS.)

LOUIS: (*piano behind*) A boy hears sound. He hears sound before he has a name. He hears gurgling, pounding underwater. He hears an ocean of blood swimming around him. Through his veins. Through his mother. He breaks into the light of day. He's shocked that he has a voice. He finds his voice and screams. He hears it screaming as though coming down through ancient time. Like it belongs to another body. He hears it that way. He hears the crack of his own flesh. His own heart. His skin sliding on rubber mats. Squeaking. He hears his own bones growing. Stretching his skin in all directions. Bones moving out. Organs expanding. The sound of cells booming through his brain like tiny intergalactic missiles. Atoms. Nuclear rushes of wind through his nose holes. Toenails rubbing blankets in the dark. Books falling on pianos. Electricity humming even when the lights are off. Internal combustion engines. Turbo jets. Then one day he hears what they call music. He hears what they call "music" in the same way he hears what they call "noise." In the same stream. Music as an extension of sound. An organization. Another way of putting it. He's disappointed. He's disappointed and exhilarated at the same time. Exhilarated because he sees an opening. An adventure. A way inside. He sees that putting any two things together produces sound. Any two things. Striking, plucking, blowing, rubbing, dropping, kicking, kissing. Any two things. He has a revelation. Or rather, a revelation presents itself. Stabs at him. Enters into him and becomes part of his physiology. His physiognomy. His psychology. His paraphernalia. His makeup. He puts it to use. He's driven toward it in a way most men consider dangerous and suicidal. His production is abundant. Nonstop. Endlessly winding through un-heard-of-before symphonies. Concertos beyond belief. He organizes quintets. Soloists rush to him just to be in his presence. The best ones are rejected. He only takes on apprentices. He only plays nightclubs although he could pack out the Garden in a flash. He shakes the sidewalks with his compositions. Every city in the world is calling his name. He invents totally new chord progressions and scales. New names for notes that not even the Chinese have heard of. Instruments that he makes in the bathtub. His music is sweeping the country. And then one day he disappears. Just like that. He goes. Not dead. Just gone. No one can figure it. Rumors are spread that he's kidnapped. Abducted and taken to Sweden. Then it switches to murder. Talk of him being involved with particular ladies of particular gentlemen. Then his body is found. His body is found but his face is blown off. His fingerprints are tested and they check out completely. His one-of-a-kind fingerprints. The case is closed.

PABLO: (*short pause, still looking through papers*) Is that it?

LOUIS: No.

PABLO: There's more?

LOUIS: Yes.

PABLO: Well what is it?

LOUIS: He's fooled them all.

PABLO: How do you mean?

LOUIS: He's just laying low.

PABLO: (*crossing, begins to pace,* LOUIS *crosses to chair*) That doesn't make any sense at all! He's got nothing to lay low for.

LOUIS: Aha! We don't know that for sure. That's where the case gets interesting.

(LOUIS *sits in chair and starts going through papers as* PABLO *paces back and forth.*)

PABLO: He was at the top of the bill. Maybe not as high up as you depict but pretty goddamn high up there. Why disappear when things are going so good. It's crazy.

LOUIS: But Possible.

PABLO: It's a crazy theory! (*sees* LOUIS *with papers*) Stay away from those papers!

(PABLO *rushes over to* LOUIS *and grabs the papers out of his hands.*)

PABLO: Just keep your hands off!

LOUIS: Look, I'm on this case too. This stuff's not confidential.

PABLO: Oh yeah! Not confidential, huh? Who the hell called me up in the middle of the goddamn night, worried sick, and wanted to know if these papers were under lock and key? Who do you suppose?

LOUIS: I haven't the faintest.

PABLO: The governor! That's who, wise ass! The governor! Not confidential my ass. They're Super-Confidential! They're so confidential, they're even classified. That's how confidential they are. Classified by a top-flight agency. I'm not at liberty to say any more about it.

LOUIS: You've become a blithering idiot, Pablo. A total meatball. Those papers are as valuable as yesterday's *Daily News.* There's nothing in there but palilalia. Do you know what "palilalia" is?

PABLO: I'm not talking.

LOUIS: Well "palilalia" is what you've got. "Palilalia" is what you've got right there in your hamburger hands. And that's all you've got.

PABLO: I know you've been trying to sabotage this project right from the start. Right from the very beginning. There's something in you that wants to destroy me.

LOUIS: You're a turkey, Pablo. A total turkey.

PABLO: I don't see any possible way that we can work together. I just don't see how it's possible. It would be hard enough working with someone who's compassionate and sensitive and at least showed an interest in the case but you're totally negative.

LOUIS: Indifferent.

PABLO: That's worse than negative!

LOUIS: I'm trying to remain objective about this.

PABLO: Objective my ass! You're dead weight, Louis! Dead weight!

(LOUIS *stands suddenly, listening intently for a noise. No sound.*)

LOUIS: What was that?

PABLO: What was what?

LOUIS: That.

(*They both listen for a second. Again nothing.*)

PABLO: Not only are you dead weight but you're a lunatic.

LOUIS: No, listen!

PABLO: I'm not going to listen! I'm through listening.

LOUIS: Like a woman screaming. A terrible screaming. Like a woman being tortured.

PABLO: It's your ears, Louis! Your ears are telling you stories.

LOUIS: (*crossing toward outline on floor*) I don't like the idea of having this outline of a dead man on the floor with us. It's primitive. There's something creepy about it.

PABLO: Don't touch it until the Squad gets here!

LOUIS: I'm not going to touch it.

PABLO: What is it with you anyway? Have you completely lost touch with your vocation?

LOUIS: I'm wasting away. At least half of me is wasting away.

PABLO: Pull yourself together.

LOUIS: You didn't hear a voice?

PABLO: Of course not.

LOUIS: Don't be so smug about it. You're totally ignorant of what's going on here. You're blundering around in here as though this was just another ordinary old homicide. You're blinded by your career.

PABLO: I'm not distorting the facts yet, if that's what you mean.

LOUIS: You don't have any facts!

PABLO: And you don't have any sense! (*pause as they stare at each other*) Now let's get to work.

LOUIS: What now?

PABLO: A stabbing. We haven't tried a stabbing yet.

LOUIS: His face was blown off.

PABLO: There's no report from ballistics!

LOUIS: You don't need a report when someone's face is blown away.

PABLO: It could've been carved off. Now you stand over there where the body was found and I'll come at you with a butcher knife.

LOUIS: Have you got a butcher knife?

PABLO: I'll get a butcher knife. Now you just stand there and wait.

(PABLO *exits up left.* LOUIS *stands center stage. Simultaneously with* PABLO'S *exit,* PETRONE *enters from stage right. He's tall and extremely skinny, wearing baggy pants, T-shirt and suspenders. He has an alto saxophone strapped to his neck. He bites down on the mouthpiece and mimes blowing it. No sound comes from the sax but a high shrill scream of a woman is heard offstage. It should be delivered like a musical note but definitely be a scream. It stays on one note for ten full seconds as* PETRONE *keeps blowing silently into the horn.* LOUIS *does not hear the scream. He just stands there. Suddenly* PABLO *rushes on very fast from stage left holding a butcher knife high above his head as though he's going to stab* LOUIS. *He stops just short of* LOUIS *with his arms still raised holding the knife. Scream stops.* PETRONE *takes his mouth off the sax.*)

PABLO: I can't do it.

LOUIS: You're not supposed to do it. If you did it, I'd be dead.

(PABLO *drops the knife to the floor and goes to the chair and collapses into it.* LOUIS *bends over and picks up the knife.* PETRONE *crosses into the center area.*)

PETRONE: (*to* LOUIS) You seen Niles?

LOUIS: Niles? No. Why?

PETRONE: We were supposed to get together.

PABLO: (*still in chair*) I can't get it up. I can't get it up for this. What's happening to me? I've waited a lifetime for a case like this. And now I can't get it up.

PETRONE: (*crossing toward chair, to* PABLO) Do you mind if I sit in that chair? That's the chair I always sit in.

PABLO: Yes I do mind. I'm having a nervous breakdown as a matter of fact.

PETRONE: Well do you mind if I sit on your lap then? I've gotta sit down. My bones are snapping.

PABLO: (*to* LOUIS) Who is this guy? (*to* PETRONE) Sure! Sure, sit on my lap! What the hell! The whole case is going to pot anyway.

(PETRONE *sits down on* PABLO'S *lap. He smiles at* LOUIS, *who is still handling the knife.*)

PETRONE: (*to* LOUIS) You guys are awful nice. You know that? Awful nice. I'm part of the scum of the earth. You know what I mean. Low DOGS. Lower in fact. It's a caste system. Don't you agree? Wouldn't you guys agree to that?

LOUIS: Sure.

PETRONE: Same as they got in India. Wouldn't you say? Same story over here. No different.

LOUIS: No different. That's for sure.

PETRONE: There's more disguises over here I guess. More ways of covering it up. But I have a theory that it's something we're born with. You know what I mean? I mean it seems like I'll never get out of it.

LOUIS: You're right. You won't.

PETRONE: You won't either.

LOUIS: I might. But you definitely won't.

PETRONE: You're right.

PABLO: Would you mind shifting a little bit?

PETRONE: (*shifting his weight on* PABLO'S *lap*) Oh sure. Sorry about the bones. This time of year they get particularly menacing. One time it got so bad they came right out at the elbows. Right straight out like two white fish.

LOUIS: You mean out of the skin?

PETRONE: Sure. Like two white fish. I almost blinded people in the daytime. The sun bounced right off them like ivory. Right into people's faces. People bounced back, holding their eyes, screaming in pain. It was a great feeling of power it gave me. A great feeling. Like I possessed certain laser rays within my elbows and if anyone fucked with me I just pointed them in the right direction.

PABLO: Get off my lap please.

PETRONE: No.

LOUIS: (*after pause*) You were supposed to meet Niles here?

PETRONE: I am meeting him. That's what I'm here for. We're going to play.

LOUIS: He's dead.

PETRONE: No he's not.

LOUIS: Yes he is.

PETRONE: No he's not.

LOUIS: Yes he is.

PETRONE: No he's not.

LOUIS: (*after pause*) Get off my partner's lap please.

PETRONE: (*laughing*) Your partner? This is your partner? Like Gabby Hayes? You remember Gabby Hayes?

LOUIS: Yes I do remember Gabby Hayes as a matter of fact.

PETRONE: What're you guys doin' here anyway? This isn't your house.

PABLO: We probably have more of a right to be here than you do. In fact we're fully within our rights.

LOUIS: We're investigating a murder.

PABLO: A possible murder.

PETRONE: You're detectives?

LOUIS: That's right.

PETRONE: Like Dick Tracy! You remember Dick Tracy?

LOUIS: (*after pause, fondling knife*) If you don't get off my partner's lap (*pause*) I don't know what I'm going to do.

PETRONE: I remember Dick Tracy. (*he gets off* PABLO'S *lap and crosses upstage*) I remember all about him. Two-way wrist radio. His yellow hat. His black Mercury.

LOUIS: Are you part of Niles' band?

(PETRONE *turns to* LOUIS *and stares at him. He puts the saxophone to his mouth and starts to finger the keys. No sound from the sax except the rhythmic tapping of the keys. He keeps this up.* LOUIS *crosses over to* PABLO.)

LOUIS: (*confidentially to* PABLO) Are you all right?

PABLO: Don't be ridiculous.

LOUIS: (*under his breath*) We've got to get out of here. This is worse than I expected.

PABLO: Don't panic. It could be our big break. I'll try to have a talk with him.

(PABLO *gets up and crosses to* PETRONE, *who continues fingering the sax.*)

LOUIS: It's too dangerous, Pablo! You don't know what you're getting into.

PABLO: (*to* PETRONE) You've known Niles for some time I take it?

(PETRONE *keeps blowing silently into sax and fingering keys.*)

LOUIS: He's burned out, Pablo. You won't get anywhere with him. I say we go back to headquarters and file a report.

PABLO: Do you know if he had any girl friends?

(PETRONE *stops "playing" sax for a second and looks hard at* PABLO.)

PABLO: Any lady friends that we might be able to have a talk with?

(PETRONE *puts the sax back in his mouth and "plays" silently again.*)

LOUIS: Leave him alone and let's get out of here!

PABLO: (*to* PETRONE) Any rackets?

(LOUIS *suddenly puts the butcher knife up to his own neck as though about to kill himself.* PABLO *and* PETRONE *pay no attention.*)

PABLO: (*to* PETRONE) Was he involved in any side activities? Poppy seeds? Pari-mutuels? O.T.B.? Anything like that?

(LOUIS *starts to struggle with one hand against the hand that's holding the knife against his neck.* PABLO *and* PETRONE *continue without noticing.*)

PABLO: It could be important. You see, I have a strong inclination that he didn't kill himself. I have the feeling he was under the influence of macabre overtones. A victim of odious events that spiraled toward his eventual downfall.

(PIANO PLAYER *breaks in here, strong forceful bass line.* PETRONE *keeps playing silently.* LOUIS *struggles more desperately with the knife hand, moving all over the stage;* PABLO *keeps talking.*)

PABLO: A victim of circumstances beyond his control. He got in over his head. He bought off more than he could chew. He began dallying with power figures. He was sinking in a sea of confusion. His music was driving him mad. His improvisations were lasting for days on end. He had to be dragged from his piano and strapped to his bed. Fed intravenously to keep him from starving. He forgot how to speak and only uttered noises of varying pitch. His gestures were all in slow motion as the shock of fast movement was too loud for his ears. He began to feel certain that he was possessed. Not as if by magic but by his own gift. His own voracious hunger for sound became like a demon. Another body within him that lashed out without warning. That took hold of him and swept him away. Each time with more and more violence until his weaker side began to collapse. He was desperate for some kind of help so he turned to religion. Superstition. Cultism. There were plenty of self-proclaimed "healers" ready to take him on. Waiting like hyenas in the wings. He gave himself over to them willingly. Anything that promised to deliver him from this nightmare. He followed their every demand. His music was written to their specifications. His money was put in their hands. His thoughts were geared to their dogma. And his demon began to be tamed. It changed its attitude completely and started to toe the line. His music turned into boring melodics. Slowly he noticed the change. He liked the new feeling of freedom. He thanked his masters and told them that now that the demon had left him he would go off on his own again. But they told him he couldn't. That he was still in danger. That as long as he was within their power he'd be all right. He'd be safe. He argued with them for weeks on end. His mind would go back and forth between submission and rebellion. His music was turning to pablum. Finally he decided to leave them completely. And that's when they killed him.

(*Piano stops.* PETRONE *stops.* LOUIS *falls to the floor, exhausted from the struggle. The knife falls from his hand.*)

LOUIS: (*breathing heavily, on floor*) Pablo, we've got to get out of here!

PABLO: (*to* LOUIS, *crossing back to chair and papers*) Get up off the floor. We're through with simulating events now. Now we've got some real evidence.

PETRONE: (*to* PABLO) That's not the way it happened at all. You guys are really off the deep end.

PABLO: Ah! Then you admit something did happen! That's more than you were admitting before.

LOUIS: There's no evidence, Pablo!

PETRONE: You guys better get outa' here before Niles comes back.

PABLO: Where's he gone to?

PETRONE: He went out to get some toasted English muffins. That's the only thing he eats when he's working.

PABLO: Where did he go to get the toasted English muffins?

PETRONE: Hey, lighten up, buster. This is my day off.

PABLO: (*suddenly intent, crossing slowly toward* PETRONE) What do you know about improvisation?

PETRONE: You talkin' to me?

LOUIS: (*still on floor*) Pablo, will you leave him alone!

PABLO: (*to* PETRONE) Yes. You claim to be one of Niles' musicians. I haven't heard a sound come out of your horn yet.

PETRONE: You haven't?

PABLO: No, I haven't.

PETRONE: Well, it takes a while to attune your ears to the frequency we're playing in. It's extremely high. Dogs can't even hear it. That's why Niles has trouble selling it.

PABLO: I see.

PETRONE: It's also an attempt at visual music. You'll have to wait

for Niles to come so he can explain it to you. I know how to play
it but I can't explain it.

PABLO: I can't wait for Niles.

(LOUIS *starts struggling with his hand again as it tries to reach for the
knife. He grabs it with the other hand, pulls it back. The hand reaches
out again for the knife, etc.*)

PETRONE: You guys are very pushy, you know that? I'm not even
used to talking and you're trying to force me into explanations.

PABLO: What do you know about improvisation?

PETRONE: Will you get off that kick! That's not something to mess
around with. That's private!

PABLO: How does it relate to breaking with tradition! To breaking
off with the past! To throwing the diligent efforts of our forefathers and their forefathers before them to the winds! To turning
the classics to garbage before our very eyes! To distorting the
very foundations of our cherished values! (*piano breaks in with
loud atonal chords at random intervals*) To making mincemeat out
of brilliance! To rubbing up against the very grain of sanity and
driving us all to complete and utter destruction! To changing the
shape of American morality! That's where it's at! That's where
it's at isn't it! You've snuck up on us through the back door.
You're not strong enough to take us over by direct political
action so you've chosen to drive us all crazy. Then, when we're
all completely within your control, you'll take us over. That's it
isn't it? You're getting back at us after all these years. I wasn't
born yesterday you know! I know a thing or two! I know when
I'm being bushwhacked!

(*Piano stops.*)

LOUIS: (*from floor, reaching for knife*) Pablo! Could you reach me the
knife?

(LAUREEN *enters from stage right dressed in a bathrobe and wheeling an
acoustic double bass fiddle in front of her. The bass is contained in a
canvas case. As soon as she enters she screams on a high note and
continues the scream until she's crossed to center stage. She stops center
stage and ends the scream. She unzips the canvas case, takes out a bow
and starts bowing the bass on random notes. It makes no difference if
she knows how to play.* PABLO *circles around her, taking note of the new
development.* PETRONE *crosses down to the chair and sits in it. He
starts going through* PABLO'S *papers.* LOUIS *keeps reaching for the knife
on the floor. There is a while that passes with no talk.*)

PETRONE: (*to* PABLO, *in chair as he browses through papers*) There was a time when I felt like that myself. As though a particular group was at the heart of it. As though secret organizations were constantly plotting against me. Not just against me but against all members of my particular caste. The Low Dogs. Gang warfare on an international scale. It got so that I felt they were personally responsible for a bad count of smack.

LAUREEN: (*as she bows the bass, to* PABLO) Your partner is reaching for the knife.

PABLO: (*as he circles around her*) Yes, I know.

LAUREEN: (*to* PABLO) You should tell him that everything's all right. There's no need for that kind of stuff now. He's extending himself needlessly.

PABLO: (*still circling* LAUREEN *as she plays*) How long have you known Niles?

LAUREEN: We've gone through that particular era. Something new is called for now. There's no need for remorse. He's defeating the purpose.

PABLO: Just answer the question!

LAUREEN: (*still playing*) You should tell him not to jump to conclusions. There's no organization strong enough to make you crumble. There's no system stronger than a single man. He should just stand up and forget about the whole thing. What's he killing himself for anyway? An audience? There isn't any audience. Tell him there isn't any audience. Tell him that.

PABLO: HOW LONG HAVE YOU KNOWN NILES! ANSWER THE QUESTION!

(*She stops playing and looks at* PABLO.)

LAUREEN: (*to* PABLO) Long enough. (*she looks at* LOUIS) Will you get up off the floor please? It's distracting.

(LOUIS *stops reaching for the knife. He looks at her.*)

LOUIS: (*to* LAUREEN, *from floor*) Isn't the nation broken in half?

LAUREEN: No way of telling.

LOUIS: Aren't we leaderless? Jobless? Destitute? Forlorn?

LAUREEN: Just get up.

LOUIS: Not until I get some guarantees!

PETRONE: (*from chair, with papers*) Let him kill himself. Who gives a fuck.

(PABLO *rushes over to* PETRONE *and grabs the papers out of his hands.*)

PABLO: (*to* PETRONE) Stay away from those papers!

LAUREEN: (*to* LOUIS) Personally, it doesn't matter to me one way or the other if you kill yourself. It just seems pointless.

(LAUREEN *goes back to bowing the bass*, LOUIS *stays on floor*, PABLO *goes through his papers*, PETRONE *sits in chair*.)

LOUIS: (*to* LAUREEN) To you it would seem pointless! You've got a particular calling. You've got an obsession. The whole structure can collapse around you and you wouldn't mind. You'd just sit there fiddling away like Nero or something. (*suddenly hysterical, throwing himself around on the floor*) IT'S DIFFERENT WITH ME! I'M DOWN HERE ON THE GROUND! I'M WAY DOWN HERE! YOU CAN'T EVEN SEE ME I'M SO LOW!

PETRONE: (*to* PABLO) I'm lower than him.

LAUREEN: (*casually to* LOUIS *as she plays*) Pick yourself up.

LOUIS: Stop saying that to me! I'm a detective! I should be ordering you around! I should be the strong one!

LAUREEN: But you're not.

LOUIS: Pablo, call her off! She's trying to destroy my opinions!

PABLO: (*calmly to* LAUREEN *and* PETRONE) It's time for you people to leave now. You've been very helpful. We'll call you if we need any further information.

PETRONE: (*to himself*) We need another martyr like a hole in the head.

LOUIS: I'M NO MARTYR! I'M A DETECTIVE!

PABLO: Louis, get up.

LAUREEN: (*still playing*) This music has no room for politics. It answers to nobody. It plays by itself even when we're not playing it. Even when we're not there to listen. It has no boss. Even when the boss is dead it keeps playing.

PABLO: (*suddenly lunging toward* LAUREEN) Was Niles the boss? Was that it?

LAUREEN: (*still playing*) Even when idiots surround it on all sides.

(PETRONE *stands suddenly*. LAUREEN *stops playing*.)

PETRONE: (*to* PABLO) I'll tell you the whole story. You wanna' hear it? I'll tell you the whole thing. It's no secret.

PABLO: (*rushing to* LOUIS) Louis, get up! He's going to spill the beans. Get up! Get up!

LOUIS: Right now?

PABLO: Get up! Come on. We've finally forced their hand.

(PABLO *helps* LOUIS *to his feet and takes him over to the armchair. He sets* LOUIS *down in the armchair and then sits on his lap.* PETRONE *moves center stage.* PIANO PLAYER *begins to play behind* PETRONE. LAUREEN *accompanies on the bass.*)

PETRONE: The story of Niles from the top:

LOUIS: Is he going to tell us a story?

PABLO: (*sitting on* LOUIS' *lap*) He's going to tell us the whole story.

LOUIS: I could've easily killed myself, you know.

PABLO: It's all right now. It's going to be all right. We've got them just where we want them. They're playing right into our hands.

PETRONE: (*to* LOUIS *and* PABLO) Niles was a big man. A huge man in fact. The kind of man you'd take to be a brakeman before anything else.

(NILES *enters from up right with a flashlight. He's accompanied by* PAULETTE, *a skinny young girl in a skimpy dress with a blanket over her shoulders. She carries a large suitcase.* NILES *is very big, dressed in a crumpled black suit, dark glasses and a black hat. They both sneak on tiptoes very slowly toward center stage. The others do not relate to them. Piano accompanies them.* PETRONE *narrates but does not direct anything to* NILES *and* PAULETTE.)

NILES: (*half whisper*) You sure it's not too soon, Paulette? They could be waiting around in there.

PAULETTE: No, it's perfect. If you waited any longer you'd give them time to figure it out.

NILES: Don't the streets smell funny?

PAULETTE: They smell wet.

PETRONE: (*to* LOUIS *and* PABLO) His hands were so huge they could stretch two octaves in a single stroke. Not even Art Tatum could boast such hands. Not even Joe "Fingers" Carr. The kind of hands that looked capable of breaking a young calf in half.

(NILES *and* PAULETTE *approach the center playing area and stop at the edge of it.*)

NILES: (*whispering*) You better take a look inside, just to make sure.

(PAULETTE *goes up on her tiptoes as though looking through a window.*)

NILES: See anything?

PAULETTE: Nothing. Just an outline of your body on the floor.

NILES: Nothing else?

PAULETTE: Nope.

(NILES *and* PAULLETTE *sneak their way into the center stage area, amongst the other players, who ignore them.* PETRONE *keeps narrating. Piano keeps playing.* LAUREEN *accompanies on bass.* LOUIS *and* PABLO *are spellbound watching* PETRONE *tell the story.*)

PETRONE: As a child he was held in contempt by the other children because of his giant proportions. The kids called him "Brontosaurus Morris" and other nasty things. He was totally awkward as an adolescent and couldn't even speak a full sentence until the age of eighteen.

(*Suddenly the music stops, the stage lights go black. Only* NILES' *flashlight is seen. Then a pale follow spot comes on, illuminating* NILES *and* PAULLETTE. *The others stay motionless.*)

NILES: What happened?

PAULLETTE: (*in a heavy whisper*) We're inside. It's all right. We're inside now.

NILES: No one's here?

PAULLETTE: Just us.

NILES: Did you hear someone screaming?

PAULLETTE: No, Niles. It's okay now.

NILES: I just want to do it and get out of here.

PAULLETTE: We don't have to rush. We got plenty of time.

NILES: I feel like I shouldn't have come back. I already escaped. How come I came back?

PAULLETTE: (*setting suitcase down center on the ground and opening it*) We just gotta' do this one thing and then we'll be gone.

(PAULLETTE *starts taking different pieces of clothing and masks out of the suitcase as* NILES *moves around the stage with the flashlight, shining it in different areas. Once in a while the flashlight crosses somebody's face but he doesn't linger on it. The stage lights stay dark. Just the flashlight and the follow spots.*)

NILES: It's not so easy to leave a life. It's not the easiest thing in the world. I can still smell myself in this place. It feels like I never left.

PAULLETTE: It'll be different.

NILES: When?

PAULLETTE: Just take it easy.

NILES: (*shining flashlight on outline on floor*) Why do they still have this outline of my body on the floor? Maybe they're not convinced.

PAULLETTE: Stop worrying. They're convinced all right.

NILES: They've gone through all my papers! Look at my papers all over the place!

PAULLETTE: Go make yourself some coffee or something.

NILES: I just had a nightmare. I just had a nightmare while I was standing here.

PAULLETTE: What?

NILES: What if it turns out to be harder playing dead than it was playing alive?

PAULLETTE: That's not the way it works. You've got to give yourself time to settle into this thing, Niles. I'll explain the whole thing to you.

NILES: How come I'm trusting you? How come? All of a sudden I'm wondering that. I never questioned that before.

PAULLETTE: You know why.

NILES: I know you're not one of those big city models. I know that much. I know you're not hooked up to the politicians. The gangsters. The rackets. Dope syndicates. Numbers. Private Foundations. Federal Granting Organizations. C.I.A. Code Scanning. I know that much. I checked all that out. You're clean on that score.

PAULLETTE: Okay.

NILES: What I haven't checked out is the more insidious groups. The Mind Benders. The Chromatic Persuaders. The Psychic Transfusions. The Cult Mongers. All forms of ritualistic terrorism. That area is completely in the dark!

PAULLETTE: Don't shout.

NILES: (*suddenly screaming*) THERE'S VOICES COMING AT ME!

(PAULLETTE *jumps up and goes to him.*)

PAULLETTE: Niles, quiet down! If they catch you here now, it's all over.

NILES: (*screaming*) THERE'S VOICES FROM ALL SIDES!

PAULLETTE: There's nothing here now. You've shot yourself in the head and it's all over.

NILES: IT'S NOT! IT'S NOT OVER!

(LAUREEN *lets out her shrill high scream again. Stage lights stay dark through this. Just follow spot. Piano comes in strong. Sax is heard live here, high wailing sounds.* LAUREEN *bows the bass in sharp rasping sounds.* NILES *moves frantically around stage to get away from the sound.* PAULLETTE *tries to calm him down. This lasts a short time and ends with a gunshot offstage and sound of body falling. Music stops. The*

lamp comes on, illuminating the shade. NILES *stands and stares at it.
Pause.*)

NILES: (*suddenly cooled out*) Do you know why I bought that
lampshade?

PAULLETTE: Why?

NILES: Because I was born on an island. I wasn't born in America
you know. I was born way far away. I was imported. I lived in a
tin house with a corrugated roof that sounded like Balinese
cymbals when it rained. It rained tropical rains there. The kind
that sound like they'll never end. And you'll be washed away.
And you'll all be washed away. And at night the laundry flaps.
The sheets snap like wet whips. They're all tied down by ropes
so the Japanese don't steal them. And your mother has a .45
automatic Colt revolver with an extra clip in her pocketbook just
in case. And she takes you to the movies in an Army Jeep. Right
through the monsoons in a Jeep to the drive-in movies to watch
Song of the South. (*sings*) "Mr. Bluebird on my shoulder. It's the
truth. It's actual. Everything is satisfactual. Zippety doo-da.
Zippety ay. My oh, my oh what a wonderful day." (*back to talk*)
And the rain is pouring down in a sheet of green jungle water.
Right over the movie screen. Like watching a movie through a
waterfall. Right over the windscreen of the Jeep. And Mom has
the .45 sitting right there loaded on her lap in case any gooks
stick their heads in the window. She'd blow their heads right
off. Blow them right back out into the rain again.

PAULLETTE: That's why you got the lamp?

NILES: That's why I got the shade. I already had the lamp.

PAULLETTE: You wanna' lie down for a while?

NILES: No, I want to listen.

PAULLETTE: To what?

NILES: Whatever there is.

PAULLETTE: You want me to leave you alone for a while?

NILES: Doesn't matter. (*continuing*) I got on a boat then. A tin boat
with big holes in the deck that showed the ocean way down
below. Sharks flashing by beer cans. Coral reefs. Island kids
diving for American money. Silver dollars sinking to the deep
blue seas.

PAULLETTE: Niles, you gotta' get your head together now. You have
to be clear about what you're doing. No fuzziness.

NILES: I know, I know. That's important. It's a good thing you
stopped me. I was about to go off the deep end again.

PAULLETTE: (*moving toward suitcase*) Now come over here and try some of these things on.

(NILES *moves to suitcase with* PAULLETTE. *The stage lights come back up as* NILES *starts taking off his clothes, one piece at a time and putting on pieces of a costume that* PAULLETTE *hands him from the suitcase. The costume is a kid's cowboy outfit. This change of costumes should be slow and deliberate as the focus switches to the others in the scene.*)

LAUREEN: (*to* PABLO) Petrone shouldn't be telling you anything actually.

PABLO: (*still sitting on* LOUIS' *lap*) How come? We're entitled to some information. We've been working for weeks on this case.

LOUIS: Could you move a little, Pablo? My knees are going to sleep.

PETRONE: (*to* PABLO) You know how Raymond Chandler worked? He always started out knowing who the killer was first and then spent the rest of the time covering it up. He always worked backwards. That's how you guys should do it.

PABLO: Just keep telling the story or I'm taking you all down to headquarters!

LAUREEN: This is headquarters.

PABLO: Don't get smart with me, sister!

PETRONE: (*moving slowly toward* PABLO) What exactly do you guys know anyway? Do you guys know anything?

PABLO: We know plenty.

PETRONE: Do you know anything about the nature of a nation?

PABLO: Don't try to dance around me with half-baked intellectual notions, mister! I've been to school too!

LOUIS: Let him talk, Pablo. He's smarter than you.

PABLO: He's not smarter than me! He comes on like he's smarter but he's not. I've got a master's degree!

PETRONE: Small nations. Nations within nations.

LAUREEN: Don't give them too much rope, Petrone.

PETRONE: (*to* PABLO) What's a musician to you?

PABLO: You're trying to confuse the issue but what you're not counting on is our singlemindedness. My singlemindedness. All this stuff doesn't matter. All this periphery. Extra frills. I'm here to discover what's at the heart of it. That's all that matters to me. The investigation.

PETRONE: What's a guy doing up there in front of dozens of people blowing his brains out on a horn for? What's he doing it for?

PABLO: How should I know! That's not my job to know that!

LOUIS: Pablo, get up!

PABLO: (*to* LOUIS) No.

LOUIS: (*suddenly hysterical*) GET UP! I'M GOING CRAZY UNDER HERE! GET OFF ME!

(LOUIS *throws* PABLO *off him.* PABLO *lands on the floor by the outline.* LOUIS *stands.*)

LOUIS: I gotta' get out of here, Pablo! Something's not right! We've gotten ourselves into deep water here! Can't you feel it? Everything's crazy! I've got to get my bearings back. It feels like we're involved in something we'd be better off not knowing about. I never wanted to kill myself before. I've always had a good relationship with myself. A solid footing. I feel like I've slid into somebody else's head here or something. I'm used to Tommy Dorsey, the Mills Brothers, Benny Goodman. All this free-form stuff is disturbing to my inner depths. It leaves me feeling nauseous. Like I'm going to throw everything up. Everything that's ever come into me. (*starts moving frantically around stage, others stay still*) I'm a Republican by nature! That's what I am. I'm not ashamed of that! Eisenhower was my main man! We went through the war together. The Real War in the Real World! Why do I have to go through everything again! I'M NOT GUILTY! Am I guilty, Pablo? Answer me that!

PABLO: (*from floor*) You're not guilty.

LOUIS: Of course not! Of course I'm not! These dues belong to somebody else. Somebody else has to pay for this. IT'S NOT MY FAULT! I can't help it if things are in a state. I had to go to night school in my spare time to earn my diploma. The war took my time away. Took all my time away. I have shrapnel scars on the back of my neck. Pieces of hand grenade still embedded in my knees. I'm entitled to a little dance music! A nice waltz now and then. Three-quarter time!

PABLO: (*still on floor*) Louis, don't go crazy. The Squad needs you. You're one of our best men.

LAUREEN: (*to* LOUIS) You could always kill yourself.

LOUIS: You'd like that wouldn't you? It would be a mark of your success. There was a time when death was looked upon as a defeat!

PETRONE: When was that?

LOUIS: You're all so twisted around that you even have sane people thinking they're crazy. You've driven me and my partner to utter distraction! Look at my partner on the floor there! Once he was a proud man. He walked erect like the rest of us. Now he's groveling around on the floor!

LAUREEN: Pick him up.

LOUIS: You've made us lose track of our mission. We came here to get to the bottom of an evil act. We're working for the right side!

PETRONE: Suicide?

LOUIS: Murder in the first degree! A man doesn't blow his face off if he wants to kill himself. His face is something personal right up to the end. Even if he shot himself in the mouth it wouldn't blow his whole face off.

PETRONE: He wanted to remain mysterious. Anonymous.

LOUIS: You want him to remain mysterious! It's you that's hiding him from us.

LAUREEN: He's right here now.

LOUIS: I know he is. You've got him tucked away somewhere and we're going to drag him out!

PABLO: (*from floor*) Louis, maybe we bit off more than we can chew. I'm even starting to hear voices now.

LAUREEN: (*listening. Starts to play bass softly*) Listen to that. He's doing away with dominant sevenths.

PABLO: (*ear to floor, rubbing the outline softly with his hand*) Listen, Louis! Can you hear that? He's a virtuoso.

LOUIS: I don't hear a thing! Wind is blowing through my head.

(PETRONE *starts to play sax silently*.)

PABLO: (*from floor*) His body was right here. Right where I'm laying now.

LOUIS: I can't hear a thing.

PABLO: Listen. It's incredible. (*puts his ear to the floor*)

(*Lights fade. Follow spots up on* NILES *and* PAULLETTE. NILES *is all dressed in the cowboy outfit now.* PAULLETTE *turns him around in a circle, checking out the costume.* NILES *sings softly to himself as* PAULLETTE *keeps circling him, adjusting his costume.*)

NILES: (*singing softly*) Pecos Bill, Pecos Bill

> Never died
> And he never will
> Oh, Pecos Bill

NILES: (*to* PAULLETTE, *talking*) I hate killing this one off first, Paullette. Can't we save this one till last?

PAULLETTE: They'll all be painful. Doesn't matter what order you do them in.

NILES: Then let's do this one last.

PAULLETTE: No.

NILES: But there's no guarantee I won't die along with him.

PAULLETTE: I guarantee it.

NILES: But you don't know how attached I am. I feel as though his skin is my skin.

PAULLETTE: He doesn't have any skin.

NILES: He has a heart doesn't he?

PAULLETTE: He's a parasite. He's sucking your blood.

NILES: But I used him all these years. It only seems fair that he'd take something out of me.

PAULLETTE: Wait a second. You're making it sound like this was all my idea. It was you who was going down the tubes, remember?

NILES: Yeah.

PAULLETTE: It was you who was looking for a way out. I'm only supplying the means.

NILES: But how can we be sure we're going about it in the right way. I mean it already backfired once on us.

PAULLETTE: That was a mistake.

NILES: His whole face was blown off!

PAULLETTE: That was a mistake, all right!

NILES: I don't want my face blown off!

PAULLETTE: Your face isn't going to get blown off! Now turn around.

NILES: What?

PAULLETTE: Turn around. You're not supposed to see the weapon.

NILES: Oh, Jesus, now I'm really scared.

PAULLETTE: Just turn around.

NILES: I need some time. Just let me work through this a little first. Just a little while longer.

PAULLETTE: Okay, take as much time as you want. I don't care. You're only giving them more time to catch up to you.

NILES: You said they were convinced!

PAULLETTE: For a while. It doesn't mean we can stand still. We gotta' keep moving.

NILES: Just let me walk through this a little.

PAULLETTE: Go ahead.

(NILES *starts moving around*. PAULLETTE *stands watching him. Soft piano builds under this*.)

NILES: I want to be clear about this. I was clear before but now I'm not so sure. I want to be sure. I want to get rid of all these ones so I can start over. Is that it? Is that what it was?

PAULLETTE: That's it.

NILES: All these ones have to go because they're crowding me up. They've gotten out of control. They've taken me over and there's no room left for me. They've stolen their way into my house when I wasn't looking.

PAULLETTE: You invited them.

NILES: I invited them but I forgot to ask them to go. If I don't get rid of them they'll strangle me or something.

PAULLETTE: Something.

NILES: They'll do me in.

PAULLETTE: They're doing you in right now.

NILES: Yes. I can feel that. But I'm not sure what I'll do without them either. I'm not sure that if I get rid of all of them that I won't be lonely.

PAULLETTE: You will be for a while.

NILES: I don't want to be lonely.

PAULLETTE: You'll get over it.

NILES: I will?

PAULLETTE: You'll go through it.

NILES: I'm afraid to be lonely. I can't stand the idea of it even. It's almost worse than dying.

PAULLETTE: It is dying.

NILES: That's the reason I invited them in to begin with. So I wouldn't have to feel that loneliness. That's the reason I invented music. It filled me up. I got so filled up that I couldn't go on. Now I gotta start over.

PAULLETTE: You gotta start from scratch.

NILES: But they showed me their music too. I borrowed from them. They showed me everything I know.

PAULLETTE: But now you can't get to anything new. It's always the same. You're repeating yourself.

NILES: I'm repeating myself, again and again. It's not even myself I'm repeating. I'm repeating them. Over and over. They talk to me all the time. (*suddenly screaming*) THERE'S VOICES COMING AT ME!

PAULLETTE: Keep it together, Niles.

NILES: (*calmer*) You'd think in a nation this big there'd be someone to talk to.

PAULLETTE: You talk to yourself.

NILES: You talk to yourself and other people talk to themselves. I wonder where my voice is.

PAULLETTE: Inside. Coming out.

NILES: Where? I don't hear a thing. Now there's nothing inside. They've all gone home.

PAULLETTE: They've just shut up for a while.

NILES: They're hiding?

PAULLETTE: They're waiting to jump on you. Any second they can jump on you.

NILES: And that's why I gotta do them in?

PAULLETTE: One at a time.

NILES: They aren't gonna' like it.

PAULLETTE: They won't know what hit them.

NILES: They're gonna' start screaming when they find out.

PAULLETTE: Don't let them know.

NILES: I feel like a traitor.

PAULLETTE: Turn around.

NILES: Not yet. I want to know this one first before he goes.

PAULLETTE: You already know him.

NILES: Not well enough. Is he King of the Cowboys or something? Does he make his women walk in ditches because he's so short? Does he wear elevator cowboy boots? What's so terrible about him?

PAULLETTE: Nothing.

NILES: What have I got against him?

PAULLETTE: Nothing.

NILES: Then why does he have to go?

PAULLETTE: He's burning your time.

NILES: He's a hero Paullette! He discovered a whole way of life. He ate rattlesnakes for breakfast. Chicago wouldn't even exist if it wasn't for him. He drove cattle right to Chicago's front door. Towns sprang up wherever he stopped to wet his whistle. Crime flourished all around him. The law was a joke to him. State lines. He sang songs to the Milky Way.

PAULLETTE: Turn him around, Niles.

NILES: You can't kill a hero!

(*Piano building through this.*)

PAULLETTE: He's no hero! He's a weasel! He's a punk psychopath built into a big deal by crummy New England rags.

NILES: He's a myth!

PAULLETTE: So are you!

NILES: You can't kill a myth!

PAULLETTE: Turn him around, Niles! Show me his back side.

NILES: He doesn't want to die!

PAULLETTE: Do you?

NILES: YES!! I mean no! NO!

PAULLETTE: Any way you want it.

NILES: (*after pause, staring at* PAULLETTE) All right. But do it easy.

(NILES *turns his back to her. Piano builds.* PAULLETTE *goes to suitcase and pulls out a bow and arrow.* NILES *speaks with his back to her as she loads the arrow in the bow very slowly.*)

NILES: (*to himself*) It's a bright day. The kind of day you'd never expect to die in. He's got one foot up on the brass rail. The worn elbows of his rawhide jacket are digging into the mahogany bar. The bartender used to be his barber when he was a kid. The dirt streets outside are full of life. Girls of every color are doing their afternoon shopping. Newspapers are printing the news.

(PAULLETTE *aims the bow very slowly and trains it on* NILES' *back. She pulls the arrow back inch by inch as he keeps talking.*)

NILES: Farriers are hammering iron. Dogs are pissing on horses' legs. Scaffolds are being constructed. He sees the nation being built in every small activity. Everything looks like progress to him. Nothing looks like it could ever die. He doesn't see it coming. He never even knew what hit him. It was over in a flash.

(PAULLETTE *lets the arrow go. It strikes him dead center in the back.* LOUIS *screams in the dark as the second arrow strikes* NILES. NILES *stays standing with the arrow stuck in him. He makes no reaction. Follow spots out. Stage lights up.* NILES *starts taking off his cowboy outfit and* PAULLETTE *helps him on with another costume from the suitcase. Focus switches to others on stage.* LOUIS *is staggering around with an arrow stuck in his back, moaning and trying to pull it out.* PABLO *jumps up from the floor and starts searching the stage for possible attacker.*)

LOUIS: (*moving all over, trying to reach the arrow in his back*) I knew he was around! I knew it! We should've left someone on the door, Pablo!

PABLO: Don't anyone move!

PETRONE: We aren't going nowhere.

PABLO: Don't anyone touch anything! Don't anyone even breathe! We've got a psychopath on our hands!

LAUREEN: Aren't you guys going overboard a little with this whole thing? I mean, Christ, the poor guy's dead. Leave him lay.

LOUIS: He's not dead! He just shot me in the back! Look! I've been shot!

LAUREEN: It's just an arrow. Pull it out.

LOUIS: I can't reach it!

LAUREEN: Bring it here. I'll pull it out.

PABLO: Stay where you are! All of you!

LOUIS: Even me?

PABLO: Especially you. We have to determine the exact angle of projectory. You'll mess everything up if you start moving around.

LOUIS: Call a doctor, Pablo. I'm not kidding. I've got an arrow stuck in my back.

PABLO: I can appreciate that but we can't have everyone moving around and destroying the evidence.

LOUIS: Call the Squad then. We need extra help! There's too many of them for us to handle. They're coming at us through the woodwork! I didn't even see it coming.

PABLO: We can handle it. We've been on tougher assignments than this. We've been to Cuba, Louis! You forget that! We've both been to Cuba and back.

LOUIS: No one's supposed to know about that.

PABLO: It's all right now. Now we can pull out all the stops.

LOUIS: Am I bleeding?

PABLO: It's a superficial abrasion. You'll pull through. I guarantee it. "Intelligence" is a risky business. You knew that when you joined up.

LAUREEN: How did you two get in here anyway?

PABLO: I'll do the questioning, sister, if you don't mind.

LAUREEN: Stop calling me sister. I'm not your sister.

PABLO: You're as fishy as a cat in heat, lady.

LAUREEN: Very flattering.

PABLO: First you slink in here—you and your friend—and claim to be waiting for this Niles character to show up.

LAUREEN: That's right.

PABLO: And then you turn around and tell us to lay off the case because the guy's dead. Now which is it? Dead or alive? What's the story?

PETRONE: I was in the midst of telling you the whole story but you guys are hysterical.

PABLO: (*to* PETRONE) Just shut up until you're spoken to! My partner's been shot, in case you haven't noticed. This whole thing has taken on a new dimension.

LAUREEN: That's what we're after.

PABLO: What?

LAUREEN: A new dimension. What's the point in messing around in the same old dimension all the time.

LOUIS: Because it's safe, that's why! You don't get shot in the back when you're not looking! You don't get sudden sweeping surges of terror coursing through your blood! You don't get the urge to end the whole thing right here and now!

LAUREEN: Yes you do but it just comes later. It comes at the end of your life instead of the middle.

LOUIS: I'm in my prime! I deserve better than this.

PABLO: Louis, shut up! I can't hear myself think. (*puts his fingers in his ears*)

LAUREEN: It comes when all your friends have died off and you're just laying there with the radio playing. Just going in circles. Same old thoughts, just repeating themselves. Over and over. It's too late then. All the doors are shut. But you can still hear your life going on. Somewhere outside. Somewhere way outside.

LOUIS: I'm not listening anymore. I can't take it! (*puts his fingers in his ears*)

(LAUREEN *starts bowing bass as* PETRONE *mimes sax.* LAUREEN *speaks as she plays.* PABLO *and* LOUIS *keep their fingers in their ears as she speaks.*)

LAUREEN: You struggle to the window. You hold yourself up by both elbows and stare down at the street, looking for your life. But all you see down there is yourself looking back up at you. You jump back from the window. You fall. You lay there gaping at the ceiling. You're pounding all over. You crawl back for another look. You can't resist. You pull yourself up to the windowsill and peer down again. There you are, still standing down there on the street. Still looking straight back up at yourself. Your terror drops for a second. Long enough to start getting curious. You look hard at yourself on the street. You check out all the details. You examine yourself in a way you never have before. Not to resolve any conflicts but only to make an absolute identification. You check the face, the hands, the eyes, the turns in the mouth. You look for any sign that might give him away to you as an imposter. A man in disguise. But then you see him signaling to you from the street. He's pointing to his head, to his own head, then pointing back to you. He keeps repeating this over and over as though it's very important. As though it's something you should have understood a long, long time ago but never did. You pick up the gesture from him and start repeating it back to him. Pointing at your head first then pointing down to him on the street. He starts to nod his head and smiles as though you've finally got the message. But you're still not clear what he means. You pry open the window with the last strength you've got and the shock of cold air almost kills you on the spot. "If only I don't die before I find out what he means!" you say. "Just let me live five minutes longer." Then you see him more clearly than before. You see for sure that he is you. That he's not pretending. He yells up to you in a voice you can't mistake. He yells at you so the whole street can hear him. "YOU'RE IN MY HEAD! YOU'RE ONLY IN MY HEAD!" Then he turns and walks away. You watch him go until you can't see him anymore. Then you make a clean jump all the way to the bottom. And your life goes dancing out the window.

(LAUREEN *stops playing the bass abruptly*. PABLO *and* LOUIS *take their fingers out of their ears. Lights go black onstage. Follow spots up on* NILES *and* PAULLETTE. NILES *dressed this time in black tails, puffing on cigar while* PAULLETTE *circles him again, checking out the fit of the costume.*)

NILES: (*to* PAULLETTE) I'm not sure if I have the theory straight. I'm not even sure where the theory came from.

PAULLETTE: It came from you.

NILES: Are you sure? I remember having some ideas about all this and then you took it further. You found someone who knew about this stuff.

PAULLETTE: If you have visitors you don't want, you should get rid of them.

NILES: (*to himself*) Never give your address out to bad company.

PAULLETTE: What?

NILES: Nothing. I agree about getting rid of them but what I question is the means; the technique.

PAULLETTE: It's no technique. It's a ritual.

NILES: Yeah, but it seems so stupid. So primitive. I mean I'm not a kid. I know that if you dress up funny, like another person, and then you pretend to shoot that person—

PAULLETTE: I wasn't pretending. I shot him.

NILES: Yeah, but I didn't die. I'm not even wounded. Look.

PAULLETTE: He died. That's the whole point. You don't want to kill yourself, do you?

NILES: No. Yes. No.

PAULLETTE: Just these other ones.

NILES: Yeah, but I'm not really sure if there actually are these other ones or if I'm making it all up.

PAULLETTE: Doesn't matter.

NILES: Why not?

PAULLETTE: It's the same. They're the same thing.

NILES: That's crazy. You can't just invent someone and have them appear.

PAULLETTE: Sure you can. You did.

NILES: (*suddenly terrified*) Is that the one we killed!

(PAULLETTE *backs away from him.*)

NILES: (*after pause*) Is that the one whose face we blew off! (*no answer from* PAULLETTE) Is it, Paullette! WHOSE FACE DID WE BLOW OFF?

PAULLETTE: Somebody else's.

NILES: WHO WAS IT?

PAULLETTE: Look, we're messing with something that's very tricky. I can't help it if an accident sneaks in here and there.

NILES: I'll kill myself before I go to jail! I'm not going to jail, Paullette.

PAULLETTE: In this state they hang you.

NILES: I don't mind getting hung but I'm not going to jail.

PAULLETTE: You won't.

NILES: Was it someone important we killed?

PAULLETTE: Who knows.

NILES: You know!

PAULLETTE: I don't know everything. It was an experiment. It just so happened it worked. We fooled them. They took it as suicide. Clean and simple. Leave it at that.

NILES: It was someone important. I can remember his face now. The kind of face that looks overfed. Too much rich food and not enough exercise. What was he doing here?

PAULLETTE: Knock it off, Niles! We can't backtrack now. There's not enough time.

NILES: He was pleading with us. I remember him pleading. Chewing on his tie. It was cruel beyond belief.

PAULLETTE: Turn around and let's do the next one.

(PAULLETTE *moves to the suitcase.*)

NILES: He was miserable. He was surrounded by everything he ever wanted. What was he doing with us? Why us?

PAULLETTE: He knew we'd cooperate.

NILES: I remember what he said! I remember exactly what he said! He said, "Look now at the state of things. Look closely at the state of things. You won't ever see it again exactly as it is now. This is it. If you don't catch it now, it'll all be gone tomorrow. You have to look with a penetrating vision in order to catch it because everything lies in the name of the truth. Everything is trying to convince you it isn't what it is." Why did he say that?

PAULLETTE: He was lying.

(*She turns suddenly towards him with an automatic pistol which she's taken from the suitcase and fires a full round of ammunition into him. He just stands there. Stage lights up as spots go out.* PABLO *staggers around the stage doubled over, holding his stomach.* PABLO *screams.*)

PABLO: (*staggering*) THEY GOT ME, LOUIS! THIS TIME THEY REALLY GOT ME! I'M GUT-SHOT! RIGHT THROUGH THE SMALL INTESTINE! CALL THE SQUAD! TELL THEM WE DID OUR BEST! WE ACTED BEYOND THE CALL OF DUTY! WE USED EVERY MEANS POSSIBLE TO COME TO TERMS WITH THE ENEMY! WE TRIED TO REASON! WE TRIED TO CONNIVE! BUT NOTHING WORKED! IN THE END WE WERE DEFEATED BY GHOSTS! AN UNSEEN ENEMY! IN THE END WE WERE NOT CERTAIN! WE COULD MAKE NEITHER HEAD NOR TAIL OF THE PREDICAMENT! WHETHER OR NOT WE WERE DESTROYED FROM WITHIN OR WITHOUT! NOW IT MAKES NO DIFFERENCE! THERE IS ONLY THE REALITY OF MY DYING! TELL THEM THAT! WRITE IT DOWN! LOUIS! WRITE IT DOWN BEFORE YOU FORGET!

(PABLO *falls to the floor on top of the outline. The others stand watching him lie there.* PABLO *gasps heavily as though going into a coma.*)

LOUIS: (*to others, watching* PABLO) What did he say?

LAUREEN: (*setting down the bass on the floor*) I couldn't make it out.

(*She crosses to the armchair and collapses into it.*)

PETRONE: Too bad Niles didn't show. He would've liked this.

Sometimes it was hard for us to even get him to eat. He'd go for days just staring straight ahead of himself. I'd try to tell him it wasn't all that bad. Nothing's all that bad. I'd try to tell him the worst was imaginary. But it wouldn't penetrate. He'd just sit there and stare.

LAUREEN: (*in chair*) I'm exhausted.

PETRONE: I knew, ya' know, because I'd been there before. I could recognize his state. I could see it in his eyes. A kind of deadness. Like he'd died inside. Given up.

LOUIS: (*still staring at* PABLO *on the floor*) Is there a telephone?

PETRONE: I'd been like that so I knew. The difference was that I went through it. Clear on through it. But he never made it. He had no idea that things would change. He took it to the end.

LOUIS: (*to* PETRONE) I've got to make contact with the outside world. Isn't there a phone somewhere?

LAUREEN: (*to* LOUIS) You're mistaken if you think it's different out there. It's just the same.

PETRONE: It's worse.

LAUREEN: It's just the same.

LOUIS: WHY ARE WE BEING SYSTEMATICALLY BUMPED OFF BY AN UNSEEN ENEMY! IT'S NOT FAIR!

LAUREEN: The planet is going crazy.

LOUIS: That's no explanation! I've got an arrow in my back and Pablo's been gut-shot! Don't blame it on the planet!

PETRONE: I have a feeling you'll never get to the bottom of it. He never did. That's one thing he couldn't understand. The one thing that killed him.

PABLO: (*still on floor, ear to floor, listening, gasping*) I can hear him breathing still, Louis. He's still with us! Still around! Check the next room! Check all the exits! We're not alone!

LOUIS: I'm paralyzed, Pablo! I never thought it would be this tough.

LAUREEN: (*in chair*) He had that kind of quality. That kind of presence. He'd move into a room and everything would change.

PABLO: (*on floor*) He's after us, Louis! Right now he's after us! He thinks we're out to get him.

LOUIS: I never even met him!

PETRONE: I can remember him the very first time. Moving through the streets like a Kodiak bear. I followed him for blocks. An umbrella half-hid him from behind but his shape was unmistakable.

(*Spot comes up on* NILES *down left walking slowly with* PAULLETTE *clinging to his arm like a little girl.* NILES *carries a small black umbrella. They move silently across the stage as* PETRONE *narrates in half-light. Piano music comes in softly.*)

PETRONE: A small girl played at his sleeves like a puppy pulling at its mother's tits, trying to get a grip then falling back then trying again. I was mesmerized by his progress. His immense size only added to the sense of awe. The entire city stood out around him like a miniature replica. A backdrop to his steady walking. Now and then he'd stop and buy a bag of green grapes which he'd share with the girl. It wasn't raining but he kept the umbrella perched on his shoulder as though he'd forgotten it was there.

LAUREEN: (*still in chair*) That was spring, I remember. City spring. The mayor was negotiating with the street gangs to keep the city cool for the coming summer heat wave. His "men in blue" were buying off the leaders with laundry bags of raw opium.

PETRONE: (*moving slightly toward* NILES *downstage,* NILES *keeps talking with* PAULLETTE) That was it! The weather. The change in the season. The city change. Not like the country where you see it coming on gradual, bit by bit. Every day a slightly different color to the trees. A slow emerging. This was sudden. Abrupt. Bang. There it was. Now I connect it!

PABLO: (*on floor*) To what? Don't leave us, whatever you do!

PETRONE: (*to* PABLO) To the feeling I was feeling. I didn't make the connection then but now it's clear. A raw despair.

LOUIS: With spring? What age are we living in? Spring is full of promise! Spring has always been full of promise! Arrows can't change that! Terrorism can't change that!

LAUREEN: (*to* LOUIS) Pipe down, you dope. Have respect for a man's reveries.

PETRONE: (*moving closer to* NILES, *watching him intensely,* NILES *pays no attention, just keeps walking*) The lateness of the day. The "daylight savings time." Still not dark at eight P.M. Everything was adding up. Piling up. Brothers were jumping off apartment buildings into broad daylight. Sisters disappeared down elevator shafts. Methadone programs were taking their toll. Coltrane was gone. Dolphy was gone. But Niles was right there. Right there in front of me. Walking. Still moving. His music wrapped up and carried inside him. Protected. Hidden from all the pedestrians. I followed him closely. I watched his every move as though some magic would escape his gestures and plunge into me. As though his music would start playing from his skin and jump back to my skin, transforming me, changing me, filling me up. Taking away everything deadly. Taking all this awful, empty loneliness and making me whole again. Making me feel alive.

(NILES *turns abruptly on* PETRONE, *who's been following him closely.* PAULLETTE *hides behind* NILES.)

NILES: Are you following me? Is that it?

PETRONE: (*stepping back*) Sorry. I didn't realize I was getting so close.

NILES: You're too close for comfort.

PETRONE: It was just that I recognized you and—

NILES: You recognized me? How could you recognize me when I don't even recognize myself?

PETRONE: I don't know. I've seen you play.

NILES: That was someone else.

(NILES *turns sharply away from* PETRONE *and walks away with* PAULLETTE *trying to hide behind him.* PETRONE *follows.*)

PETRONE: No! It was you. You're so big I could never mistake you.

(NILES *stops suddenly again and turns to* PETRONE.)

NILES: Did you listen or just watch?

PETRONE: What do you mean?

NILES: Did you listen to the music!

PETRONE: Yeah. Sure.

NILES: What did it say?

PETRONE: What?

NILES: What did the music say? Did you hear it?

PETRONE: Yes. It wasn't words. I mean it wasn't words like we're talking now.

NILES: Of course not! What did it say?

PETRONE: It said that there was a chance.

NILES: What kind of chance?

PETRONE: A slim chance but still a chance.

NILES: And you'd given up hoping and this chance you heard filled you with hope and now that you've seen me on the street you think that just by coming in contact with me that your asslicking life will be saved from hopelessness.

PETRONE: Yes.

NILES: No chance.

(NILES *turns again and walks away from him*, PETRONE *follows*.)

PETRONE: Just saying that doesn't make any difference. It doesn't change it.

NILES: Get away from me! The sidewalk's not big enough for the three of us!

PETRONE: I know where you live, Niles!

(NILES *stops dead*. PETRONE *stops*. NILES *turns slowly toward* PETRONE. PAULLETTE *trembles behind* NILES.)

PAULLETTE: He's lying! He's working for any number of malevolent organizations! You can see it in his eyeballs!

PETRONE: I know, Niles.

NILES: (*moving slightly toward him*) What do you know?

PAULLETTE: This is a trick! I've seen it a million times! They sucker you. They promise you! They "yes" you to death and then they slam you in the "Tombs." Don't buy it, Niles!

NILES: (*to* PETRONE) What do you know!

PETRONE: I know that you sold it all down the river. The whole fandango.

NILES: Sold what?

PETRONE: I know that you were rewarded before your time. Before your "coming of age." That you "bought it" from the big boys. You swallowed it whole.

PAULLETTE: This is lying claptrap! I can recognize an evil force when I see one!

NILES: (*to* PAULLETTE) Shut up!

PETRONE: I can take you home, Niles. Back to the scene of the crime.

NILES: What for? I'm safe now. I'm on the streets. Anonymous. Why should I go back.

PETRONE: To clean house.

NILES: Who's there? Is there someone there in my house? Who is it!

PETRONE: I'll show you.

PAULLETTE: Don't follow him, Niles! He'll nail you for sure.

NILES: What're they doing there? Why can't they leave me alone?

PETRONE: (*motioning to others upstage*, NILES *sees them*) Take a look. They're crawling all over your furniture, across your floor, inside your walls. Take a look, Niles.

(*Lights up bright on upstage people.*)

NILES: Get them out of there! I'm already dead! Don't they know that. (*yelling at them upstage*) I'M ALREADY DEAD!

PETRONE: Now's your chance, Niles. You can clean the slate.

You've got them all in one place at the same time. It's perfect.
You can wipe them all out.

NILES: (*to* PETRONE) What's your interest in this. What's in it for
you?

PETRONE: I'm a fan. A fanatic. I live for revenge.

NILES: (*after short pause*) Take me inside.

(NILES *follows* PETRONE *into the upstage area with the others.* PAULLETTE
follows them at a distance.)

PAULLETTE: Niles! It's a trap! It's worse than a trap! THEY'LL
TEAR YOU APART, NILES!

(PAULLETTE *watches* NILES *for a second then runs off stage, right. The
others watch* NILES *closely as he strolls through the space. Silence.*)

NILES: What's happened to all of you?

LAUREEN: (*still in chair*) We've been waiting.

NILES: For me?

LAUREEN: We've been waiting to play.

NILES: You don't need me for that.

LOUIS: (*to* PETRONE) Is this him?

PETRONE: This is him.

LOUIS: Alive?

PABLO: (*on floor*) I knew it! I knew it! I could hear him breathing!

NILES: (*to* PABLO) Get up off my floor.

(PABLO *stands slowly.*)

NILES: (*to* PABLO) Does everyone grovel in your profession?

PABLO: I wasn't groveling. I was on the verge of prayer.

NILES: Religious? Something drove you to get religious?

PABLO: It's my last hope.

NILES: (*turning to* LOUIS) How about you? Religious?

LOUIS: I have no faith. I subscribe to no system of thought. I'm on
the verge of total madness.

NILES: The verge. Only the verge?

LOUIS: What's the point in going further!

NILES: (*turning to* PETRONE) What's the point, Petrone?

PETRONE: No point.

NILES: No point. (*starts moving through space*) Petrone's been over
the edge on several occasions and he confirms your suspicion.
No point. Absolutely nothing to be gained by going off the deep
end. Right, Laureen?

LAUREEN: Absolutely.

NILES: Laureen herself is a confirmed basket case and even she agrees. Madness sucks.

LOUIS: (*bursting out*) I'm dedicated to the pursuit of truth at whatever cost! Where's the telephone!

NILES: What a position we're in. We've all lost our calling. How could that be?

PETRONE: We're ready to play, Niles. Just say the word.

NILES: There is no word to say. If you feel like playing go ahead.

(PETRONE *picks up saxophone and begins playing silently again.*)

NILES: What's everyone waiting for? Are you here to arrest me? Is that it? In my own house? Am I dead or alive? Is that it? Is this me here, now? Are these questions or answers? Are you waiting for the truth to roll out and lap your faces like a bloodhound's tongue? Are you diving to the bottom of it? Getting to the core of the mystery? Getting closer? Moving in for the kill? Waiting for one wrong move when they're all wrong moves? Sifting through the reams of corruption? Toppling politicians in your wake?

(LAUREEN *stands and starts bowing the bass in long mournful notes. Piano fills softly behind.* LOUIS *and* PABLO *start to move in on* NILES *very slowly, almost unnoticed, as he raves on.*)

NILES: Are you martyring yourselves with your own criminal instincts? Are you inside me or outside me? Am I inside you? Am I inside you right now? Am I buzzing away at your membranes? Your brain waves? Driving you berserk? Creating explosions? Destroying your ancient patterns? Or am I just like you? Just exactly like you? So exactly like you that we're exactly the same. So exactly that we're not even apart. Not even separate. Not even two things but just one. Only one. Indivisible.

(PABLO *and* LOUIS *arrive simultaneously on either side of* NILES *and snap handcuffs on both of his wrists. The other half of each pair of handcuffs is locked onto their own wrists so that all three are locked to each other.* NILES *makes no move to protest. The sound of the snapping handcuffs should happen in a moment of silence between the language and the music.*)

NILES: (*after short silence*) Someone was killed here for sure. I saw him face to face. I saw his whole life go past me. Someone should pay for that. That's for sure. Someone should be made to pay for that. A life's not cheap, that's for sure. You guys know that. You've seen enough to know that. You've been around. You've been through the war. You're nobody's fool. He had his whole face torn off. Beyond recognition. Right down to the bone. I think he was alive at the time. Right up to the last. He stayed alive right through it. Right up to the point where he died. He was alive to the very last moment. You know what that's like.

(PABLO *and* LOUIS *lead* NILES *off stage-right. Piano music swells along with sax and bass. Lights fade very slowly on* PETRONE, LAUREEN *and* PIANO PLAYER. *Lampshade stays lit in dark then goes out.*)

SEDUCED

Seduced was first produced at the American Place Theater in New York City. It was directed by Jack Gelber with the following cast:

HENRY HACKAMORE:	Rip Torn
RAUL:	Ed Setrakian
LUNA:	Pamela Reed
MIAMI:	Carla Borelli

ACT 1

SCENE: *In the dark, Randy Newman's song "Sail Away" from the album of the same name (Reprise) is heard over the sound system. Very slowly, in the tempo of the song, the lights start to come up onstage. The stage is basically bare and empty but for two lone palm trees, each one situated at the extreme downstage left and right corners of the playing area, not in the apron. They are very lush, well-cared-for trees about seven feet tall and each planted in a large, black clay Mexican pot. The entire upstage wall is covered from floor to ceiling by a jet-black velour curtain which can be mechanically raised until it's unseen in the flies above. Dead center stage is an old black Naugahyde reclining chair which resembles a dentist's chair. It's raised off the ground about a foot. The chair is situated horizontally onstage with the head toward stage left.* HENRY HACKAMORE *is seen lying flat out on the chair as the lights come up. He is naked except for a baggy pair of white boxer shorts with a drawstring. His hair is shoulder length and white, long white beard, long corkscrew-shaped fingernails and toenails. He is old to the point of looking ancient. His body is extremely thin and emaciated. The general impression is a cross between a prisoner of war and an Indian fakir. As the song continues,* HENRY *slowly extracts single sheets of Kleenex from a large box on a nightstand beside his chair and slowly spreads the sheets on different parts of his body, starting with his feet and working toward his chest. He continues this action over and over until the song ends. The song ends and* HENRY'S *attention seems to be pulled toward the palm tree in the down-right corner. He moves himself up to a more vertical position on his elbows and scrutinizes the tree. He squints his eyes. He pulls himself up even more. The sheets of Kleenex flutter to the floor.*

HENRY: (*sitting up, looking hard at palm tree down right; calling to someone off*) Raul!

(RAUL *enters quickly from left. A heavyset, middle-aged man, dark hair. Wears a brightly colored Hawaiian print shirt with a black shoulder holster and snub-nosed .38 over the top of the shirt. White pants, black shoes. He crosses to the bed beside* HENRY.)

RAUL: Sir?

HENRY: Don't "sir" me. (*pointing to palm down right*) You can see the state of the palm. Without even looking. You can feel that something's off.

(RAUL *looks at the palm and then back to* HENRY.)

RAUL: It's out of place, sir?

HENRY: Out of place! It's off the deep end! Look at the position it's in! Do something about it.

RAUL: Yes, sir.

(RAUL *crosses down right to the palm and squats down, prepared to turn the base to suit* HENRY.)

HENRY: What are you doing! Why are you squatting down like a Filipino houseboy! I didn't ask for that.

(RAUL *stands quickly.*)

RAUL: I'm sorry, sir.

HENRY: Can't you see what's called for. Can't you perceive it on your own without me guiding you every step of the way. Take a step back. Step away from it!

(RAUL *steps back from the palm and looks at it, then looks back at* HENRY.)

HENRY: There. Now look. Can't you tell now.

RAUL: I'm not sure what you want, sir.

HENRY: What *I* want? What I want is for you to know instinctively what I want. Without any coaching. Without hints. For you to be living inside the very rhythm of my needs.

(RAUL *moves to the palm tree and turns it slightly.*)

HENRY: Now what are you doing! Put it back! Put it back like it was!

(RAUL *turns the palm back to its original position.*)

HENRY: That's not it! That's not it. It's getting worse. I can't believe it.

(RAUL *keeps turning the palm trying to restore it to its original position.*)

HENRY: After all these years! Still out of touch. Get away from the damn thing! Stand back away from it!

(RAUL *stands back from the palm.*)

HENRY: Now just look at it. Just stand there and look at it.
RAUL: I am, sir.
HENRY: Now try to see it in relationship to the space around it. Try to see the space it's consuming.
RAUL: I am.
HENRY: Now try to see the space it's not consuming. Can you see that?

(*Long pause as* RAUL *stares at the palm.*)

HENRY: No, you can't see that. See? That's where it goes wrong. All right, all right. I was asking too much. I was pushing it. I was hoping that after so many years you might have picked up a trick or two but I can see I was mistaken.
RAUL: I'm willing to try, sir.
HENRY: Trying's not enough. Just forget it.
RAUL: If you just describe to me how you want it, I'll move it.
HENRY: No! Descriptions don't describe the picture I have in my head. I need some turning now. Come and turn me.
RAUL: (*moving to* HENRY) Yes, sir.
HENRY: Left side first. Left side.

(RAUL *moves to the upstage side of the chair and rolls* HENRY *onto his left side and holds him in that position as* HENRY *speaks.*)

HENRY: We'll have to get a palm specialist in here. Probably hard to find in this country.
RAUL: Oh, I don't think so, sir. We could dig one up.
HENRY: No Americans, though. That's what we need. An American to deal with it. Someone who understands the urgency. Down here they have a different sense of time or something. Things go on forever without getting done.
RAUL: We could fly one in.
HENRY: Never mind. I'll deal with it later. I'll have you walk me over to it.
RAUL: No walking, sir.

HENRY: Don't keep repeating my limitations to me as though I've forgotten. As long as I've got them I can't forget them. (*pause*) Rock me. Back and forth.

(RAUL *gently rocks his body back and forth, still keeping* HENRY *on his left side.*)

HENRY: Oh, that is stupendous! What a motion! Suddenly I'm flooded with wonderful pictures.

RAUL: Of what, sir?

HENRY: Of this place. Of the outside. Of how the outside must find us. This is a new place, isn't it?

RAUL: Yes, sir.

HENRY: Of course it is. A new place in a series of new places. A stepping-stone. You're trying to sneak me back in, isn't that it? Didn't I give orders to that effect?

RAUL: We're trying to get you closer to the border, sir. In case of an emergency.

HENRY: Closer? The women are still coming though?

RAUL: Oh yes, sir.

HENRY: That's still in the plan.

RAUL: Yes, sir.

HENRY: (*still being rocked*) I've got to see them. Every last one of them. Oh, these women, Raul! Wait till you see them! Fifteen years it's been. Wait till you see the way they carry themselves. Like visions. Like moving pictures. How are they coming?

RAUL: Jet, sir.

HENRY: Individually?

RAUL: Yes, sir.

HENRY: We have that many planes left?

RAUL: I think so.

HENRY: Good. Do my feet. My feet.

RAUL: Jet, sir.

(RAUL *rolls* HENRY *onto his back.*)

HENRY: Move me up first. Pull me up!

RAUL: Yes, sir.

(RAUL *moves to the head of the chair, grabs* HENRY *under the arms and pulls him up to a semisitting position. He props pillows behind his back, then moves down to* HENRY'S *feet and starts massaging his toes.* HENRY *keeps talking.*)

HENRY: Pictures, Raul. Pictures! Every shift of the body brings a new wave. It's amazing. Almost a rejuvenating effect, although I shouldn't go overboard in my expectations. (*pause*) We came here at night, didn't we?

RAUL: Yes, sir.

HENRY: Always at night. Pitch black. Wrapped in a gray stretcher. Theoretically I shouldn't have seen a thing. Numb to the world.

RAUL: There was a full moon.

HENRY: I was asleep?

RAUL: You'd awake in fits.

HENRY: Fits?

RAUL: Spurts.

HENRY: Oh yeah. Short bursts. Short bursts of waking. Still, that doesn't account for these vivid details. Golden beaches. Black-headed kids. Shimmering, silver water. How do you account for that?

RAUL: You're seeing that now?

HENRY: Off and on. It must come from the touching. Do my feet.

RAUL: I am, sir.

HENRY: You are? You're doing them now?

RAUL: Yes, sir.

HENRY: That's funny. I can't feel a thing.

RAUL: Well, it comes and goes, doesn't it, sir?

HENRY: That's right. Comes and goes. Can't depend on it. But why all those images then?

RAUL: We could raise the curtain.

(HENRY *jerks his feet away from* RAUL *and struggles to a sitting position.* RAUL *tries to calm him.*)

HENRY: No! Nothing from out there comes in here! Nothing! No life! Not sun, not moon, not sound, not nothing!

RAUL: I know, sir. I'm sorry.

HENRY: That's the law! That's the absolute law!

RAUL: I know, sir.

HENRY: What a suggestion! Curtain up in the middle of the day.

RAUL: I just thought you might want it for a second. A minute or two.

HENRY: Stop trying to make your desires mine. If you need a vacation it can be arranged. Don't piddle around in here trying to figure out what's best for you in the disguise of what's best for me. We've been together too long for that.

RAUL: I just thought if you were seeing things it might be good to open up the room a little.

HENRY: I'm always seeing things! The room's got nothing to do with it. I was seeing things before you were born. Before I was born I was seeing things. I prefer seeing things to having them crash through my window in the light of day. It's a preference, not a disappointment.

RAUL: (*pause*) Would you like something to eat, sir?

HENRY: (*pause*) Why do you always do that? Why do you constantly switch the areas of my concern? Food is not on my mind. Food has nothing to do with what's on my mind. Pictures are on my mind and you put food in there. They don't mix! Pictures of food don't mix!

RAUL: I'm sorry, sir.

HENRY: You have to be more sensitive, Raul, to the subtle shifts in my intellectual activity. The mind covers a wide range of territory. Sometimes simultaneously traveling several different hemispheres in a single sweep and then diving suddenly for the prey.

RAUL: I understand, sir.

HENRY: You do? You understand what the prey is? The prey is an idea. A single, lonely, fleeting idea trying to duck into a rabbit hole and the mind comes sweeping in for the kill.

RAUL: It's a beautiful idea, sir.

HENRY: That's not an idea! It's a description. An idea is something useful. (*pause*) Do my back. My back!

(RAUL *moves around to the head of the chair and starts massaging* HENRY'S *back. Pause.*)

RAUL: It would be great to fly over America in the daytime though. Just once. Somewhere over Nevada.

HENRY: Where did that idea come from? Out of the clear blue sky. Flying? What an idea.

RAUL: Just to see it. I haven't seen it in ten years.

HENRY: That's not true. Anyway, nothing's changed. I guarantee it. All it would do is tempt you. Fill you with a lot of aching. Desire again. Desire all over the place. Land of lust.

RAUL: These women—

HENRY: What about them?

RAUL: I'm not to touch them. You don't have to worry about that.

HENRY: Something in your need to remind me, fills me with trepidation. You should take it for granted that you won't touch them.

RAUL: I do, sir.

HENRY: Don't take it as a taboo. That will only lead to trouble. It should be deeply rooted in your blood.

RAUL: What should?

HENRY: Your lack of lust! Haven't you learned anything from me! I should be a living testimony. Of course it would help if I was living more. More alive. Nevertheless you should be able to see where desire leads just by looking. That not only goes for the body, Raul, but the spirit, the soul. The body's the least of it.

RAUL: (*still massaging*) I can't see your soul, sir.

HENRY: Of course not. Good point. But take it from me, there are certain unseen parts that are thoroughly ravaged beyond recognition. Worse than what you see. Far worse.

RAUL: Can you feel my hands?

HENRY: Vaguely. Keep rubbing.

RAUL: Yes, sir.

HENRY: (*pause*) I want you to keep something in mind, Raul. When these women begin to fill up my room I want you to keep something firmly in mind.

RAUL: Yes, sir.

HENRY: I want you to constantly remember, as you're taking them in with your eyes, that at one time or another I've penetrated every single one of them. Every last one. Right to the core. Straight to the heart.

RAUL: I will, sir.

HENRY: Promise?

RAUL: I'm not to touch them, sir. You can be sure of that.

(HENRY *violently pulls himself away from* RAUL'S *touch*.)

HENRY: Stop saying that! Stop telling me that!

RAUL: Should I leave, sir?

HENRY: No!

RAUL: Should I take a vacation?

HENRY: No vacation! Not at this point in the game. I might need you at any minute. At any minute we may have to evacuate. You're aware of that.

RAUL: Yes, sir.

(*Pause.* HENRY *looks hard at* RAUL.)

HENRY: You're more aware of it than I am in fact. That's why you've brought me here. Closer to the border. My lucidity is not without its bounds, Raul. It comes and goes like the rest of it. But that's no reason to assume that I'm a total blathering fool.

Crisis is a normal state of affairs. Emergency is the seed of great decisions. I'm not blind to the fact of my dying. I'm living it while you're on the outskirts. While you're hanging around in a holding pattern dreaming about America in the daylight. While asshole doctors visit me in my sleep. Sneaking in here in the dark and shaking their heads over my bed. Waiting across the border for me, in a hospital I built myself with excess cash.

RAUL: No one's gone over your head sir. No decisions without your approval.

HENRY: That's obvious! The decisions are mine! It's a foolproof organization although at times I wonder how it could be when the very ones closest to me seem farthest away.

RAUL: You are the sole stockholder, sir.

HENRY: Your forthrightness fills me with suspicion, Raul. Now why should that be? How could that be the case? Has my body poisoned my mind along with everything else? Why does it seem like every nuance in your verbal patterns is designed to hide some sneaky truth? Like you're standing there watching me through a one-way mirror when I can see you plain as day. It is you, isn't it? (*suddenly panics, screaming*) RAUL! IT IS YOU ISN'T IT?

(RAUL *rushes to him and holds him firmly.* HENRY *grabs onto his arms in terror.* RAUL *strokes his head and calms him down.*)

RAUL: (*stroking his head*) Yes sir. It's me. It's always me.

HENRY: Rub my head! My head!

(RAUL *eases him back into the pillows, rubbing his head.*)

RAUL: Try to be calm, sir.

HENRY: Calm? Have you ever known terror to be calm?

RAUL: No, sir.

HENRY: Don't let them take me while I'm sleeping, Raul. Promise me.

RAUL: I won't, sir.

HENRY: Even if they think I'm dead I won't be.

RAUL: No, sir.

HENRY: I'll just be sleeping.

RAUL: Yes, sir.

HENRY: Last time they took me while I slept.

RAUL: It was your orders, sir.

HENRY: My orders?

RAUL: Yes, sir.

HENRY: Where do my orders come from, Raul?

(*Pause as* RAUL *strokes his head.*)

RAUL: Would you like a drink, sir?

HENRY: What is there?

RAUL: Pineapple, coconut, papaya, mango, tangelo.

HENRY: A paradise. America never had such things. Not the America I knew.

RAUL: Oh, I'm sure they have all the juices up there by now, sir.

HENRY: I'm sure. If I didn't travel by night I'd see some of these things.

RAUL: You might.

HENRY: I'd see more than I bargained for probably. (*pause*) Why is daylight so terrifying, Raul?

RAUL: I don't know.

HENRY: Pineapple. Make it pineapple. Pineapple seems the least dangerous.

RAUL: Yes, sir. (*moving away from* HENRY) Try to sleep if you can.

HENRY: Don't be stupid.

(RAUL *exits stage left.* HENRY *lies there a while silently. He starts to sing to himself, repeating the same phrase over and over again.*)

HENRY: (*singing to himself*) Hey ba ba re bop. Hey ba ba re bop. Hey ba ba re bop. Hey ba ba re bop.

(*He stops singing and sits up abruptly in the chair. He looks around the space as though remembering something, then carefully gets up and pulls out a large cardboard box from underneath the reclining chair. He next pulls out a roll of paper towels and starts tearing off sections and laying them on the floor. He starts singing again as he does this, repeating the phrase.*)

HENRY: (*singing*) Hey ba ba re bop. Hey ba ba re bop. (*etc.*)

(*He sits on the floor and pats the towels firmly, then pulls out several thick manuscripts from the cardboard box. He picks up each one and pounds it on all four edges on top of the paper towels, examines the edges for straightness then stacks them neatly on the floor beside the box. He goes through this process like a private ritual which has lost its original purpose. As he continues repeating this action while singing, the large black curtain upstage begins to slowly ascend up into the flies revealing a slightly raised platform. As the curtain continues to rise, without* HENRY'S *knowing, Venetian blinds are revealed which cover the entire upstage wall from floor to ceiling. The blinds are open and through the cracks can be seen a huge silver full moon with a long reflection cast on what appears to be the ocean. Directly in front of the blinds, standing on the platform, upstage center is a beautiful young woman named* LUNA. *She has black hair and is dressed like a Hollywood starlet of the thirties. Furs, high heels, stockings with seams, patent leather purse, etc. She just stands there looking down at* HENRY *until the black curtain has disappeared above.* HENRY *continues with his manuscripts and singing, unaware of her presence. His back is always to her. She speaks from the platform.*

HENRY: (*singing*) Hey ba ba re bop. Hey ba ba re bop. (*etc.*)

LUNA: (*from the platform*) So, the real Henry Hackamore is taking guests?

(HENRY *stops singing immediately and struggles to his feet but does not turn upstage to see her. His body seems unable to turn around. He scrambles for a brass bell underneath the reclining chair. He pulls it out and starts ringing it frantically for help and calling* RAUL. LUNA *stays on the platform and smiles down at him.*)

HENRY: (*ringing the bell*) Raul! We've been penetrated! They've found their way in!

LUNA: (*giggling but staying behind him on platform*) Visitors from the outside world. Alien life.

HENRY: (*ringing bell*) Raul! Drop the pineapple and get in here!

(HENRY *drops the bell and starts frantically putting all the manuscripts back into the cardboard box and shoves it under the chair.*)

LUNA: Sweeping it under the table Henry? You are the real Henry, aren't you?

HENRY: (*ringing bell again*) RAUL!

(HENRY *keeps scrambling with the manuscripts, cleaning up the paper towels.*)

LUNA: I'd hate to have come all this way to be in the company of a stranger.

(RAUL *charges on from left with his pistol drawn. He sees* LUNA *and stops. He looks at* HENRY *and then puts his gun back in the holster.*)

HENRY: (*to* RAUL) Where have you been! There's someone in here! Right now, there's someone in here! I can't see them but I hear them!

RAUL: It's one of the ladies, sir.

HENRY: What ladies! Help me up on the chair! Help me!

(RAUL *goes to* HENRY *and lifts him onto the chair so that he's facing front with his back to* LUNA, *legs hanging over the side. He starts pulling sheets of Kleenex out of the box and covering his legs with them.*)

RAUL: (*as he helps* HENRY) One of the guests.

HENRY: There are no guests, only visitors!

RAUL: She's a visitor then, sir.

HENRY: How did she get in!

(LUNA *giggles and walks back and forth on the platform.*)

RAUL: I don't know sir.

HENRY: Ask her!

RAUL: (*to* LUNA) Mr. Hackamore would like to know how you got in, ma'am?

LUNA: It wasn't easy.

RAUL: (*to* HENRY) She won't give a straight answer, sir.

HENRY: Well get her around here in front of me for God's sake! I can't see through the back of my head.

RAUL: (*to* LUNA) Mr. Hackamore is unable to turn around, ma'am. Could you come down here in front of him so he can see you?

LUNA: Mr. Hackamore is unable to turn around?

RAUL: Yes, ma'am.

LUNA: He can hear me, can't he? Isn't that enough? He doesn't have to see me. He hasn't seen me for fifteen years. Why stop now?

HENRY: Who is this one? I don't like the sound of her.

RAUL: (*to* LUNA) Could you tell Mr. Hackamore your name?

LUNA: Oh, he knows my name. Just leave us alone. You're very charming but unnecessary. I'm not going to hurt him. I'm just teasing him a little.

HENRY: I can't stand this!

LUNA: He's getting excited.

RAUL: (*to* HENRY) Try not to scream, sir.

HENRY: Why won't she come around here! Raul, use your influence.

(RAUL *moves upstage toward* LUNA. *She stops him.*)

LUNA: (*to* RAUL) Easy. Easy. I'm not alone.

HENRY: She was told to come alone! Everything's falling apart.

LUNA: (*to* RAUL) Just go away and leave us. I'll be nice to him. Don't worry.

HENRY: (*still facing front*) Don't leave, Raul! Not until I see her face.

RAUL: Please, ma'am. All you have to do is let Mr. Hackamore see you and then I'll go.

HENRY: Is she beautiful, Raul?

RAUL: Yes, sir.

HENRY: Very beautiful?

RAUL: Yes, sir.

HENRY: You're not getting worked up, are you?

RAUL: No, sir.

HENRY: You're remembering what I told you?

RAUL: Yes, sir.

LUNA: (*to* RAUL) You two have an agreement, is that it?

HENRY: Don't talk to her, Raul! Don't get involved.

(LUNA *laughs*.)

RAUL: Please, ma'am.

LUNA: Oh don't beg me. You can see I'm harmless.

RAUL: I can't leave him alone.

LUNA: All right. All right. I'll reveal myself. Slowly. A step at a time.

(*She starts to move slowly off the platform, down toward* HENRY *as she speaks*.)

RAUL: She's coming, sir.

HENRY: Wonderful!

LUNA: Anticipation is delicious, isn't it, Henry? Truly delicious. The best part in fact.

HENRY: I recognize this line of thinking.

RAUL: You know her now, sir?

HENRY: Not yet.

LUNA: (*to* HENRY) Isn't your whole body thundering? Mine is.

HENRY: Oh God, Raul! What'd I tell you! Didn't I tell you this would be terrific!

RAUL: Do you want me to leave you now, sir?

HENRY: No! There's still a possible danger. There's always that slim chance of danger. Just when you let your guard down.

LUNA: It's true. That's when it happens. Just when you let your guard down.

HENRY: It's almost worth the risk, though.

LUNA: (*still advancing, coming left toward* HENRY *from behind*) This *is* risky, Henry. Very risky.

HENRY: I don't care. I've been in jams before. Jams of an international stature. This is nothing.

LUNA: Peanuts.

HENRY: Just come around so I can see you! Just show yourself!

LUNA: Easy, Henry.

HENRY: Don't make a fool out of me in front of my bodyguard!

LUNA: Oh please, Henry. It's you that won't let him go. All this could be avoided.

RAUL: I'll turn around, sir.

HENRY: Yes! Yes, turn around. Cover your eyes. Plug up your ears. This is between me and myself.

(RAUL *turns around upstage right and covers his eyes.* LUNA *keeps advancing. She comes up almost parallel with* HENRY. *Stage left of him.*)

LUNA: Silly. It's very silly.

HENRY: It's not silly! It's desperate. Show yourself!

(LUNA *suddenly walks out directly in front of* HENRY *and smiles at him. She opens her furs. She is wearing a slinky blue evening gown, diamond necklace and earrings. She lets the furs fall to her elbows and turns herself seductively in front of him like a high fashion model. Henry stares in awe.*)

HENRY: Oh God. Oh my living God. Oh my Christ. Raul, did you see this? Don't look!

(RAUL *drops his hands from his eyes then quickly covers them again.*)

HENRY: (*stretching his hand out toward* LUNA) Oh.

(LUNA *moves toward him, smiling, and reaches for his hand.* HENRY *pulls it back quickly.*)

LUNA: You are a demon, Henry.

HENRY: I was.

LUNA: Anyone with nails like that should have been dead long ago. What're you raising, corkscrews or something?

HENRY: Rub my head.

(*She moves toward him.* HENRY *pulls back.*)

HENRY: No!

RAUL: Can I leave now, sir?

HENRY: Yes. No! Wait a minute. (*to* LUNA) Empty your purse out.

LUNA: Henry, this is insulting. It's not enough that I liquidate my affairs overnight after not hearing from you for years, leave without telling a soul my destination in an unmarked jet, for an unmarked island, but on top of it all I have to empty my purse out on your bed?

HENRY: Do it.

(LUNA *rips open her purse and dumps the contents on the chair beside* HENRY, *to his right.*)

HENRY: Raul, check it.

(RAUL *moves to the chair and looks through the objects quickly.*)

RAUL: It's all right, sir.

HENRY: Nothing that could be construed as a weapon?

RAUL: Nothing.

HENRY: No daggers? Poison? Bombs? Even the most innocent looking things are potential killers.

RAUL: No, sir. She's clean.

HENRY: Good. Put the contents in a plastic bag. Take the bag to the parking lot. Drive the Chevrolet back and forth over the bag sixteen times. Collect the smashed remains and put them in another bag. Take that bag to the beach. Rent a small boat. Row out to the twenty-mile limit. Dump the bag. Abandon the boat and swim to shore.

RAUL: (*starts to move*) Yes, sir.

HENRY: Oh, before you do that bring us in a chaise longue and two tall drinks.

RAUL: Yes, sir.

(RAUL *sweeps the objects off the chair into his shirt and exits left.* LUNA *watches* RAUL. HENRY *watches her.*)

HENRY: (*after pause*) Don't be insulted. Everyone gets the same treatment. Some are even flattered.

LUNA: Flattered?

HENRY: Yes, flattered. The innocent crave to be guilty. There's a certain pride in having one's dormant criminal instincts beckoned up by suspicion. It's not even that I'm particularly suspicious.

LUNA: Just cautious.

HENRY: Just careful.

LUNA: Just nuts. That was harmless stuff. A bunch of harmless makeup!

HENRY: Nothing's harmless till it's squashed.

LUNA: If you expect this meeting to go on for any length of time you might try lightening up your act, Henry.

HENRY: I'm sorry but I don't even know you.

LUNA: That's it!

(*She moves as if to go then stops when* HENRY *speaks.*)

HENRY: No please! I thought I'd recognize you immediately but it's taking some time. You are beautiful though.

LUNA: Thanks.

HENRY: There'll be something for you to sit on in a minute. I don't like keeping anything extra in here. Just more surfaces for things to collect on. Microscopic things. That's the worst. What you can't see. I'd have you sit on my chair—(*pauses*) Just a minute.

(*He starts pulling off sections of paper towel and spreading them on the chair beside him.*)

LUNA: Don't worry about it. I like standing.

HENRY: (*continuing with towels*) Did you like the plane?

LUNA: The plane?

HENRY: The jet. I designed it from scratch. The very latest.

LUNA: Yes, it's fine.

HENRY: It's yours. You can take it back with you.

LUNA: Thanks.

HENRY: Were you expecting more?

LUNA: Look, Henry, Just relax, all right? I'm here out of curiosity more than anything else. Don't jump to conclusions.

HENRY: Sorry.

LUNA: I have a life already. I don't need more.

HENRY: Good. One of the satisfied. One of the few.

(RAUL *pushes on a green-and-white-striped bamboo chaise longue from stage left. He pushes it across the stage behind* HENRY'S *chair and places it down right facing left. He exits left again.*)

HENRY: There we are. Just in the nick of time. Bamboo. My favorite, bamboo. (*to* LUNA) Now you won't have to sit on my chair after all. You won't have to deposit unseen, invisible plant life.

(*He pushes all the paper towels onto the floor and slaps his hands together.* LUNA *smiles at the chaise longue then looks at* HENRY.)

LUNA: (*looking at chaise*) If I sit does that mean I'm staying?

HENRY: You want to stay, don't you? You wouldn't have come if you didn't want to stay.

LUNA: You don't seem to have any trouble staying. How long have you been here anyway?

HENRY: None of that stuff!

LUNA: Too sticky, huh? Too filled with reverberations? I could be working for anyone now, right?

HENRY: You're still on the payroll.

LUNA: Are you kidding? You think I've been sitting there by the pool, waiting for your next whim all these years?

HENRY: Don't tell me about it! Times have changed. I've lived through earthquakes, disasters, corruptions, fallout, wives, losses beyond belief.

LUNA: Poor baby.

HENRY: I don't need that! I'm not responsible now for your naive beliefs in what I was then. Anything I might have told you was a lie.

LUNA: True.

HENRY: So why needle me?

LUNA: Then you do recognize me? You do remember?

HENRY: I remember something. Parts of something.

LUNA: You're lucky I still recognize *you*.

HENRY: I'm sorry. I didn't have a chance to clean up. We lost track of the planes.

LUNA: Planes? You mean there's other ones coming?

(HENRY *pauses*.)

LUNA: There are, aren't there? Same old shit as it always was. All the "dollies."

HENRY: I've been in the company of men for twenty-one years and in all that time I've never raised my voice so much as I have in the past ten minutes!

LUNA: (*in sex-kitten voice*) I'm sorry, Henry. Let me comply. Anything you want. Just tell me. Tell me once and it's yours.

HENRY: Anything?

LUNA: The world.

HENRY: I have that.

LUNA: Something else?

HENRY: What else is there?

LUNA: Heaven?

HENRY: Oh my God!

LUNA: Heaven, Henry?

HENRY: You're being sarcastic! It's uncanny how you lose touch with female elusiveness.

LUNA: I'm not, Henry. I'm not now and I wasn't then.

HENRY: Wasn't what! My mind's a jumble from all this.

LUNA: Sarcastic.

HENRY: Oh.

LUNA: I'm not. Anything you want.

HENRY: Don't confuse my body. My mind can take it but not the body.

LUNA: Are you actually dying, Henry?

HENRY: I suppose. I suppose I actually am. They tell me I'm actually not but actually I am. I know it. They wouldn't have moved me here if I wasn't. I look it, don't I?

LUNA: You look like something from another world.

HENRY: I am. That's true. I can't take the sun anymore.

LUNA: Do you want me to rub you like I used to?

HENRY: No! I have a man for that! Nothing from outside touches me! Go sit down!

(LUNA *goes down right and sits on the chaise, facing toward* HENRY. *She preens herself, pulls her dress up and crosses her legs.*)

HENRY: (*struggling to get up from the chair*) It's a mutual arrangement. I don't touch it, it doesn't touch me. That's what happens when you rape something, isn't it?

LUNA: Rape?

HENRY: Yes! Rape. After that you don't touch. There's a repulsion between both sides.

LUNA: I wouldn't know.

HENRY: Really? That clean, huh? That above it all?

LUNA: Don't fall, Henry.

HENRY: (*still struggling to stand*) I'm not falling! I'm standing! There's certain machinery at work that thinks I can't even move. Some even think I'm dead. Others don't know. Most others don't know. That's the best of all. Keeping them all in the dark. That's the best.

(LUNA *stretches herself out on the chaise as* HENRY *tries to walk inch by inch toward her.*)

LUNA: Like me?

HENRY: You're the least of it. Harmless. The worst is invisible. They know that. That's why they fear me. That's why they can't put a finger on me. A stab in the dark.

LUNA: Are you coming toward me, Henry?

(LUNA *stretches herself seductively for him.* HENRY *inches his way toward her.*)

HENRY: (*trying to walk*) They comb the cities for me. Little American towns. Fortunes are spent on hired assassins. Presidents fear me. International Secret Agencies, Internal Revenues. Secretaries of Defense. Mobsters. Gang Lords, Dictators, Insurance Detectives. None of them can touch me. None of them.

LUNA: (*stretching, arms over her head*) You're a master, Henry. A wizard!

HENRY: I'm invisible!

LUNA: (*giggling*) I can see you.

HENRY: Untouchable!

LUNA: (*holding out her arms to him*) Touch me.

(HENRY *tries painfully to get closer to her. Puts out his arm.*)

HENRY: I can't.

LUNA: Can you see me, Henry? Look.

(*She rolls herself from side to side.*)

HENRY: Something. Something's there.

LUNA: What do you see?

(*She rakes her fingers through her hair and lets it fall over the chaise.*)

HENRY: I see you moving.

LUNA: Keep watching.

HENRY: I am.

(*She writhes on the chaise as* HENRY *keeps getting nearer.*)

LUNA: Do you see me breathing?

HENRY: Yes! I see your skin moving. It's incredible.

(*She arches her back and smiles at him.*)

LUNA: Do you see my teeth?

HENRY: Yes! Your teeth. Your pearly gates.

LUNA: What else?

HENRY: Your femaleness. It's an awesome power.

(LUNA *squirms with delight.* HENRY *is getting closer to her.*)

LUNA: Henry, it's only me.

HENRY: It's not only you! It's a force. With men I was always a master. They'd lick my heels. Men become dogs in a second. It's the female that's dangerous. Uncontrollable. Catlike.

LUNA: Henry.

(*She runs her hands over her stomach and hip.*)

HENRY: Your pearly gates. Look at them spreading for me. Shining. Calling me in. It's exactly how I pictured it. Exactly. The gates of heaven! You were right.

LUNA: I was?

(*Her actions get more and more erotic.*)

HENRY: They never counted on this. My private salvation. My ultimate acquisition. No spy in the world could ever see what I really had my eyes on. Where my real hunger lay. My ravenous appetite. Beyond private holdings. My instincts were right. At the front door to death I needed women! Women more than anything! Women to fill me up. To ease me into the other world. To see me across. To bring me ecstasy and salvation! Don't let me fall! Don't ever let me fall!

(HENRY *collapses on top of* LUNA *and goes unconscious.* LUNA *screams and tries to struggle out from under him but he stays lying across her.* RAUL *rushes on from left with two tall tropical-looking drinks. He sees the situation and puts the drinks down on the night table beside* HENRY'S *chair. He rushes over to* HENRY *and* LUNA *on the chaise.*)

LUNA: Get him off of me! Get him off!

RAUL: Mr. Hackamore!

LUNA: Jesus Christ!

(RAUL *sweeps* HENRY *up in his arms and rushes him over to his chair and lays him down.* LUNA *stands and brushes herself off.*)

LUNA: If he thinks I flew all the way down here to get jumped on, he's crazy.

RAUL: (*to* LUNA *as he attends* HENRY) How did this happen! What've you been doing to him?

LUNA: Me? I didn't do a damn thing! He collapsed on me. Started mumbling about salvation and ecstasy, next thing I knew, wham, he's on top of me. The guy's a maniac.

(RAUL *turns away from* HENRY *and approaches* LUNA *slowly. She backs up from him slightly.*)

RAUL: I want to tell you something, ma'am. You haven't seen the boss in fifteen years, right?

LUNA: Yeah. So what?

RAUL: In fifteen years a lot of things happen. A whole lot of things. Now he may have invited you down here for some reason. But whatever that reason is it don't mean shit on shinola if it gets in our way. You understand?

LUNA: I think so.

RAUL: I think so too. Now you just string him along with whatever he wants. He may want a lot of funny things but you just play the ball game. Just like all the rest of us. We've been doing it for all these years. It won't hurt you to do it for a few days.

LUNA: A few days?

RAUL: Maybe less. Don't worry, it won't be that long.

(RAUL *turns and exits left.* LUNA *is left alone with* HENRY, *who is still unconscious, breathing heavily. She crosses up to him slowly and looks at him. She reaches out to touch him, then pulls her hand away.*)

LUNA: Henry?

(*No response from* HENRY.)

LUNA: Henry, don't die, okay?

(HENRY *stays unconscious.* MIAMI *enters from up right on the upstage platform, looking out through the blinds then down toward* LUNA. *She is a voluptuous young blonde women dressed in the same style and era as* LUNA *but in pale orange and salmon colors. The effect of both women should be that they've stepped directly out of* HENRY'S *past without aging. She crosses downstage toward* HENRY *and* LUNA.)

MIAMI: (*to* LUNA) Cripes, how many floors they got in this crib? I come up twenty-five on the elevator and the lights go blank. No numbers. Thing's still shootin' up. Pickin' up speed. Feel like to puke.

LUNA: (*motioning to drinks*) Have a drink.

MIAMI: (*taking off her coat*) You kidding? That'd do it for sure. That'd put it right over the top. I gotta get my sea legs first. (*looks at* HENRY) Who's this old dude?

LUNA: Don't you recognize him?

(MIAMI *tosses her coat over* HENRY'S *legs and takes a closer look at him.*)

MIAMI: Am I supposed to? Looks like he's half dead.

LUNA: He is. At least half.

(LUNA *picks up a drink and crosses back down right to the chaise and sits.* MIAMI *moves around* HENRY'S *chair.*)

MIAMI: Weird place to die in, if he's dyin'.

LUNA: He's dying, all right.

MIAMI: Somethin' about your tone of voice gives me the feelin' that you know somethin' more than me. I don't like that feelin'.

LUNA: Tough.

MIAMI: Nasty.

LUNA: I can back it up.

MIAMI: Hold it, hold it. I'm still in the grips of jet-lag. I'm not here for a slug-out. I've got an appointment.

LUNA: (*laughing*) An appointment!

MIAMI: For some reason I had the idea I was gonna' be met with bowls of roses. Little guys dressed up like Philip Morris relieving me of my wrap.

LUNA: Well, there's nothing like disappointment for broadening one's character.

MIAMI: Hey, look, don't use words like "one's" around me, okay? Gives me the creeps. Just talk like a person. I mean if we're gonna' be spendin' any time together.

LUNA: I doubt if we will be.

MIAMI: Swell. What is this, the waiting room or something?

LUNA: What's your name?

MIAMI: Miami.

LUNA: Miami, this is not the waiting room. This is *the* room. The main room. The innermost chamber room. The secret nucleus that everything springs from. The Pharaoh's crypt. And lying in state, at the very heart of things, is the Pharaoh himself.

MIAMI: (*pointing to* HENRY) He's the Pharaoh?

LUNA: He's the Hackamore. *The* Mr. Henry Malcolm Hackamore.

(MIAMI *looks at* HENRY *then back to* LUNA *then crosses closer to* HENRY *and takes another look.*)

MIAMI: No shit. This is him, huh?

LUNA: The one and only.

MIAMI: Whew! Got a little unravelled, didn't he?

LUNA: He's let himself go.

MIAMI: I'll say. I don't know if I can handle this.

(MIAMI *picks up the other drink and takes a sip.*)

LUNA: This is nothing. Wait till he wakes up.

(RAUL *enters from left pushing an intravenous rack with a bottle of blood hanging upside down and a long tube attached.* MIAMI *backs off down left and watches as* RAUL *inserts the needle in* HENRY'S *arm and tapes it down.* MIAMI *looks over to* LUNA, *who shrugs her shoulders.* HENRY *suddenly speaks but stays still. The women listen.*)

HENRY: Raul?

RAUL: Yes, sir.

HENRY: That's you?

RAUL: Yes, sir.

HENRY: Whose blood is it this time?

RAUL: Only the best, sir. Guaranteed.

HENRY: Genius blood? Only genius blood?

(RAUL *looks uneasily at the women, then answers* HENRY.)

RAUL: Yes, sir. Only genius.

HENRY: Good. Because I've made my decision.

RAUL: What's that, sir?

HENRY: To fly. I'm going to fly again.

RAUL: Fly, sir?

HENRY: Straight to Nevada. I'm going to land in Nevada in the middle of the day. I'm going to land with my women. All of us. We're going to disembark in the blazing sun. We're going to appear out of nowhere. We're going to climb into sixteen black Chevrolets and drive straight out across the Mojave Desert.

RAUL: You think you're capable of flying again, sir?

(*The women move in closer to the couch to hear* HENRY.)

HENRY: I'm capable of anything. At any moment anything is possible. Now I want you to find me the proper equipment. The jacket I used to wear. The helmet. The scarf. I'll need all those things.

RAUL: Yes, sir.

HENRY: (*noticing curtain is up*) And lower the damn curtain! How long has it been up like that?

RAUL: Not long, sir.

HENRY: Lower it! Anything could be out there trying to get in. Anything! Have you got any idea what's out there, Raul? Any idea at all?

RAUL: No, sir.

HENRY: The world at large! That's what's out there. Wild. Undominated. Ravenous for the likes of us. Ready to gobble us up at the drop of a hat. We can't allow penetration. Not at any cost. Whatever the price we have to pay it to insure our immunity. You have to insure that for me, Raul. It's in your hands. These

women will deliver me. These two women. Nobody else. I
don't want anybody else in here.

RAUL: Nobody's getting in here, sir.

HENRY: (*to himself as he lies back on chair*) This time I'll escape for
good. It's guaranteed. A clean sweep. A slice of the atom.
Cataclysmic. Perfect timing. Absolutely perfect timing.

(HENRY *beckons the women toward him. They start to move very slowly
and hesitatingly toward* HENRY. *Randy Newman's song "Lonely at the
Top" from the* Sail Away *album (Reprise Records) comes on over the
sound system. The big black curtain upstage starts to slowly descend,
covering the blinds, moon, etc. The descent of the curtain is very slow
and timed to touch the stage floor just as the song ends. The stage lights
are fading in the same tempo as the curtain.* HENRY *keeps slowly
beckoning the women toward him. Song ends. Lights go to black.* RAUL
exits.)

ACT 2

SCENE: *In the dark, Randy Newman's "You Can Leave Your Hat On" from the* Sail Away *album is heard. Lights come up onstage. The big black curtain is down.* HENRY *is seated on his chair facing front to audience, legs hanging over the side. He is rubbing his entire body with alcohol from a bottle on the nightstand. He seems to be entirely absorbed in this process and continues in a slow rhythmical way in time to the music. The two women are standing upstage facing the audience.* MIAMI *to stage right,* LUNA *to stage left. They each have on a lush fur coat. A small black chair is beside each of them. They move seductively to the music.* HENRY *stays front without turning around to them. They follow the instructions in the song and each let their coats fall to their elbows then drop them to the floor. They pick up their chairs and move downstage in time to the music. They set their chairs downstage right and left then they each take off their dress and let it fall to the floor.* LUNA *mimes the line in the song about turning off the light. They both stand on the chairs. They don't take off their high heels as the song suggests. All they are wearing is bra, panties, garter belts, silk stockings with seams, black high heels and whatever jewelry they had on. They raise their arms up above their heads and move to the music.* HENRY *keeps rubbing himself with the alcohol. Now and then he looks up at the two women but his gaze seems indifferent. After the verse which ends, "You give me reason to live,"* HENRY *gets up from the chair with the bottle of alcohol and moves downstage center looking at the women and rubbing his arms. He crosses slowly to each of them through the last verse as they keep undulating to the music.* HENRY *crosses back up center to his chair and sits again facing the audience as the song ends. He keeps rubbing himself as the women get down off the chairs and put their dresses back on.*

HENRY: (*as women dress*) Very impressive. Very interesting little rendition. Choice of music's a little off the wall but aside from that I'd say you two make a nifty combination.

LUNA: Thanks, Henry. You were always more than generous.

HENRY: I was never more than generous! I was never guilty enough to be more than generous.

MIAMI: Henry, what's the scoop here anyway? What've you got planned for us?

HENRY: Planned? (*laughs to himself*) You girls believe in destiny don't ya'? To a certain extent? Prophesy of one kind or another?

(*The women look at each other then back to* HENRY.)

HENRY: I mean you're not gonna' tell me that you map out every move you make in a day. Calculate your every word. There's still a spark of the sense of adventure left? Am I wrong?

MIAMI: It's always good to see you, Henry.

HENRY: That's right. I've never let you down in the past.

LUNA: Well—

HENRY: Well what!

LUNA: Maybe once.

HENRY: When was that? You're not gonna' drag up a lot a' dreary reminiscences for me now are ya'? A lot a' false accusations over circumstances beyond your control!

LUNA: Beyond *my* control?

HENRY: And mine! Certain moves had to be made. Without hesitation! Certain disclosures. Immediate decisions.

LUNA: All right! It's too far gone now anyway.

HENRY: Don't play magnanimous with me!

LUNA: Well, shall we go tooth and nail with it then, Henry? Shall we really get into it?

MIAMI: (*crossing to* LUNA) Look, let's not go and get worked up about the past, okay?

HENRY: She started it! She's the one!

LUNA: (*laughing*) Henry, you're wonderful! You're absolutely wonderful! I always felt like I was ten years old around you and I still do.

HENRY: I'll resist the temptation to take that as a slur. My visions were always of you reveling in the luxury of hotel rooms. Sinking up to the neck in bubble baths. Blanketing your naked body with Pomeranians. All at my expense!

LUNA: (*laughing*) Yes! That was me! That was me!

HENRY: Hardly the environment that would foster complaint! Let alone accusations. You, high on the hog and me, risking my life in a desert junkyard!

LUNA: (*laughing harder*) Oh! Risking your life! Yes! For me!

HENRY: That's right! Shadowboxing with the underground isn't my idea of a kid's game. There was danger at every turn!

LUNA: (*still laughing*) Danger!

MIAMI: Knock it off will ya'! (LUNA *stops laughing*) Jesus, I didn't fly all the way down here to get treated to this.

(HENRY *goes silent, starts pulling out sheets of Kleenex and putting them on his legs. Pause.*)

MIAMI: Henry?

(HENRY *stays silent, absorbed in the Kleenex action.* MIAMI *and* LUNA *look at each other.*)

MIAMI: (*crossing to* HENRY) Henry, look, it's all right with me if you want to keep this thing a secret. I'm game. It's kind of exciting not knowing what to expect. (HENRY *stays silent with Kleenex*) We don't want to upset you or anything. I'm just a little curious about why you asked us down here. That's all.

LUNA: I don't think he even remembers.

MIAMI: (*to* HENRY) Sure he remembers. Don't you, Henry? Didn't you say you wanted to take us flying?

(HENRY *looks up at her. Pause.*)

HENRY: (*stares into space*) There was a song about that.

MIAMI: A song?

HENRY: A silver plane.

MIAMI: What song was that, Henry?

(HENRY *goes back to putting Kleenex on his legs.*)

HENRY: (*referring to* LUNA) She knows what song it was. She used to try to sing it. Used to think she was a singer. Even had me convinced. Spent a lot a' money on that voice.

MIAMI: (*to* LUNA) You remember a song?

LUNA: Not me. Musta' been one of his rural discoveries. One of his quaint little waitress-types.

HENRY: Turns out she could only sing two lines. That's all she could memorize. Two lines.

MIAMI: I could sing something for you if you want me to.

HENRY: You? (*looks at* MIAMI) You can't sing, can ya'?

MIAMI: Sure.

HENRY: You can't sing a note. I remember you. You could barely even talk.

MIAMI: (*moving away from him*) Boy, Henry, you really are a pisser! You know that? A real charmer.

HENRY: Okay, go ahead and sing something. Thrill me.

MIAMI: I think the moment's past! All the inspiration went right out the window!

HENRY: (*laughs*) Inspiration! That's great! Inspiration. Well, that's what ya' get for relying on inspiration, sister!

LUNA: Henry, is this going to be just another opportunity for you to indulge in insults? What do you want from us? Here we are. You sent for us and here we are. I'm not willing to hang around here while you bombard us with your twisted little versions of injury. I didn't even know you were still alive until I got your telegram.

HENRY: (*smiling to* LUNA) There's still no way to be sure about that, is there?

(*Long pause.* LUNA *stares at him. He stares back.*)

LUNA: Well, you're not are you? Henry, don't try to scare me, all right? This situation is already getting me a little bit on edge. I think you owe us some kind of an explanation.

HENRY: That'd be nice, wouldn't it. A little explanation. That'd be real nice. I tell ya' what. We'll have an exchange. You do a little explaining then I'll do a little explaining. Stroke for stroke. That way none of us will be left out on a limb.

LUNA: Well, there's nothing to explain. You know all about me already.

MIAMI: What do you wanna' know from us?

HENRY: I want to know what it's been like.

MIAMI: What what's been like?

(*Pause.*)

HENRY: Life. Living. That's simple enough, isn't it?

LUNA: Life in general, you mean?

HENRY: No. Life in particular. What it smells like. What it tastes like. What it sounds like.

LUNA: Jesus Christ.

HENRY: That's not so unusual, is it?

LUNA: You mean you've been that cut off all these years?

(HENRY *suddenly goes back to the Kleenex and starts putting it on his legs again. The women move in toward him.*)

LUNA: (*after pause*) Henry, I'm sorry. I'll tell you anything you want to know.

(HENRY *quickly looks up at* MIAMI.)

HENRY: What about her?

LUNA: What *about* her?

HENRY: I need a commitment! A pact. We all have to come into agreement. It's no good if two of us are willing and the third one isn't. It's the third one that always spoils everything! It's the third one that stabs you in the back! That's the one you have to watch out for!

MIAMI: I agree already!

HENRY: It's no good just saying it. The words mean nothing. The words just fly out and disappear into thin air. (*to* LUNA) Isn't that right?

LUNA: Yes. I guess so.

HENRY: You're not sure. If you're not sure we can't proceed. You have to be absolutely sure. You have to be convinced beyond a shadow of a doubt! We have to be in communion. Completely in communion!

LUNA: All right! What do you want, a contract!

HENRY: (*short pause*) A contract.

LUNA: Maybe we should all slash our wrists and drink each other's blood or something! I mean how far do you want to carry this thing?

HENRY: A contract sounds good. I'll agree to that.

(*The women look at each other and stifle a laugh.*)

LUNA: All right, Henry. Let's make a contract. You got a piece of paper or something?

HENRY: Paper's filthy! I don't keep the stuff around.

LUNA: (*moving toward his manuscripts under chair*) You've got papers underneath your chair there.

HENRY: You stay away from that! (LUNA *stops*) Just stay away! That's no concern of yours.

(LUNA *backs away.*)

MIAMI: Henry, maybe we could skip the contract thing.

HENRY: No! (*to* MIAMI) See, it's you! You! You're the one! You're the one who wants to stifle the project! Turn around in fifty years and you'll be sittin' at the head of the table! That's the way you'd like it, isn't it? A flimsy verbal agreement. That way you can manipulate and twist things up any way you like. Well, I'm not puttin' one cent into this thing unless we have a contract.

LUNA: And we can't have a contract unless we have paper!

HENRY: Write it in the air!

LUNA: (*short pause*) What?

HENRY: Write it in the air.

(*The women break into laughter.*)

HENRY: Shut up! (*they stop laughing*) Neither one of ya's got the sense God gave a chicken! City girls. Couple a' dumb-ass city girls. You laugh at air! You think air's funny, huh? Well I happen to have built an entire legacy on nothin' but air!

(*Silence.*)

HENRY: That's right. Thin air. Invisible. Tiny little invisible molecules. Jet propulsion! Whad'ya' think about that? The wings of a plane?

(*He stretches his arms out horizontally and slowly tips them from side to side. He smiles at the women.*)

HENRY: Now, what happens when a thing moves through space? What happens?

(*He lowers his arms very slowly. The women seem almost hypnotized by his movements now.*)

HENRY: Do you see anything? Do you see anything leaving a trail? A path? a ghost? A memory of the movement? It's all being recorded. Isn't that something? It's all being left behind and you can't even see it.

(*His arms finally come to rest at his sides.*)

HENRY: Put your hand out in front of you. Your finger.

(LUNA *stretches her right arm with her finger pointed in front of her.*)

HENRY: Both of you!

(MIAMI *does the same.*)

HENRY: That's right. Now—write the words. Write the words I tell you. In plain English. Bold print. I want to see the letters speak. Write this: "We agree—." Write! "We agree—."

(*The women write simultaneously in the air.* HENRY *squints to make out the invisible letters.*)

HENRY: That's right. "This day." Go ahead. Write, "This day—."

(*The women continue writing the words in the air.* HENRY *watches closely.*)

HENRY: "We agree—this day—to everything." Write that! "To everything."

(*The women finish writing the sentence.*)

HENRY: Good. Now sign it. Both of you.

(*They sign their names in the air.*)

HENRY: Now each of you sign the other one's.

(*They look at him, not understanding.*)

HENRY: As a witness! Countersign it! Go ahead.

(*They switch places and sign their names again.*)

HENRY: Good. Now I'll put my sign here.

(HENRY *makes a strange writing mark in midair and dots it.*)

HENRY: There. Now that was painless, wasn't it? Perfunctory and painless. These things have to be taken care of. Now we can breathe a little more freely. Now that we know we're protected.

LUNA: Henry, do you think we could get something to drink? I'm feeling a little bit dizzy.

HENRY: Drink? We don't have anything to celebrate yet. A contract's nothing to celebrate. I never went in for that stuff.

MIAMI: All right, let's get this over with. What do you want us to do now?

HENRY: That's not the attitude. This has to be a voluntary endeavor, otherwise it won't work.

LUNA: Couldn't we raise the curtain or something? It's so claustrophobic in here. I don't know how you stand it.

HENRY: The curtains? No! It's too distracting.

LUNA: Just to get a little sunlight in here.

HENRY: No! (*pause*) This is no vacation! I didn't call ya' down here just to dress up the furniture. There's plenty a' others I could've called for that. You don't seem to recognize the importance of this meeting. You two are my last link. My very last possibility.

MIAMI: For what?

HENRY: For remembering. For bringing something back. Raul's no good for that anymore. I used to depend on him. He used to

give me regular reports. But now he's gone sour. I need a
woman's version. Two women. Two is always better than one.
Now let's start with Las Vegas. That's as good a place to start as
any. How 'bout it?

MIAMI: Vegas? (*she looks at* LUNA)

HENRY: Yeah. What'sa' matter with Vegas?

MIAMI: I haven't been to Vegas since nineteen fifty-two.

HENRY: (*to* LUNA) What about you?

LUNA: (to HENRY) The last time I was there it was with you.

HENRY: Me? You were never there with me! I woulda' remembered
that.

LUNA: Henry, this is going nowhere fast. Can't we play cards or
something?

HENRY: No! There's no time for cards! I'm not lookin' for diversions!
What'sa' matter with you two? Maybe you don't have any
experience. Nothin'. Nothin' to relate. Is that it? A couple a'
zombies?

MIAMI: All right. Las Vegas, nineteen fifty-two.

HENRY: You don't have anything more recent, huh?

MIAMI: Well, yeah. Sure. I got uh—New Orleans. I got some good
Memphis stories. St. Louis. Take your pick.

HENRY: Vegas.

MIAMI: Vegas it is.

HENRY: It has to be Vegas. (*pointing downstage right, by palm*) Go
down there and tell it. Down there. I wanna' see you in the
proper setting.

MIAMI: By the tree?

HENRY: Right. By the tree. (*to* LUNA) You come here. Come here
and stand next to me. Over here. That's right.

(LUNA *crosses to* HENRY, *stands next to him.*)

HENRY: (*to* LUNA) Not too close.

(LUNA *moves slightly away from* HENRY, MIAMI *has crossed down right
to the palm tree.*)

HENRY: (*to* MIAMI) Move a little bit to your left (MIAMI *moves*) Not
too much. Good. That's it. Right there. Good. (MIAMI *stops*) Now
when you tell this—when you start tellin' this I want you to get
real animated. Almost like uh—almost like you were in a movie.
Ya' know what I mean?

MIAMI: A movie?

HENRY: Yeah. Except more than a movie.

MIAMI: More?

HENRY: Much more. More like you were actually stepping back in time. Sort of reliving the experience of having been in Vegas. Ya' see what I mean?

MIAMI: I think so.

HENRY: I don't want you to just tell me some dumb story about some vague memory. I want to feel like I'm actually there.

MIAMI: Okay.

HENRY: If I don't actually get the feeling of it then there's no point in tellin' it. Am I right?

MIAMI: Right.

HENRY: Okay. Now just relax. Are you ready?

MIAMI: Ready.

HENRY: Good. You may begin.

MIAMI: Thanks. (*takes deep breath, starts to tell story*) Well—uh— actually I remember the day I got hired as a chorus girl.

HENRY: Tell about that.

MIAMI: I was in the hospital. I mean I'd just gotten out of the hospital from hepatitis. I was still yellow. And my friend. This friend I had then. Her name was Ellen. She picked me up and we drove to this Shell station. And we went into the rest room and she started slapping makeup on me. She put rouge all over my face to take the yellow out. And she got me this dress. And she got me all dressed up and everything. So then we drove to this casino.

HENRY: Wait a second! Wait a second! I'm not getting the feeling of this at all. I mean you've gotta' move around a lot more and make believe you're actually there.

MIAMI: But I'm not there!

HENRY: I know you're not there. Just make believe you're there.

MIAMI: But I can't make believe I'm there when I'm not there.

HENRY: Just pretend. It's easy. You can pretend anything.

LUNA: (*to* MIAMI) Go ahead. You might as well.

HENRY: You've just got to get into it a lot more.

MIAMI: All right! Jesus, I didn't think I was coming here to do a fucking audition!

HENRY: Well, just do your best.

(*Pause.* MIAMI *starts to tell the story again and tries to "act it out" for* HENRY.)

MIAMI: So we drove up to the casino. And we went inside. And there was this guy. He was a great big guy.

HENRY: Wait! Start over.

MIAMI: What're you talking about!

HENRY: Start from the beginning again.

MIAMI: From the hospital?

HENRY: Right.

(MIAMI *takes a deep breath and starts again, trying to "act it out."*)

MIAMI: I was in California. In the hospital. I'd just gotten over having hepatitis. And this girl friend of mine picked me up and drove me to the airport.

HENRY: The airport? Last time it was the gas station.

MIAMI: (*crossing toward* HENRY *and* LUNA) I'm not doing this! Are you kidding?

HENRY: I'm sorry. I didn't mean to stop you but you did say the gas station the first time around.

MIAMI: I don't care what I said. I'm not doing it anymore! I'm gone. I'm tellin' you, this guy is out of erasers as far as I'm concerned. I didn't come down here to get rousted! I don't care whose charge account it lands on. Who in the fuck does this sonofabitch think he is! Chargin' around accusing me of double espionage! The guy's totally whacko! (*she whips up her coat from the platform*) I came down here for a little vacation not a goddamn brain bath!

LUNA: (*crossing down center*) I'll do it!

HENRY: Good! That's the spirit! That's exactly the kind of enthusiasm we need around here. That's what's been missing. (*to* MIAMI) You come and stay here and we'll watch her do it.

LUNA: (*to* HENRY) You want another Vegas story? Is that it?

HENRY: I don't want another Vegas story. I want the same Vegas story.

LUNA: But that's her story.

HENRY: What difference does it make? It's a good story. One story's as good as another. It's all in the way you tell it. That's what counts. That's what makes the difference.

LUNA: You want me to tell you her story?

HENRY: Why not?

LUNA: Because I don't know what her story is.

HENRY: Make it up. It's all the same.

LUNA: You want me to pretend that I'm her?

HENRY: Just take a plunge and stop pussyfooting around!

(LUNA *starts "acting out" the story for* HENRY.)

LUNA: All right. Let's see. I'd just gotten out of the hospital and I was very yellow. Still very yellow. And a good friend of mine named Ellen picked me up and drove me to a Shell station.

HENRY: (*to* MIAMI) She remembers it better than you.

LUNA: (*continuing story*) First of all she washed off my face. And I remember her face while she was doing it. She looked like she felt sorry for me. Like she was taking pity on me. Then she started putting makeup on me. All kinds of makeup. Green eye shadow and rouge and lipstick. I looked like a different woman.

HENRY: (*to* MIAMI) Now we're getting somewhere. You see? You see what it takes?

LUNA: (*continuing*) Then she drove me out to the airport and put me on a plane for Montreal.

MIAMI: (*interrupting*) No, it wasn't Montreal. It was Vegas. First it was Vegas.

HENRY: (*to* MIAMI) Let her tell it the way she wants to tell it!

MIAMI: Look, it's my story! If she's gonna tell my story she's gotta' tell it right.

HENRY: (*to* LUNA) All right. Just change it to Vegas.

LUNA: (*checking with* MIAMI) It was Vegas first?

MIAMI: That's right. Vegas first. Then Montreal.

LUNA: (*continues story*) Okay. First it was Vegas. I went into this casino and there was this great big guy sitting on a tall red stool in the bar. I told him I'd come for the auditions. He sent me into a back room. Introduced me to this ballet instructor who teaches me a few basic steps. Then they send me into another room where the guy who does the hiring is. And he looks at my legs. All the usual stuff. Says, "Fine." And I'm on my way to Montreal.

HENRY: What about the airport?

LUNA: First I went to the airport and got on a plane and flew to Montreal.

HENRY: No, no, no!! It doesn't make sense! It's gotta' make some kind of sense! It's too confusing. First you're in Montreal then you're in Vegas. What the hell's goin' on here! (HENRY *suddenly gets alarmed*) Wait a second! Who are you people! (MIAMI *moves away from* HENRY *down toward* LUNA, HENRY *starts yelling offstage*) RAUL! RAUL! SOMEBODY'S BROKEN IN HERE! RAUL!

(HENRY *scrambles for the brass bell as he continues yelling for* RAUL. *He enters and carries a World War I leather aviator's jacket, leather helmet, blue silk scarf and goggles over one arm.* HENRY *continues ringing the bell with his back to the platform, unaware of the activity behind him. Stops ringing the bell.* RAUL *holds out the jacket, helmet and goggles to* HENRY. HENRY *stares at them.*)

HENRY: (*to* RAUL) What the hell's that?

RAUL: It's the best I could come up with. Hard to find this stuff nowadays.

(HENRY *grabs the gear out of* RAUL'S *hands, moves back on his chair.* HENRY *glares at the two women then turns to* RAUL.)

HENRY: Did you invite these women in here?

RAUL: No, sir.

HENRY: I want them out of here! Right now! I want them outa' here!

RAUL: Yes, sir. (*to women*) Sorry, ladies.

LUNA: (*stepping towards* HENRY) Wait a second—

HENRY: (*violently, trembling with rage*) Out! Out! Out! Out! Out!

(HENRY *is gasping for breath and passes out.* RAUL *moves to him, tries to calm him down, rubbing his shoulders.*)

HENRY: Who in the hell's making the decisions around here anyway!

RAUL: Only you, sir.

HENRY: Only me?

RAUL: Yes, sir.

HENRY: There's no one over my head somewhere? Somewhere lurking?

RAUL: Not a soul, sir.

HENRY: How can you be sure of that, Raul? How can you be absolutely positive? These women didn't come on my invitation! That's impossible!

RAUL: It may have been an oversight, sir.

HENRY: An oversight! I can't afford an oversight! Not now.

RAUL: We won't let them out of the building without a thorough interrogation.

HENRY: Something's happening, Raul. Something's happening that I can't put my finger on.

RAUL: How do you mean, sir?

HENRY: I mean—the earth. Is the earth shaking? (*sudden panic*) Is that the earth shaking, Raul!

(RAUL *presses firmly on* HENRY'S *shoulders.*)

RAUL: There's nothing shaking, sir.

HENRY: That sound! There's a sound! Down here the earth opens up sometimes. From time to time it swallows people. I've heard of that.

RAUL: It's all right, sir. There's no sound.

HENRY: Don't tell me there's no sound! Listen to that! Just listen.

(RAUL *and* HENRY *listen. Silence.*)

RAUL: There's nothing, sir.

(HENRY *keeps listening. Long pause.*)

HENRY: Is there someone watching me, Raul? Is that what it is?

RAUL: No one's watching you, sir.

HENRY: Someone has to be watching me. I wouldn't feel this uneasy otherwise.

RAUL: Would you like some more plasma, sir?

HENRY: Yes! Anything. Give it a mix. Give it a stir before you bring it in here.

RAUL: Yes, sir.

(RAUL *rushes off to get the blood. Women follow.* HENRY'S *left alone. He puts the blue scarf around his neck. He stares out at his palm trees. His eyes go from one palm to the other. He climbs off his chair and makes his way down to the stage-right palm slowly, his arm reaching out in front of him. He talks to the palms.*)

HENRY: (*as he walks toward palm*) Stop that shaking! Stop that! It's not necessary at a time like this. I'll tell you when to shake. You shake when I shake! The earth's not shaking so why should you.

(HENRY *reaches the palm and grabs it with both hands as though to hold it still. He releases it and stands back. Looks at palm. Looks across at the other one.*)

HENRY: That's better. Both of you. It's not my time yet. You'd agree to that. Both of you'd agree to that. I'm not completely at the end of my rope. There's other lives yet. More to come.

(*He darts a look at the stage-left palm.*)

HENRY: (*to palm*) Stop that shaking! (*he crosses quickly to the down-left palm*) Stop it! There's no reason for it. No reason at all.

(*He grabs the stage-left palm and steadies it the same as he did to the other one. When he's satisfied with the palm's stability he stands back and talks to it.*)

HENRY: (*to palm*) I have enough premonitions already without you creating more. The earth is firm. Temporarily firm. Once I take off, then it can fall apart. You can shake all you want to then. (*pause.* HENRY *slowly tilts his head back and stares up at the sky*) What's that moving? You feel that? There's something moving. Clouds. A fleet of planes. You hear that? You hear that sound? Thundering. Blue steel. They're trying to leave without me!

(HENRY *suddenly panics. Moves center stage.*)

HENRY: (*yelling*) Raul! They're evacuating the country without me! The President's leaving! The generals! They're trying to maroon me again! Abandon me to the elements! Raul! Where are my women! Get me my women before it's too late! Raul!

(RAUL *comes rushing on with the intravenous rack and a fresh bottle of blood. He leaves the rack by the chair and moves down to* HENRY, *helping him back center stage to the chair.*)

RAUL: (*helping* HENRY *walk*) You shouldn't get out of your chair, sir.
HENRY: Where are my women! What's happened to my women!
RAUL: I brought you some fresh blood, sir.
HENRY: We've got to get out of this place before the tidal wave. There is a tidal wave. You know that, don't you? Widespread devastation. Nevada's the only safe ground. Only Nevada. I have inside information. Tribal information.
RAUL: Yes, sir.

(RAUL *helps him back onto the chair, inserts the I.V. needle into* HENRY'S *arm and tapes it down.* HENRY *continues talking.*)

HENRY: Las Vegas is on holy ground. Proof positive. I have definite verification on that.
RAUL: Just relax, sir.
HENRY: Problem is the transit. Keeping it secret. Absolute secret. A black plane. Do we have the black plane?
RAUL: Yes, sir.
HENRY: The jumbo?
RAUL: Yes, sir.
HENRY: No markings of any kind?
RAUL: None, sir.
HENRY: Radar spoiler?
RAUL: Yes, sir.
HENRY: Zero to touchdown?

RAUL: That's right, sir.

HENRY: So I'm to believe you've covered all the variables then?

RAUL: Who else can you believe, sir?

HENRY: (*pause*) That's right. Who else. (*he picks up leather jacket and helmet*) This is my gear?

RAUL: Well, it's just like what you used to wear.

HENRY: You mean this is stand-in gear? Dummy gear?

RAUL: Your original stuff exploded with that pilot over Nebraska.

HENRY: We don't talk about that!

RAUL: I'm sorry, sir.

HENRY: I'm not supposed to hear about that!

RAUL: I forgot.

HENRY: Help me on with this stuff. You put it on me.

RAUL: Yes, sir.

(RAUL *puts the goggles on over* HENRY'S *eyes, then the helmet. He helps* HENRY *on with the jacket, leaving the one sleeve loose over the intravenous arm.*)

HENRY: Why am I shaking, Raul? Why am I constantly shaking?

RAUL: You're shaking less than you used to, sir.

HENRY: I'm not getting better, am I? I'm getting worse.

RAUL: You'll be fine once we get across the border.

HENRY: Why should the border make any difference? I won't be safe until I hit Vegas. Sacred ground. Get my feet on sacred ground.

RAUL: You'll be fine, sir.

HENRY: You think I can still handle that plane? After all these years?

RAUL: It may be a little ambitious, sir.

HENRY: Ambitious? Of course it's ambitious! What's that got to do with it?

RAUL: I just meant physically, sir.

HENRY: Physically? Physically. It's hard to believe I've still got a body left.

RAUL: The doctors say you're on the upswing.

HENRY: The doctors! Those Mexican goons?

RAUL: They're not Mexican, sir.

HENRY: They're not American, either! This country's not fit for a man to get sick in. There oughta' be a law against falling ill in a foreign country. A man's got a right to die in his homeland.

RAUL: You're not dying yet, sir.

HENRY: How can you live down here with monkeys crawling all

over your food! Mosquitoes poisoning the water. We've gotta get outa' here!

RAUL: We will, sir.

HENRY: Those women are probably already contacting the papers. Blabbing about my whereabouts.

RAUL: They haven't left yet, sir.

HENRY: Good. Keep them under surveillance. Constant surveillance. This is an evil time, Raul. Much worse than what I grew up in. Much, much worse. You've lost touch with things but I've still got the old inner radar to depend on. Still got the jump on the world at large.

RAUL: I've always respected your vision, sir.

HENRY: My vision? That's right. My vision. I still see. Even in the dark, I still see. Do you want to know what I see, Raul? It's the same thing I saw in Texas when I was a boy. The same thing I've always seen. I saw myself. Alone. Standing in open country. Flat, barren. Wasted. As far as the eyes could take in. Enormous country. Primitive. Screaming with hostility toward men. Toward us. Toward me. As though men didn't belong there. As though men were a joke in the face of it. I heard rattlesnakes laughing. Coyotes. Cactus stabbing the blue air. Miles of heat and wind and red rock where nothing grew but the sand. And far off, invisible little men were huddled against it in cities. In tiny towns. In organizations. Protected. I saw the whole world of men as pathetic. Sad, demented little morons moving in circles. Always in the same circles. Always away from the truth. Getting smaller and smaller until they finally disappeared.

RAUL: I think your plane is ready, sir. Is there any business you want to finish before we leave?

HENRY: Business? What business? My business is finished.

RAUL: Your will, sir?

HENRY: My will? That's been decided. Everything goes to you, Raul. That's already been decided.

RAUL: But there's nothing on paper, sir.

HENRY: Paper's transient! Write it in the air. Air's the only thing that'll last forever.

RAUL: But the lawyers won't honor that, sir.

HENRY: The lawyers! All the lawyers are good for is stealing you blind! They all work for the government. They're the ones who took my planes. Stole my planes right out from under me!

(RAUL *suddenly pulls his pistol on* HENRY, *points it at his chest.* HENRY *stares at him. Pause.*)

RAUL: (*quiet and firm*) I want something written on paper. Proof positive. I want it written in blood.

HENRY: What is this!

(RAUL *moves into him suddenly and violently rips the intravenous drip from his arm.* HENRY *screams.* RAUL *holds the needle as blood spurts from it onto the floor. He holds the gun on* HENRY *with the other hand.*)

RAUL: Get your papers out, Henry. Under the bed.

HENRY: You can't do this to me! There's others over your head!

RAUL: There's no others, Henry. Just me.

HENRY: You're nothing but a bodyguard. A servant! What're you doing this for? I already told you it all goes to you. Don't you take me at my word?

RAUL: Nobody takes you at your word, Henry. Your word means nothing.

HENRY: I can have you annihilated in a second!

RAUL: By who? By what? You're nothing. You're not even a ghost. You don't even exist, Henry. You've disappeared off the face of the earth. Nobody can trace you. We've made sure of that.

HENRY: I still have my executives! My trustees.

RAUL: Nobody. Nothing. It all stops at me.

HENRY: What've you done behind my back! What've you done to me!

RAUL: I've kept you alive for years and years. I've carried you on stretchers. I've cooked your spinach. I've bought you ice cream cones in the middle of the night. I've held you while you screamed. I've saved you from yourself, Henry. That's what I've done.

HENRY: I'm not signing anything! I'm not making anything final!

RAUL: You still don't believe it, do you?

HENRY: Believe what?

RAUL: That you're dying. You're finished. This is it, Henry.

HENRY: You can't kill me! You can't murder me!

RAUL: I can do anything I want, Henry. Anything. I can fabricate any story. Make up any lie. Have you disappear in London. Reappear in Brazil.

HENRY: That wasn't you! It was me! I was making the decisions! Only me!

RAUL: That's why it worked so beautifully, Henry. Because you believed it. Every suggestion we made, you believed it was your idea. That everything originated from you. The sole stockholder! The one and only Henry Malcolm Hackamore.

HENRY: I invented everything! My planes! My hotels!

RAUL: But not your life! Your life you left to us. To me. I shaped it for you. At first to suit your needs. And then to suit mine.

HENRY: You're a maniac!

RAUL: You can't make a move without me. Stand up! (*pause.* HENRY *stares at him, still sitting on chair*) STAND UP! (HENRY *stands.* RAUL *smiles*) That's right Henry. That's right. Now pull out your papers and put them on the chair.

(HENRY *pauses, then does what he's told. He pulls out the box of manuscripts and sets it on the chair. He turns to* RAUL.)

HENRY: I can't understand why you don't trust me. I can't understand it. I already told you I'd give you everything.

(RAUL *moves to the box and starts pulling out the manuscripts. He hands the intravenous needle, still spurting blood, to* HENRY. HENRY *takes it.*)

RAUL: (*handing needle*) Take this. (*thumbing through manuscripts*) This is where it counts, Henry. In these pages. This is where you give it away. All the secrets. All the treasures. This is what the world will believe. When they see it in black and white. (*he spreads manuscripts out on chair*) Now sign it. Every copy. Sign it with the needle. (WOMEN *enter*) I've arranged for a few witnesses. I hope you don't mind.

(MIAMI *and* LUNA'S *laughter is heard offstage, then the soft background sound of 40's dance music. The* WOMEN *come onto the upstage platform slowly, dancing cheek to cheek with the two* DOCTORS. *The* GANGSTER *follows behind, peering down from the platform at* HENRY. *The music is* "You Belong to Me" *where the lyrics go* "Fly the ocean in a silver plane," *etc.* HENRY *watches the group on the platform then turns to* RAUL. *He still holds the needle with the blood dripping out of it.*)

HENRY: (*to* RAUL) Will I still be able to fly?

RAUL: Anything you want, Henry. I've never refused you yet.

HENRY: I want to see Nevada again. Vegas. Vegas is the only place that makes sense. I can't die without seeing Vegas.

RAUL: You'll see it, Henry. Don't worry.

(HENRY *starts signing the manuscripts with the dripping needle. The* WOMEN *look down at him over the shoulders of the doctors. The* GANGSTER *watches* HENRY *closely.*)

HENRY: I've never signed my life away before. There's nothing to it. No pain. Nothing.

RAUL: It should be a great relief.

HENRY: I don't feel a thing. It's as though it never happened. A whole life. Where's the proof, Raul? Where's the proof?

RAUL: Just sign. Just keep signing.

(HENRY *continues signing the papers. The blood pours across the pages onto the floor.*)

HENRY: I could've made the whole thing up. Any story I wanted. It's not even my blood, is it?

RAUL: By now it is. Your blood was used up a long time ago, Henry.

HENRY: (*starts to panic again*) It's not even my hand! My body! Whose body is this!

RAUL: (*moving in with gun*) Just sign, Henry. Just settle down and sign.

(HENRY *continues signing papers.* RAUL *hovers around him. The platform action continues to the music.*)

HENRY: (*signing*) In a second I see it. I see it now.

RAUL: What do you see?

HENRY: I see how I disappeared. It happened a long time ago. A long, long time ago.

RAUL: Where was it, Henry?

HENRY: Texas. That's the last time I lived on this earth. Texas. I disappeared in a dream. I dreamed myself into another shape. Another body. I made myself up.

RAUL: Keep signing, Henry.

HENRY: It happened in a second. In a flash. I was taken by the dream and all the time I thought I was taking it. It was a sudden seduction. Abrupt. Almost like rape. You could call it rape. I gave myself up. Sold it all down the river.

RAUL: It's too late to regret it now, Henry.

HENRY: But I still get to fly, don't I? You're still going to let me fly?

RAUL: Climb into the cockpit, Henry. Everything's waiting.

(HENRY *starts climbing onto his chair to a standing position facing the audience as* RAUL *collects the manuscripts and piles them into the* GANGSTER's *arms who's waiting on the platform. The blood drips from them onto the floor. The* WOMEN *keep dancing slowly with the* DOCTORS *as the music continues underneath. As* HENRY *climbs the chair,* LUNA *starts singing the words of the song, softly, as she dances.*)

LUNA: (*singing softly*)
"Fly the ocean in a silver plane

See the jungle when it's wet with rain
Just remember till you're home again
You belong to me
See the pyramids along the Nile."
(etc.)

(LUNA'S *singing continues softly underneath* HENRY'S *voice.* RAUL *stays by* HENRY, *looking up at him, his pistol still drawn. The full moon in the background starts to slowly turn orange as the sky grows darker to the end of the act.*)

HENRY: (*standing on the chair*) It's pitch black out here. Perfect. Perfect for escape. I think we did the right thing, Raul. I can slip back in. No one will ever know the difference. They'll say I existed somewhere. A face. A name. No one will ever know for sure. You can take my place now. You can have it.

RAUL: You'll never escape, Henry. You're standing on your bed. You'll never get out of here.

HENRY: (*slowly spreading his arms as though flying*) I've already left. I've gone. Come and gone. Just like that. Every seed I ever planted is growing. Look! (*he points far below him*) Look at it growing! Hotels! Movies! Airplanes! Oil! Las Vegas! Look at Las Vegas, Raul! It's glowing in the dark!

RAUL: You're nowhere, Henry!

HENRY: I'm everywhere! All at once I'm everywhere! I'm all over the country. I'm over Nevada!

(RAUL *points the pistol at* HENRY *as* HENRY *soars on the chair with his arms spread. The sky gets darker. The moon grows red.* LUNA'S *singing fades out.*)

HENRY: I'm high over the desert! Invisible. A ghost in the land. No voice. No sound. A phantom they'll never get rid of.

RAUL: You're dead, Henry! You're dead! Lay down and die!

(RAUL *fires the pistol at* HENRY. *The* WOMEN *and the* DOCTORS *rush offstage. The music continues softly.* HENRY *doesn't die. He keeps flying.* RAUL *points the pistol at* HENRY'S *head.*)

HENRY: I'm the demon they invented! Everything they ever aspired to. The nightmare of the nation! It's me, Raul! Only me!

(RAUL *fires again.* HENRY *keeps raving and flying. He seems to get stronger with every blast of the pistol.* RAUL *goes down on his knees below* HENRY, *keeps firing at him but can't kill him.*)

HENRY: I can move anywhere I want to now. Freer than life.
Flying. My body's gone. You can't even see me now. Nothing
can see me.

I'm dead to the world but I never been born.
I'm dead to the world but I never been born.
I'm dead to the world but I never been born.
I'm dead to the world but I never been born.
I'm dead to the world but I never been born.
I'm dead to the world but I never been born.

(*repeat-fade with lights*)
(*As* HENRY *chants the lines, repeating the rhythm, his body slowly sways
from side to side as his arms drop slowly to his sides. This should be a
very slow, hypnotic movement as his voice fades in the chant.* RAUL
*finally gives up firing the pistol and collapses forward on his knees in a
gesture of supplication. The lights fade to black with the full moon
remaining dark red behind the silhouette of* HENRY *standing on the
chair. The voice of* HENRY *fades in the dark.*)

GEOGRAPHY OF A HORSE DREAMER

A Mystery in Two Acts

Geography of a Horse Dreamer was first performed at the Theatre Upstairs in London on February 21, 1974, directed by the author with the following cast:

CODY:	Steven Rea
BEAUJO:	Bob Hoskins
SANTEE:	Kenneth Cranham
FINGERS:	Neil Johnston
THE DOCTOR:	George Silver
THE WAITER:	Alfred Hoffman
JASPER:	Bill Bailey
JASON:	Raymond Skipp

ACT 1: THE SLUMP

SCENE: *An old sleazy hotel room. Semirealistic with a beat-up brass bed, cracked mirror, broken-down chairs, small desk, etc. It's the dead of winter. A small paraffin heater provides the only heat.* CODY *lies spreadeagled on his back on the bed with his arms and legs handcuffed to each bedpost. He's asleep with dark glasses on. He wears jeans and a cowboy shirt.* SANTEE *sits in a chair stage right of the bed reading the* Racing Form. *He wears a long dark overcoat, shiny black shoes and a gangster-type hat. In his lap is a Colt .45.* BEAUJO *is practicing his pool shots with a cue and three balls on the floor. He wears a forties-type pinstriped suit with white shoes. His clothes are very wrinkled like he's been sleeping in them for a month. The stage should be dark or hidden before the opening. In the darkness the sound of horses galloping at a distance is heard. A slow-motion color film clip of a horse race is projected just above* CODY'S *head on the rear wall. No screen. The film begins out of focus and slowly is pulled into a sharp picture as the sound of galloping horses grows louder. The film clip lasts for a short while with the sound then* CODY *wakes up with a yell. The film goes off and the lights onstage bang up.* SANTEE *and* BEAUJO *continue their routines.*

CODY: Silky Sullivan in the seventh! By a neck. By a short head. Silky Sullivan in the seventh!

BEAUJO: He's got one, Santee.

SANTEE: (*without moving from behind his paper*) He's lost it. I told ya' he's lost it.

BEAUJO: Sounds very certain to me.

SANTEE: Silky Sullivan was a fly-by-night C.V. Whitney nag outa'

Santa Anita. Won a couple a' stakes back in sixty-two. Retired to stud shortly thereafter. Known chiefly for his dramatic closing rushes.

BEAUJO: I'll be darned. He's sure slippin' bad ain't he.

SANTEE: Slippin' ain't the word for it. He's almost disappeared.

CODY: (*waking up*) I need a better situation. It's too jagged in here. This wallpaper, the smell. You gotta take these things into consideration.

BEAUJO: Maybe he's right, Santee.

SANTEE: Sure he's right. I'd be the first to agree that he's right. But it's his own damn fault. We was set up pretty in California weren't we. The Beverly Wilshire. Room service. The whole fandango.

BEAUJO: Yeah. Couldn't even hear yerself walk down the halls.

SANTEE: So what're we doin' here then?

BEAUJO: Fingers.

SANTEE: Naw, you numbskull. It ain't Fingers. That's a byproduct of the situation. The reason we is here is on account of Mr. Artistic Cowboy here. Backslidin' on his system. That's the reason. If he was still dreamin' the winners we'd still be in California. In the money. Now ain't that right.

BEAUJO: I suppose so.

SANTEE: No supposin' about it. It's him that put us on the skids.

CODY: Could I have a cigarette?

SANTEE: We're runnin' low, pal.

CODY: Just a puff then.

SANTEE: All right, give him a smoke.

BEAUJO: Could I have the keys.

(SANTEE *reaches in his pocket and pulls out a ring of keys. He tosses them to* BEAUJO.)

SANTEE: Just the right arm.

(BEAUJO *unlocks the handcuffs on* CODY'S *right arm and gives him a cigarette then lights it.* CODY *smokes.*)

SANTEE: You gotta remember that I ain't the source a' this caper, Beaujo. I been askin' Fingers for a new dreamer for months now. It ain't my idea of a good time beatin' a dead horse ya' know.

BEAUJO: What's Fingers' angle keepin' Cody on then?

CODY: 'Cause I'm the best. He knows that. I'm the best.

SANTEE: (*to* CODY) Aw shaddup! (*to* BEAUJO) You know a big time gamblin' man can't forget his early wins. All those memories when it was pourin' in like a flood. A quarter of a million bucks in a day. That ain't shootin' chicken ya' know.

BEAUJO: Yeah, but he must have other dreamers workin' for him. He's gotta pay the rent.

SANTEE: Sure he does but they're all mediocre. No class. I'll have to hand it to Mr. Artistic here, once upon a time he had some class.

CODY: I could regain my form if I got some decent treatment.

SANTEE: You had your shot at the red carpet routine and you blew it.

CODY: Nothin' fancy. Just some free movement during the day. A chance to get my blood moving again.

SANTEE: A chance to escape you mean.

CODY: I been with it too long, Santee. I couldn't run out on ya' now. I'd be lost. It's been years. I been blindfolded and shuffled from one hotel to another for as long as I can remember. I ain't seen Great Nature for years now. The sun would probably blind me. Where would I go if I did escape?

SANTEE: Wherever you was headed last time you cut loose.

CODY: I don't remember that. I musta' been off my cake. I'd never try it again. I promise.

SANTEE: No dice, Beethoven.

BEAUJO: Wouldn't hurt to just let him walk around the room here, Santee. Just to get his circulation going.

SANTEE: Well if it ain't the soft-hearted gangster type. Go ahead then! Turn him loose. I'm gettin' sick of his corny mug and his crucified position. Go ahead! Just remember if he gets loose it's your ass, not mine.

BEAUJO: (*as he unlocks* CODY) Sure, sure. The last time Fingers bothered with us was last Christmas when he gave us each an Indian-head nickel. We could be mistaken about this whole deal ya' know, Santee. I mean what if Fingers has just cut out on us. Left us here like a bunch a' saps.

SANTEE: He wouldn't do that.

BEAUJO: What's to stop him. He ain't exactly a man of high morals or nothin'.

SANTEE: Don't start bad-mouthin' Fingers now. Just 'cause things get tough is no reason to commit mutiny. Fingers's been good to us right along.

BEAUJO: Yeah, well I wouldn't exactly describe our present situation as the berries.

SANTEE: You got no faith. No gamblin' heart.

BEAUJO: I figure it's more like a game a' pool. You know, the way sometimes you got the feel. You got the touch. All the practice and technique in the world can't beat ya' 'cause you got magic. There's no trace a' tension. Then it goes. Just like that. No way to pin it down. It just slides away from ya'. I figure that's how it is with Cody here.

SANTEE: Maybe.

CODY: Yeah. That's how it is all right. The dreams are jagged. I get a fuzzy picture. Sometimes the numbers blur.

SANTEE: (*to* CODY) You'd agree with anything to get yerself off the hook. Come on, take a walk, Mr. Artist. It may be yer last for a while.

(CODY *begins to get up from the bed. He struggles to gain muscular control, moving his limbs very slowly and trying to figure out how they work.* BEAUJO *backs away and lights a cigarette.* SANTEE *waves the pistol at* CODY.)

SANTEE: Just remember the old iron here. She gets very ticklish in a nervous situation.

BEAUJO: What if we was to make a real effort to treat him decent for a change. You know, steak and eggs in the morning, maybe a walk down the hallway, maybe even bring in a little chippie to warm his heart.

SANTEE: None a' that stuff. First thing you know he'll be crying about his record again. That's what got him started in his present slump if you'll recall.

CODY: My record? You still got my record don't ya', Santee?

SANTEE: What'd I tell ya'? Yeah, yeah. I still got yer record.

CODY: Just don't bust it or nothin'. You wouldn't bust it wouldya'?

SANTEE: I'll bust yer damn neck if ya' don't start walkin' around this room pretty soon. Come on, start hoofin'.

CODY: I gotta take it slow. Everything's like mush. It feels like Jell-O in my veins.

SANTEE: Yeah, yeah. The Champeen Complainer.

(CODY *finally gets to his feet and moves very slowly around the room trying to adjust to walking. Every once in a while he loses his balance and* BEAUJO *helps him stay upright.*)

BEAUJO: I know you got somethin' against art, Santee, but maybe he's right ya' know. I mean maybe his dreamin' does take on a kind of an art form, the way he does it. It might need some special stuff to get him back in top form.

SANTEE: Like what special stuff?

CODY: Like a decent bed for one thing.

BEAUJO: Yeah. I mean that's important. A thing like that. After all, the bed is where he does his work. This thing's like sleepin' on a week-old griddle cake. (*kicking the bed*)

SANTEE: We can't afford it. It's not within the budget.

CODY: Some fresh air.

BEAUJO: Now you can't begrudge a man a little fresh air once in a while.

SANTEE: We might arrange some fresh air. Maybe. He's gotta be blindfolded though. He can't know where he is. That's the chief thing that Fingers impressed upon us. He can't for a second know where he is outside the room he's locked up in. Otherwise it spoils the dreaming. He can't know the time either.

CODY: We've come a long way from the Beverly Wilshire haven't we?

SANTEE: A long way down.

CODY: No, I mean we're on a whole different continent here aren't we? I can feel it.

SANTEE: How can you feel it, Mr. Sensitive?

CODY: We took a ship.

SANTEE: Don't start guessing. There's no way you can find out.

CODY: You've blocked up all the windows again.

SANTEE: That ain't so unusual. That's standard procedure.

CODY: They speak English here though. They speak English don't they?

SANTEE: No guessing goddammit! Or it's back in the sack and no dinner!

BEAUJO: Take it easy, Cody. No need to get Santee worked up.

SANTEE: Just keep walkin', meatball.

CODY: It's all right. Fingers' theory was good for the beginning but now it sucks dogs.

SANTEE: How's that?

CODY: He don't understand the area I have to dream in.

BEAUJO: There's nothing we can do about that now.

CODY: Not this area. The inside one. The space inside where the dream comes. It's gotta be created. That's what Fingers don't understand. He thinks it's just like it was when I started.

SANTEE: So what's so different now.

CODY: He's blocked up my senses. Everything forces itself on the space I need. There's too much chaos now. He'll never get a winner out of me till the space comes back.

SANTEE: What a crock a' shit. I never heard so much gobbledygook in my whole life.

CODY: What do you dream about, Santee?

SANTEE: I don't dream. I'm one a' those rare dreamless sleepers. I got no worries, no troubles to work out. Everything's hunky-dory.

CODY: I dream about the Great Plains.

SANTEE: Well that's yer whole damn trouble! That ain't what yer gettin' paid for. Yer paid to dream about racehorses. That's all.

BEAUJO: Yeah, Cody. Shit man, you gotta get down to business. We're goin' down the tubes in this dump while you dream about the Great Plains.

CODY: It'll get worse.

SANTEE: What! It can't get worse! Put him back in the cuffs! Go on! Back in the sack! I ain't gonna tolerate that kinda' stuff!

BEAUJO: Now take it easy, Santee.

SANTEE: Back in the sack! I ain't takin' no more crap from this hick! I can't stand the sight of him. Back in the sack!

(BEAUJO *leads* CODY *back to the bed and helps him back into the position he was in before. Then he puts the handcuffs back on him and locks them all.* CODY *doesn't resist.*)

SANTEE: (*pacing around the room with his gun*) I'm goin' straight to the top. No more fartin' around. Tomorrow morning I'm gonna' call Fingers and get the lowdown. This whole situation stinks. It's driving me crazy. It's useless keepin' this creep here. He ain't gonna' come up with a horse. He ain't come up with a horse for over six months. One bum dream after another. He's lucky if he even dreams a horse in this century let alone a winner tomorrow. I can't stand it. I'm goin' down there now and call him. Right now. You got some change Beaujo? Gimme some change.

BEAUJO: All right, all right. Take it easy though, Santee. You don't want him comin' down on us too hard. You might catch him in a bad mood.

(BEAUJO *hands* SANTEE *some change for the phone.*)

SANTEE: I don't care how I catch him. We just gotta get outa' this slump somehow. I'm just goin' down the block to a phone booth. Don't let this jerk loose for a second.

BEAUJO: You got the keys.

SANTEE: (*remembering he's in a position of power*) Yeah. Right. I got the keys and don't you forget it. I got the keys.

(SANTEE *exits*. BEAUJO *speaks to* CODY.)

BEAUJO: What the hell are you tryin' to pull? You know better than to get Santee pissed off like that. We're all in this together ya' know.

CODY: Yeah. Sorry.

BEAUJO: I mean it's mostly up to you ya' know. I mean the dreaming end of it. You're actually the big shot in the situation. You can call all the shots. All you gotta do is dream right.

CODY: It ain't so easy, Beaujo. I'm dried up. I need a break.

BEAUJO: Yeah, I can see that and I'm doin' everything I can to make that happen. But in the meantime you gotta play it cool. When Santee's nerves are on edge you gotta go slow.

CODY: If I could just talk to Fingers myself maybe I could convince him. I can't talk to Santee. He hates my guts. He don't understand my position. It's very delicate work, dreaming a winner. You can't just close your eyes and bingo! it's there in front of you. It takes certain special conditions. A certain internal environment.

BEAUJO: Well how did it happen before? It used to be a snap for you.

CODY: I don't know. It was accidental. It just sort of came to me outa' the blue. You know how that is. At first it's all instinct. Now it's work.

BEAUJO: Yeah, but you can't explain that kinda' stuff to mugs like Santee and Fingers. They don't buy it. All they understand is results. The process don't interest them.

(BEAUJO *lights a cigarette and walks around*.)

CODY: If I could just listen to my record again. That's all. Just a couple of tracks off my record.

BEAUJO: No show. It drives Santee crazy. Besides, like he says, that's part of what got you goin' downhill.

CODY: He's nuts. In the beginning I came up with six fifteen-to-one shots in a row. Six of 'em. And all of 'em came from the music. It's a source of inspiration, Beaujo.

BEAUJO: It's just impossible right now. We gotta go slow. Maybe later we can sneak the music back into it.

CODY: Then tell me where we are at least. What country is this?

BEAUJO: Can't do it, Cody. It's strictly against the rules.

CODY: It's stupid! It's really stupid! I'm dreaming American horses and we're probably in Morocco somewhere. It don't make sense. I gotta know where we are so's I can adjust. I've lost track of everything. I need some landmarks.

BEAUJO: Fingers says the dreams are a gift from God. It don't matter what country you dream in.

CODY: Fuck Fingers! I'm the dreamer. I oughta' know.

BEAUJO: I could describe the general area to you maybe. The neighborhood around the hotel.

CODY: That'd help. Anything would help.

BEAUJO: It's a city. We're in a certain area of a city. The workers wear handkerchiefs around their heads. Their main concern is getting laid. They use rough language and swagger their manhood around.

CODY: That could be anywhere.

BEAUJO: It's a gambling town. Racing all year round. It's the poor people who lose. Dozens of big bookmakers for every block. A few shysters work a system. All of 'em work with high stakes. The government has hooks directly into the bookmakers. There's protection on every level except for the bums. The police are paid off by high syndicates. For the rich it's a sport. For the poor it's a disease.

CODY: That doesn't help. It don't put me in touch with anything. I need firm ground to stand on.

BEAUJO: That's all I can give you.

CODY: What kind of cars do they drive?

BEAUJO: No more. I overstepped my bounds already.

CODY: What do the cops look like?

BEAUJO: That's it, Cody. No more.

CODY: If I could just take a walk. You think you can talk Santee into letting me have a short walk?

BEAUJO: We'll see.

CODY: Oh man, I wish I was dead.

BEAUJO: It'll pass.

CODY: I got a feeling I'll never see daylight again.

BEAUJO: Now come on. Don't go gettin' morbid about it. This is just a slump we're in. Fingers'll pull us out of it.

CODY: Fingers is in the same boat as us. We're like his mirror. We never see him but we're always in touch. When he's winning we're in the Beverly Wilshire. When he's losing we're in a dump like this.

BEAUJO: He's got other dreamers. As soon as things pick up he'll move us.

CODY: Why is he keepin' me on! I wanna go back to Wyoming and raise sheep. That's all I wanna do. I got no more tips. I'm from the Great Plains not the city. He's poisoned my dreams with these cities.

BEAUJO: You want a sleeper?

CODY: Yeah. Gimme four of 'em. The blue ones.

BEAUJO: Oh no. Last time you had four you didn't come around for three days. We thought we lost ya'.

CODY: Gimme three then.

BEAUJO: Two's enough. Put you in a nice light sleep. Who knows, you might even dream a winner.

CODY: Just gimme the pills!

(BEAUJO *hands* CODY *two sleeping pills and a glass of water.* CODY *gobbles them down.*)

BEAUJO: You know your problem Cody? You don't accept the situation. There's no way out. Even if you could escape you're too weak to get very far. Even if you got very far we'd know where to find you. You gotta give in to it, boy.

CODY: Yeah. Maybe you're right.

BEAUJO: You gotta use some smarts. If you just relaxed into it and accepted it then everything would come to you. We might even let you have a little more freedom. No blindfolds. Walks in the park. All that stuff would come to you.

CODY: Yeah. I keep thinking this is temporary. How long's it been going on anyway?

BEAUJO: No time hints. Just forget about the other possibilities. This is all you got.

CODY: I can't remember how it started.

BEAUJO: You had a dream.

CODY: Yeah. I had that big dream.

BEAUJO: Then you got publicized.

CODY: Yeah. *Life* magazine. Then my folks started cashin' in. My brothers.

BEAUJO: Then half the state of Wyoming. You were the hottest thing in the West. Then we nabbed you.

CODY: I was kidnapped.

BEAUJO: Well, not exactly.

CODY: I was wined and dined. Where was that?

(*Through this* CODY *is getting drowsy until he finally falls asleep.*)

BEAUJO: Hollywood Park. Aqueduct. Yonkers.

CODY: What happened?

BEAUJO: We had to keep you secret. Too many scabbies cashin' in.

CODY: I used to wake up and not know where I was. As long as I can remember.

BEAUJO: It'll be all right now. It'll all come back to you. (*melodramatically*) You'll find that special area. A huge blue space. In the distance you'll see 'em approaching the quarter-mile pole. The thunder of hooves. Whips flying. The clubhouse turn. You'll get a sense of it again. It'll all come back just like it used to. You'll see. You got magic Cody. You'll see.

(CODY *falls into a deep sleep.* BEAUJO *gets up and walks around. He comes to a stop and looks around the room.*)

BEAUJO: (*to himself*) Huh, for a second there I thought I was lost.

(SANTEE *enters and shuts the door behind him. He goes to the heater shivering from the cold and rubbing his arms.*)

BEAUJO: Did ya' talk to Fingers?

SANTEE: More or less.

BEAUJO: What do ya' mean? What'd he say?

SANTEE: He wasn't there. I had to talk to Zonka.

BEAUJO: Zonka? What's he know?

SANTEE: He gave me a message direct from Fingers.

BEAUJO: What's the scoop?

SANTEE: Dogs.

BEAUJO: Dogs?

SANTEE: Dogs. Greyhounds.

BEAUJO: Greyhounds?!

SANTEE: We been relegated to the dog tracks. It's the most humiliatin' experience of my whole career. All on account a' that meathead!

BEAUJO: There must be some mistake.

SANTEE: Ain't no mistake. It come from the top. He's gotta start dreamin' dogs. That's all there is to it.

BEAUJO: But he don't know a greyhound from a crocodile. This kid's strictly a horse man.

SANTEE: I know, I know. It ain't my idea.

BEAUJO: He can't suddenly change his whole style a' dreaming like that. It might kill him.

SANTEE: Well he's gonna' have to or our ass is grass! Wake him up.

BEAUJO: I just gave him two sleepers.

SANTEE: Wake him up! Here, take the keys and unlock him.

(BEAUJO *takes the keys and unlocks* CODY. CODY *stays asleep.*)

BEAUJO: Jesus Christ, Santee, we're gonna kill him with this kind of treatment. I'm tellin' ya'.

SANTEE: I could care less. As far as I can tell it's him that got us into this mess and it's him that'll get us out. All my life I been proud a' my position. I've carried a certain sense of honor with me but I'll be damned if I'm gonna carry it to the goddamn dog track.

BEAUJO: He's out cold Santee.

SANTEE: Wake him up! I don't care how ya' do it. I want him on his feet. I'm gonna' drill him with dogs till he hears 'em barkin' in his ears.

(BEAUJO *slaps* CODY'S *face and tries to bring him around.*)

BEAUJO: It's no good, Santee. He's out like a light.

SANTEE: Great! That's just great. Now we're sunk. We're really sunk.

(BEAUJO *leaves* CODY *sleeping on the bed. His arms and legs are free.*)

BEAUJO: It might mean we're being let off the hook, Santee. Eased-in grade.

SANTEE: Can't you understand that this is serious business. What's a' matter with you. Zonka told me if there's no results within the week that Fingers is sendin' the Doctor over here.

BEAUJO: The Doctor?

SANTEE: Yeah. You know what that means.

BEAUJO: He can't do that.

SANTEE: Yeah, well that's what's gonna' happen if Cowboy don't pop up with some winners and fast.

BEAUJO: The Doctor? Fingers must be crazy. He was goin' to the pay window every day for a month and now he can turn on us like this?

SANTEE: That's the way it falls, Beaujo.

(CODY *lets out a loud voice then goes right back into sleep.*)

CODY: Native Dancer in the eighth!

SANTEE: He's gettin' more and more pathetic. Native Dancer musta' died in the fifties.

BEAUJO: I got faith in him, Santee.

SANTEE: Faith! What good is that gonna' do us? We need results! Right now. There's only one thing we can do.

(SANTEE *goes to the* Racing Form *and leafs through it.*)

SANTEE: We gotta take the gamble. We gotta try to pick some dogs ourselves and pass 'em off as his dreams. That's the only thing.

BEAUJO: But we don't even know how to read the form for greyhounds. You don't know the first thing about it.

SANTEE: We can learn. Look, it says here: "Black Banjo, the young Walthamstow hopeful, has been unlucky in his last six outings. With the advantage of trap one and a slow starter to his right, Black Banjo could get to the first bend and go clear."

CODY: Man o' War by a neck!

SANTEE: Can you do something about him?

BEAUJO: He'll come around in a while.

SANTEE: Look, write these down. Get a piece a' paper and write.

BEAUJO: I don't know Santee. We're takin' quite a risk.

(BEAUJO *goes to a small desk and gets a pad and pencil. He writes down what* SANTEE *says.*)

SANTEE: It's worth a try. We might even pick us some winners. Put down: "Harringay. 7.45, Sgt. Mick. 8.00, Go Astray. 8.15, Zeitung. 8.30, Lemon Castle. 8.45, Come Dark Night. 9.00—"

CODY: (*speaking in an even, cool voice*) Black Banjo will win the seventh race at Wimbledon by two and a half lengths on the trot.

SANTEE: Can you shut him up. I can't concentrate.

BEAUJO: Wait a minute! Did you hear what he said. Black Banjo! That's a dog. A greyhound!

SANTEE: I know. I just read it in the paper.

BEAUJO: He just picked him to win at Wimbledon.

SANTEE: So what. The power of suggestion. He musta' heard me read it.

CODY: Black Banjo, a young son of the great Irish stud dog Monalee Champion, has all the looks and speed of a top-class dog. His early speed and clever tracking has told the tale on more than one occasion. Although unlucky in most of his recent deciders he will definitely win by two and a half lengths tonight at Wimbledon.

BEAUJO: Listen to that! Where'd he get information like that? Look it up. See if that's his breeding.

SANTEE: What'd he say?

BEAUJO: Monalee Champion. Look it up.

SANTEE: (*looking in the paper*) Monalee Champion. Let's see. Yeah. What do ya' know. Monalee Champion. How'd he know that?

BEAUJO: He's back on, Santee! He's back on the winners! We're gonna' be in the money again!

SANTEE: You think so? I'd hate to risk it.

BEAUJO: I know it. I can feel it. He's havin' a breakthrough.

CODY: Black Banjo will break in front with Shara Dee close up at the first bend. There'll be some bad crowding going around and Stow Welcome will be thrown to the outside. From there to the wire Black Banjo will have it all his own way. Shara Dee will be closing in the final stages but will not come to terms with the winner. She will be second with another length back to Seaman's Pride.

SANTEE: Go call Fingers. If Zonka answers pass on the message. Black Banjo to win, Shara Dee to place. Forecast, one and three. Tell him it's a certainty.

BEAUJO: Right.

SANTEE: And grab me a fifth of Scotch on the way back. I'm gonna' need it if we lose.

BEAUJO: This is it, Santee. I feel it in my bones. The slump is over. Tomorrow we'll be sittin' pretty!

SANTEE: It ain't happened yet.

(BEAUJO *exits*. SANTEE *talks quietly to* CODY, *who remains asleep*.)

SANTEE: Okay Mr. Artistic. Maybe I was wrong. Maybe I was pushin' it too hard. This better be it boy or we're all gonna be cut up in little pieces and mailed to our mommas. I know you ain't used to workin' under pressure but that's how it is. It's like a snake bitin' its own tail. We keep infecting each other. The Doctor's on our back. The pressure's there. It comes from the outside. Somewhere out there. We wind up with the effects. I don't understand how you work, Beethoven, that's how come I got no patience. To me it's a lot a' mumbo jumbo. Like I said, I don't even have no dreams. All I know is that you was right once. For a solid month you was right. You was so right that you had somebody out there eatin' turtle soup and filet mignon three times a day. Being chauffeur-driven to the grocery store. That's how it is. You got the genius, somebody else got the power. That's how it always is, Beethoven. The most we can hope for is a little room service and a color T.V.

(CODY *sits up. He talks with another voice; slightly Irish, as though he's been inhabited by a spirit.*)

CODY: The main mistake is watching the race in an emotional way. As though the dog you've gambled on is a piece of yourself. That way you only see one-sixth of the race and miss the other five dogs. You might go a dozen races gambling on dogs you've seen before but never watched.

SANTEE: Say, what is this? Are you awake now or what?

(CODY *gets up off the bed and moves easily around the room.*)

CODY: You gotta take mental photographs of each dog. You gotta draw back from the race, take an indifferent attitude. Memorize forty-eight dogs a night. Don't gamble for a week of racing. Just take photographs.

SANTEE: Don't try nothin' funny! I still got the rod.

CODY: Once you've built up an interior form you attack in a calculated way. Never let the odds influence you. Go about it cold-blooded. Make definite decisions and stick to them. Forget the Quinellas and Duellas. They're for suckers. Stick with £5 reverse forecasts, tenners each way on the selection.

SANTEE: What's got into you. Get back over here on the bed!

CODY: Keep a record of the seasonal dates of bitches. One week before they're due in season back 'em to the hilt. Don't be fooled by fast-improving pups but don't be afraid to have a gamble in the middle of their form. Forget Yellow Printer sons in the Derby. They're jinxed. Too difficult to tune them up. Look at Super Rory. Donemark Printer. Tremendous class but see how fast they blew up.

SANTEE: Shaddup!

(CODY *snaps out of it back into his old self. He's barely able to stand up. A short silence then* BEAUJO *bursts in the door.*)

BEAUJO: Fingers is comin'!
SANTEE: What! Now?
CODY: Lemme talk to him.
BEAUJO: After the race. He's comin' right after the race.
SANTEE: (*threatening* CODY) You better be right, Schmoe.
CODY: I gotta talk to him.
BEAUJO: He's bringin' the Doctor if he loses.
SANTEE: Where's my Scotch?

(CODY *collapses on the floor.* BEAUJO *hands* SANTEE *a fifth of Scotch.*

SANTEE *breaks it open and takes a long swig. They both stare at* CODY
on the floor as the lights dim and the sound of an ANNOUNCER'S VOICE *is
heard over the speakers.*)

ANNOUNCER'S VOICE: The hare is running at Wimbledon. Black
Banjo breaks clear of Shara Dee in trap three followed closely by
Stow Welcome and Seaman's Pride. As they go into the first turn
it's Black Banjo by a length and a half. There's some bad
crowding. Stow Welcome is knocked out of it. Down the back
straight it's Black Banjo going four lengths clear from Shara Dee,
followed by Seaman's Pride. It's Black Banjo into the third bend
still well clear of Shara Dee who is making up ground on the
outside. Coming for home it's Black Banjo with Shara Dee
closing very fast. It's Shara Dee and Black Banjo!

(*The swelling sound of a huge crowd drowns out the* ANNOUNCER'S VOICE
as the lights go to black.)

ACT 2: THE HUMP

SCENE: *A fancy hotel room with the furniture in the same position as in Act One. A color T.V. with a flickering image, the sound off. A record player on top of a chest of drawers. The characters all have new clothes but all in the same styles as Act One.* CODY *still wears his shades and speaks with a slight Irish accent. He stands center stage holding a fishing pole at arm's length with a white rabbit skin tied to the end of the line so it just touches the floor. He turns slowly in a tight circle so that the rabbit skin drags across the floor around him. He watches a litter of imaginary greyhound pups chasing the skin. This is the method for schooling puppies to chase the mechanical hare in a circle.* SANTEE *sits on a chair in the same position as Act One, reading the* Racing Form. BEAUJO *sits at a table down-left dealing a hand of five-card stud to himself and an imaginary partner across from him. In the darkness, before the action begins, the sound of dogs yapping is heard faintly and grows louder as a color film clip of greyhounds racing in slow motion is projected on the rear wall. It's done in the same way as the film of the horses at the beginning of Act One.* CODY *yells at his imaginary puppies, the film goes off and the lights onstage bang up.* CODY *turns in a circle and talks.* SANTEE *and* BEAUJO *ignore him.*

CODY: You gotta watch that brindle. He's a devil. The biggest in the litter. Thinks he can get away with murder. It's very crucial to catch them at an early age. Once they get the taste for fightin' there's the seed of a bad habit. It's usually the big ones that get pushy. You don't want to take the fire out of 'em. Just let 'em know that you'll have none of it.

(*He strikes out at one of the puppies then goes on in a circle.*)

SANTEE: I notice he missed the fifth at Catford yesterday.

BEAUJO: Seven out of eight ain't so bad.

SANTEE: Just hope it's not a bad omen.

BEAUJO: We're in the pink, Santee. He's locked into it this time.

SANTEE: Yeah. It gives me the creeps. Like being a nurse at a flip house.

(CODY *reverses direction with the pole and keeps moving in a tight circle.*)

CODY: It's important to reverse your direction once in a while. To balance out the muscles. Too much counterclockwise action makes 'em soft on the right side. You watch the Irish dogs. You'll never see near as many dogs breaking down in Ireland as you do in England. The schooling's different. We take more time in Ireland. More patience.

SANTEE: He still don't know where he is.

BEAUJO: He's gettin' closer though.

SANTEE: If ya' ask me he's further away than ever. He's off his cake, Beaujo.

BEAUJO: Lucky for us.

SANTEE: What do ya' suppose happened to him?

BEAUJO: You got me. Some kinda' weird mental disorder. I told ya' he was a genius. There's a very fine line between madness and genius ya' know.

SANTEE: Yeah, yeah. Cut the baloney. He's gone bananas and that's all there is to it. It just happens to coincide with our needs.

BEAUJO: Well, leastwise Fingers is happy. That's all that counts right now.

(*A loud knock at the door.* SANTEE *and* BEAUJO *leap to their feet.* CODY *keeps turning in a circle and mumbling to the puppies.* SANTEE *has his gun out.*)

SANTEE: You expectin' company?

BEAUJO: Not me. Must be room service.

SANTEE: I didn't order nothin'.

BEAUJO: Me neither.

(*More loud knocking.*)

SANTEE: Well answer it! Go on!

(BEAUJO *goes to the door.*)

BEAUJO: Who is it?

DOCTOR'S VOICE: Fingers! Open up!

BEAUJO: (*to* SANTEE) Oh shit, it's Fingers!

SANTEE: Well let him in.

BEAUJO: (*to the door*) Hold on a second!

(BEAUJO *unlocks three or four locks on the door as* SANTEE *grabs the fishing pole out of* CODY'S *hand and hides it under the bed. He grabs* CODY *by the back of the neck and throws him onto the bed.* BEAUJO *swings the door open and* FINGERS *sweeps into the room with the* DOCTOR *behind him.* FINGERS *is tall, thin and rather effete wearing a bowler hat, tweed cape with matching trousers, black vest with a white carnation, thin pencil-line mustache, spats, black cane and gaudy rings on every finger including the thumbs. The* DOCTOR *is very fat and looks like Sydney Greenstreet. He wears all black in the style of the thirties and carries a doctor's ominous-looking black bag.*)

FINGERS: Good God man, you'd think it was Fort Knox in here the way you carry on with the bloody locks. Where's my boy?

BEAUJO: Sorry, Fingers. We was takin' precautionary measures.

(FINGERS *spots* CODY *on the bed and moves toward him.* CODY *runs frantically to the other side of the room. He seems terrified of* FINGERS' *every move.*)

FINGERS: Ah yes! Yes, yes, yes! I should have known he'd have the look of eagles. Absolutely. Look at him, Doctor. Just look. Splendid.

DOCTOR: Hmm. So that's him.

SANTEE: We been keepin' him good, Fingers. Three squares a day. Free movement through the room. Just like you said.

FINGERS: Those eyes. It almost hurts to look in his face.

SANTEE: You ain't kiddin'. I was just tellin' Beaujo how sick I was gettin' a' his mug.

(*The* DOCTOR *takes his coat off and throws it on the bed, then he helps* FINGERS *off with his cape.*)

FINGERS: (*to* CODY) At last we meet. Like the tail and the head of a great dragon. This calls for a celebration. Order some sherry and cognac. The finest in the house. (*to* CODY) You do drink I trust?

SANTEE: He ain't being too communicative lately, Fingers. He's slipped into some kinda' depression or something.

(BEAUJO *rings for the* WAITER. *The* DOCTOR *sinks into a chair and watches T.V. He turns the sound up very loud.* FINGERS *glares at him.*)

FINGERS: Doctor! I say, Doctor!

(FINGERS *crosses briskly to the T.V. and turns the sound off. The* DOCTOR *just stares into the screen.*)

FINGERS: Do you mind? We're trying to conduct a conversation.

(FINGERS *crosses back to* SANTEE.)

FINGERS: Now then. Where are we? Oh yes. Depression. Depression? Good Lord, we can't have that. Let me feel his temperature.

(FINGERS *moves toward* CODY. CODY *leaps over the bed and crashes into a wall trying to get away from him. The* DOCTOR *is unmoved.*)

FINGERS: Is he always this hypertensive?

BEAUJO: Only around strangers. He's only seen me and Santee for the past year and a half now. He don't know what to make of you.

SANTEE: Yeah, he should settle down in a little while. Then you can pet him.

FINGERS: I see. Poor chap. I dare say he does look a bit at odds with himself doesn't he. Has he been sleeping well?

SANTEE: In spurts. He'll fall dead asleep for fifteen minutes in the middle of the floor and then wham, he'll be up and prowling the room again.

FINGERS: I don't like the sound of that at all. Doctor, did you hear that?

DOCTOR: I wasn't listening.

FINGERS: Santee says the poor fellow only sleeps for fifteen minutes at a stretch and then he's up and about.

DOCTOR: So what? It's not unusual in cases like this. People in his state can go a week without sleeping a wink.

FINGERS: I see. I rather thought it was more serious than that.

DOCTOR: 'Course they don't live long.

FINGERS: Then it is serious.

DOCTOR: Maybe, maybe not. Depends on the particular case.

FINGERS: Well I do wish you'd examine the poor chap and make some sort of diagnosis. After all our livelihood hinges upon his well-being.

DOCTOR: Later. Right now I'm gonna' take in a little viewing.

FINGERS: Well I suppose it can wait. Now then, where's the champagne?

(SANTEE *and* BEAUJO *seem surprised by* FINGERS' *lack of authority over the* DOCTOR.)

BEAUJO: I thought you said sherry.

FINGERS: Did I? Ah yes, sherry. So I did.

CODY: Just two tablespoonsful. That's all. Otherwise you blow 'em out.

FINGERS: Is he speaking to me?

SANTEE: We're never certain Fingers. It could be any of us.

FINGERS: I see. How long has this been going on?

BEAUJO: Ever since the switchover.

FINGERS: Switchover?

SANTEE: To greyhounds.

BEAUJO: You upset something very fragile, Fingers. He may never come back from it.

FINGERS: I'm afraid I don't understand.

BEAUJO: He's a horse dreamer, Mr. Fingers. A horse dreamer. When you had us switch over to dogs something snapped in him. The mind is a very mysterious thing ya' know.

FINGERS: Yes, I see. I had no idea. Poor devil.

SANTEE: He's doin' all right though. He's still on the winners and everything.

BEAUJO: But it won't last for long.

SANTEE: Will you shut up!

BEAUJO: I'm only trying to give ya' fair warning so it don't come as too much of a shock.

SANTEE: Beaujo's talkin' through his hat, Fingers. He don't know nothin' for certain.

FINGERS: It's all my fault. I should have brought a stop to this insanity long ago. I should have known something like this would happen.

SANTEE: Nothing's happened. We've been in the money for three weeks straight now. Everything's hunky-dory, Fingers. All we gotta do is ride him out. When he hits another slump we just give him a breather. Simple as that.

(*A knock at the door.*)

SANTEE: That must be the waiter. You just set yourself down on the bed there and I'll order us some drinks. You just relax, Fingers. Everything's gonna' be okay, Beaujo, help him onto the bed. Take his shoes off, loosen his tie.

(BEAUJO *helps* FINGERS *to the bed.* FINGERS *has gone all weak and sickly now. Every time* FINGERS *moves,* CODY *moves frantically to get away from him, crashing over furniture and smashing into the walls. The* DOCTOR *remains indifferent, staring into the T.V. with the sound off.* SANTEE *opens the door and lets the* WAITER *in. The* WAITER *wears white gloves and tails. He looks a bit apprehensive about the situation.*)

WAITER: Uh, you rang, sir?

SANTEE: Yeah, get us a coupla' bottles of yer best cognac and some sherry. Nothin' but the best. Oh yeah, and some glasses. Here's a tenner. Keep the change.

WAITER: Very good sir. Thank you very much sir.

SANTEE: Don't mention it. Now scram.

(*He shoves the* WAITER *out the door and bolts it.* FINGERS *is lying on the bed as* BEAUJO *takes* FINGERS' *shoes off and massages his feet.*)

FINGERS: I had a feeling it would end like this. I've committed a terrible sin.

SANTEE: Nothing's ended. It's all going on right now. We're on top. Nothing's ended, Fingers.

CODY: The sickness is sweeping through the kennel! There's no escape! Intestinal Catarrh is on the march! Sprinters and stayers! Everyone's equal in this.

FINGERS: What in God's name is he on about?

SANTEE: It's nothin' Fingers. He's practicin' up for White City tonight.

FINGERS: Oh my God!

SANTEE: I'll have him under control in just a minute. Come here you!

(SANTEE *moves toward* CODY. CODY *leaps away again crashing into things like a frightened animal.*)

FINGERS: Don't you touch him! Don't you lay a hand on him! Enough damage has been done already.

CODY: (*panting like a dog*) Didn't you give me enough stick already! At Dundalk! Shelbourne Park! Trucked around half of Ireland like so much hamburger.

FINGERS: (*to* SANTEE) Now you've done it! You've pushed him too far. He's over the edge.

CODY: (*to* SANTEE) I kept crying for trap one. Over and over again I asked for trap one. I could've won from the inside! But no, I was forced to go wide. You couldn't understand why I'd check at the third bend. Time and again I'd check at the third bend. How stupid can you get. I was schooled on the inside hare and you put me in trap six. Trap six! Trap six! Trap six! I'm bloody tired of trap six!

SANTEE: Aw fuck off, ya' nut-case! (*to* FINGERS) I wash my hands a' this whole deal. I warned ya' right from the start about this country bumpkin. He's a weirdo. Unreliable. I coulda' found ya' plenty a' good dreamers from the city but no, we had to go to the middle of the goddamn Great Plains and bring back a dodo. A fruitcake. Well I've had it. From here on it's your ballgame. I'm watchin' T.V. with the Doc.

(SANTEE *goes and stands behind the* DOCTOR *and watches T.V.*)

BEAUJO: (*to* FINGERS) Maybe after White City tonight we should give him a rest, Fingers. Let him get his strength back.

FINGERS: (*sitting up on the edge of the bed*) There'll be no White City tonight or any other night. I'm setting him free.

SANTEE: You're what! You can't do that! He's still worth millions even though he is crazy.

FINGERS: (*getting up and moving toward the* DOCTOR) I don't care what he's worth. He's going back tonight. Doctor, would you be so kind as to arrange air passage for two to Wyoming. I'm taking him back personally.

(*The* DOCTOR *stays staring at the T.V.* FINGERS *moves back to* BEAUJO. SANTEE *follows him.*)

SANTEE: Fingers, wait a minute. I take back what I said before.

FINGERS: We must gather his personal effects together.

BEAUJO: All he's got is what he's wearing and an old beat-up record.

FINGERS: Very well. Get it.

(BEAUJO *goes to a drawer and pulls out an old album with no cover.*)

SANTEE: This is a real mistake, Fingers. Why don't we just keep him on until he starts slippin' again. No harm in that. He's a gold mine right now.

FINGERS: Gold mine. Yes. By the way, what was the name of that town we took him from. Do you remember?

BEAUJO: Somewhere in the High Mountain country. Above the Big Horns.

FINGERS: That's quite a large piece of real estate as I recall. Can't you be more specific.

BEAUJO: Something like Pawnee or Cheyenne. Something like that.

SANTEE: Cheyenne's in the southeast. It was north of there.

BEAUJO: Something like Arapahoe or Mitchell. Was it Mitchell?

FINGERS: Does anyone have a map?

SANTEE: Look, Fingers, just leave him to us for a while. Give him another chance. We'll bring him around.

BEAUJO: Well look, we can figure it out easy enough. We left Salt Lake City on a Friday night and drove all night. We crossed the Utah state line about two in the morning.

FINGERS: Yes, I remember that. I remember thinking, now we're in Wyoming, it can't be far now. On the map it looked to be no further than Brighton is from London. Then all the next day we drove and drove. I'd never seen such country. Nothing as far as the eye could see. Nothing.

BEAUJO: We hit the Wind River Reservation about noon. We had lunch in the Silver Star. Fingers bought a cowboy hat and a pair of spurs.

FINGERS: Yes! I remember that! I remember thinking this is the West! This is really The West! Then we got to that town where Buffalo Bill lived. I forgot the name of it. Oh what a town! Saloons with Winchester rifles tacked up on the walls. Real cowboys in leather chaps. Indians shuffling through the dusty streets. Buffalo Bill's name plastered on everything. And at night. At night it was magical. Like praying. I'd never heard such a silence as that. Nowhere on the earth. So vast and lonely. Just the brisk cold night blowing in through the hotel window. And outside, the blue peaks of the Big Horn mountains. The moon shining on their snowy caps. The prairie stretching out and out like a great ocean. I felt that God was with me then. The earth held me in its arms.

(*A short pause as* FINGERS *reflects.*)

BEAUJO: That was the town.

FINGERS: What was.

BEAUJO: The town we nabbed him in. That was it.

FINGERS: Yes! That's right! What was it called? Doctor, do you remember the name of that charming town. The one where Buffalo Bill lived. Doctor?

(FINGERS *turns to the* DOCTOR *who is sitting very still in a kind of trance.*)

FINGERS: For heaven's sake, man, snap out of it.

SANTEE: What's eatin' him now.

(FINGERS *goes to the* DOCTOR *and shakes his shoulder.*)

FINGERS: I say. Doctor! I asked you to go and arrange our passage to Wyoming. Doctor!

(FINGERS *shakes him again. The* DOCTOR *lets out a bloodcurdling yell and throws* FINGERS *across the room.* CODY *screams like a dog who's being whipped. He whimpers in a corner.* BEAUJO *and* SANTEE *stand facing the* DOCTOR, *who stands center stage.* FINGERS *moans on the floor holding his leg in pain. The* DOCTOR *quickly gains control of himself.*)

SANTEE: Say, look, Doc, I'm with you in this. I never wanted to let Cody off the hook. I'm with you.

DOCTOR: Yes, I can see that. Fetch my bag.

SANTEE: What?

DOCTOR: My bag!

SANTEE: Yessir. You bet. I'm with you in this.

(SANTEE *gets the* DOCTOR'S *bag and give it to him.*)

DOCTOR: And stop repeating foolish platitudes. I've grown quite tired of all this trivia. Something drastic must take place.

BEAUJO: Drastic?

DOCTOR: Yes, that's right. Something rather more adventurous. You're a man of adventure aren't you, Beaujo?

BEAUJO: Well, not exactly. I mean I been around but—

DOCTOR: You've been around?

BEAUJO: Yessir. I mean, the States, you know. I've seen the States.

DOCTOR: I see. Did you discover anything of particular interest in your travels?

BEAUJO: Well, you know, the usual stuff. Card games, pool halls, that kinda' stuff.

DOCTOR: Then you're a man who can recognize gifts.

BEAUJO: Gifts? Well, I don't—I don't exactly get what you mean.

DOCTOR: What I mean very simply is that perhaps in a card game you noticed a particular player who seemed to have more luck than the others. Perhaps even yourself. Something more than luck. A gift we might say.

BEAUJO: Yeah. You might say that.

SANTEE: Say, what's goin' on here anyway?

DOCTOR: Please be silent until you're spoken to!

SANTEE: Yessir.

(*During all this the* DOCTOR *has placed his black bag on the bed and opened it. As he talks he handles various unseen objects in the bag.*)

DOCTOR: I'm not speaking superstitiously you understand. Luck is no accident. It's a phenomenon. Luck is a living thing. The problem of course is tracking it down.

BEAUJO: Yeah, I see what you mean.

DOCTOR: Do you? You see, in Cody here we had actually tracked it down. We had placed it on the map. We combed the planet for someone like him and we finally found him. In Wyoming of all places.

FINGERS: That's enough Doctor! Enough!

DOCTOR: These dreams, these visions that he has, do you suppose they are purely accident? Mere coincidence?

BEAUJO: Well, I don't know. I couldn't say for sure. Look, I'm just a sidekick here. I don't know anything important.

DOCTOR: Fair enough, but there's no harm in investigating a few details.

BEAUJO: I'd rather you talked to Santee about it. I'm liable to get a headache and go right out on ya'!

DOCTOR: Santee has no space between his ears for anything new. I was hoping perhaps you would.

FINGERS: (*still on the floor*) You can't do this! No one's prepared.

DOCTOR: I recognized you immediately, Beaujo, as a man of adventure.

BEAUJO: You did?

DOCTOR: Yes. A man who's been around as you say. A man who's looked life in the face. You have dreams, don't you, Beaujo?

BEAUJO: Sure. Santee's the only one that don't have dreams.

DOCTOR: What do you dream about?

BEAUJO: Pool mostly. Fast cars. Money.

DOCTOR: Yes. Pool, fast cars and money. Probably women too?

BEAUJO: Sure.

DOCTOR: You can see the difference between your dreams and someone like Cody's. You can recognize that you're worlds apart.

BEAUJO: I guess so. I never thought about it too much.

DOCTOR: Of course not. No reason to think about it. That's my job. I'm the doctor. You're simply the bodyguard.

SANTEE: Could I say somethin' here?

DOCTOR: No! Be quiet! Come here and look in this bag, Beaujo. I want you to see something.

FINGERS: NO! Don't look! Don't look, Beaujo!

DOCTOR: You are a man of adventure aren't you, Beaujo? I wasn't wrong in that was I?

BEAUJO: I'm feelin' a little paralyzed, Doc. I don't know what it is. I'm afraid.

DOCTOR: There's nowhere to run. Besides, it could turn out to be something quite extraordinary. Come have a look.

SANTEE: I'll look.

DOCTOR: Stay where you are! Beaujo?

BEAUJO: What's in it?

DOCTOR: Come and look.

BEAUJO: What if I can't take it. I'm not a very strong person.

DOCTOR: It doesn't matter. Nothing will hurt you. Just come and look in the bag.

(*A moment of silence while* BEAUJO *decides.* BEAUJO *slowly crosses to the bag where the* DOCTOR *is and looks into it.*)

FINGERS: Oh God. Oh my God.

BEAUJO: What are they?

DOCTOR: Take one in your hand. Go ahead. Nothing will happen, I promise.

(BEAUJO *reaches into the bag and pulls out a small white bone the size of a large marble. He holds it in the palm of his hand.*)

BEAUJO: What is it?

DOCTOR: A bone from the back of the neck. A dreamer's bone.

BEAUJO: Human?

DOCTOR: Yes.

BEAUJO: You mean you cut it out of somebody?

DOCTOR: In a dreamer's prime he collects certain valuable substances from his dreams in the back of his neck. Even when he loses his touch these substances remain imbedded in these magical bones. A man in possession of enough of these bones becomes eternally linked to the dreamer's magic. His gift lives on.

BEAUJO: You mean these are from dead dreamers?

DOCTOR: I wouldn't say dead exactly. Out of their bodies perhaps but not dead.

BEAUJO: And they help you pick the winners?

DOCTOR: Infallibly.

BEAUJO: Then what's the point in having live dreamers all the time.

DOCTOR: Unfortunately the bones tend to fade in strength. Their power has to continually be replenished. This is where the adventure comes in. It's a very delicate process finding the correct dreamer to restore the power. It has to be one who has experienced a certain stretch of genius. One who is beginning to fade but not to such an extent as to have lost all his magic. Like Cody here for instance. He appears to be the perfect choice.

CODY: Oh no ya' don't. Not me, boy. Not this kid. I ain't gettin' cut up and put in no bag. This has gone far enough. I've played ball with you right down the line but this is the limit. No more.

DOCTOR: Santee, strap him to the bed!

SANTEE: With pleasure.

(SANTEE *goes after* CODY. *There's a mad chase around the room.* FINGERS *weeps and moans on the floor. The* DOCTOR *pulls a huge syringe out of his bag.* BEAUJO *is frozen.*)

DOCTOR: You see the territory he travels in. He's perfectly capable of living in several worlds at the same time. This is his genius.

CODY: I was just bluffin'! Honest! I made it all up! I got no magic! I was just pretending!

DOCTOR: Right now he'll do anything to deny his gifts. His gifts are poison to him now. If he knew his power he could even make us disappear. Fortunately he's just a slave for us.

SANTEE: Come here you greaseball! (CODY *keeps getting away from* SANTEE)

FINGERS: Stop it! You've got to stop it! Beaujo, do something!

DOCTOR: You see how we're each on our own territory right now. Each of us paralyzed within certain boundaries. We'd do anything to cross the border but we're stuck. Quite stuck.

BEAUJO: You're gonna' operate on him?

DOCTOR: I'm simply going to alter the balance of things. Like a great chef. A pinch of this with a pinch of that. You'd be amazed at how little it takes to create an explosion. Santee, put him on the bed.

(SANTEE *has* CODY *in a firm grip.* CODY *squeals and squirms but* SANTEE *is too strong. He hauls* CODY *over to the bed and throws him down on his back then straddles his stomach and holds his arms down.*)

BEAUJO: Maybe there's some other way. I mean maybe we could hypnotize him or something. I keep putting myself in his place.

DOCTOR: That's quite impossible, Beaujo. You see there's no way for you to be in his place. There's no way for any of us to be in any place but the one we're in right now. Each of us. Quite separate from each other and yet connected. It's quite extraordinary isn't it? Now hold him down Santee. It's important to get a direct hit.

(SANTEE *holds* CODY'S *arm and slowly injects the serum.* CODY *becomes calm and speaks very evenly.* BEAUJO *looks on.*)

CODY: The white buffalo. Approach him in a sacred manner. He is Wakan. The ground he walks is Wakan. This day has sent a spirit gift. You must take it. Clean your heart of evil thoughts. Take him in a sacred way. If one bad thought is creeping in you it will mean your death. You will crumble to the earth. You will vanish from this time.

DOCTOR: Santee, hand me my scalpel please. It's in my bag.

SANTEE: Sure thing, Doc.

(SANTEE *hands the* DOCTOR *a scalpel from out of the bag. A series of knocks at the door. The* DOCTOR *remains cool.*)

DOCTOR: Beaujo, would you mind answering that. It's probably our waiter.

(BEAUJO *crosses to the door as the* DOCTOR *cuts into the back of* CODY'S *neck with the scalpel.* CODY *makes no sound.* BEAUJO *swings the door open. A shotgun blast throws him clear across the room. He lies in a heap.* CODY'S *two brothers,* JASPER *and* JASON, *enter. They're both about six foot five and weigh 250 lbs. each. They wear Wyoming cowboy gear with dust covering them from head to foot. Their costumes should be well used and authentic without looking like dime-store cowboys. They both carry double-barreled twelve-gauge shotguns and wear side guns on their waists. The* DOCTOR *turns suddenly toward them. Another shotgun blast from* JASPER. The DOCTOR *sinks to the floor.* SANTEE *reaches for his pistol and is cut down by both shotguns at once.* FINGERS *whimpers on the floor.* JASPER *and* JASON *look at him stony-faced.* CODY *sits on the bed with the back of his neck bleeding. He doesn't know where he is.* JASPER *crosses slowly over to* FINGERS *with his spurs jangling. He peers down at him.*)

JASPER: We come fer our brother, mister. You so much as make a twitch and you can kiss tomorrow goodbye.

JASON: (*crossing to* CODY) Come on, boy. We're goin' home now.

CODY: One bad thought. A clean heart.

JASON: (*helping* CODY *to his feet*) Come on now. You gather yerself together. A little beef stew in yer gullet, you'll be good as new.

CODY: (*standing*) In a sacred way. This day. Sacred. I was walking in my dream. A great circle. I was walking and I stopped. Even after the smoke cleared I couldn't see my home. Not even a familiar rock. You could tell me it was anywhere and I'd believe ya'. You could tell me it was any old where.